Augmenting Retail Reality, Part A

Augmenting Retail Reality, Part A

Blockchain, AR, VR, and the Internet of Things

EDITED BY

BALRAJ VERMA
Chitkara Business School, Chitkara University, Punjab, India

AMIT MITTAL
Chitkara Business School, Chitkara University, Punjab, India

MURALI RAMAN
Asia Pacific University of Technology and Innovation, Malaysia

AND

BIRUD SINDHAV
University of Nebraska Omaha, USA

United Kingdom – North America – Japan – India – Malaysia – China

Emerald Publishing Limited
Emerald Publishing, Floor 5, Northspring, 21-23 Wellington Street, Leeds LS1 4DL.

First edition 2025

Editorial matter and selection © 2025 Balraj Verma, Amit Mittal, Murali Raman, and Birud Sindhav.
Individual chapters © 2025 The authors.
Published under exclusive licence by Emerald Publishing Limited.

Reprints and permissions service
Contact: www.copyright.com

No part of this book may be reproduced, stored in a retrieval system, transmitted in any form or by any means electronic, mechanical, photocopying, recording or otherwise without either the prior written permission of the publisher or a licence permitting restricted copying issued in the UK by The Copyright Licensing Agency and in the USA by The Copyright Clearance Center. Any opinions expressed in the chapters are those of the authors. Whilst Emerald makes every effort to ensure the quality and accuracy of its content, Emerald makes no representation implied or otherwise, as to the chapters' suitability and application and disclaims any warranties, express or implied, to their use.

British Library Cataloguing in Publication Data
A catalogue record for this book is available from the British Library

ISBN: 978-1-83608-635-2 (Print)
ISBN: 978-1-83608-634-5 (Online)
ISBN: 978-1-83608-636-9 (Epub)

INVESTOR IN PEOPLE

Contents

About the Editors	*vii*
About the Contributors	*xi*
Preface	*xxi*

Chapter 1   Linking Supply and Demand in Retail Through the Internet of Things (IoT)
Adeline Sneha J., Sasithradevi A., S. Brilly Sangeetha, Wilfred Blessing, Shobana Manigandan and Thavamalini Sivasamy   *1*

Chapter 2   Discovering the Wonders of Blockchain: Utilising Bitcoins for Transaction Purpose
Bernard Lim Jit Heng, Phuah Kit Teng, Siti Intan Nurdiana Wong Abdullah, Ow Mun Waei and Khoong Tai Wai   *11*

Chapter 3   Guardians of Trust: Fortifying Payment Gateway Security for Digital Prosperity
Choon Sen Seah, Yin Xia Loh, Mohammad Falahat, Wing Son Loh and Ahmad Najmi Amerhaider Nuar   *43*

Chapter 4   Industry 4.0 Technologies: Managing the Future of Smart Retail
Ritu Kumari and Vinay Pal Singh   *59*

Chapter 5   Influence Dynamism of Augmented Reality in Manufacturing Industries
John Paul Raj V., Nara Srujana Rani, Sathish Pachiyappan and Saravanan Vellaiyan   *83*

vi Contents

Chapter 6 Innovation or Intrusion? Examining Employee Willingness to Collaborate With AI-Powered Service Robots in Retail
Meenal Arora, Ridhima Goel and Jagdeep Singla   *97*

Chapter 7 Measuring the Adoption of IoT in OTT Platforms
Isha Kalra and Meenu Gupta   *117*

Chapter 8 Modern Consumerism and Retailing: The Metaverse Bound
Brian Kee Mun Wong, Foong Li Law and Chin Ike Tan   *143*

Chapter 9 Ethical AI for Retail: A Bibliometric Roadmap to Building Trust and Transparency
Divya Goswami and Balraj Verma   *167*

Chapter 10 Ethical and Social Consequences of Accelerated Technology Adoption
Anuja Shukla and Poornima Jirli   *183*

About the Editors

Balraj Verma is currently serving as an Associate Professor at the Doctoral Research Centre of Chitkara Business School, affiliated with Chitkara University, Rajpura, Punjab, India. He completed his PhD from Jaypee University of Information Technology, Waknaghat, and holds a master's degree in Business Administration, bringing with him over 16 years of combined academic and corporate experience. His teaching portfolio includes courses such as marketing management, strategic management, business statistics, and research methodology. He has successfully supervised three scholars to PhD completion under his guidance, showcasing his proficiency in academic mentorship. His research contributions are substantial, with numerous publications in respected journals indexed in SCI, ABDC, and Scopus. Additionally, he has authored and edited books and contributed chapters to leading international publishers. He is actively involved in organising international conferences and serves as a resource person for faculty development programmes, management development programmes, and workshops focussed on research methodologies. As a peer reviewer for esteemed journals including the *Journal of Knowledge Economy* (Springer), *Economic Change and Restructuring* (Springer), *Electronic Commerce Research* (Springer), *International Journal of Information Management Data Insights* (Elsevier), and *SN Computer Science* (Springer), he contributes significantly to maintaining the standards of academic scholarship in his field. His research interests span e-commerce, retail management, technology adoption, aggregator platforms models, and human–computer interaction, etc.

Amit Mittal is a Pro-Vice-Chancellor (Research Programmes), Professor of Management, Doctoral Research Centre, Chitkara Business School, Chitkara University, Punjab, India, and has over two decades of domestic and international experience in academic leadership, teaching, research, consulting, training, and mentorship. At Chitkara University, his current mandate is to manage and coordinate the PhD programmes, research publications, and international/domestic research collaborations. Seventeen scholars have been awarded PhD degrees under his guidance, and he has published over 120 Scopus-/SSCI-indexed papers with a number of these included in the ABDC/ABS journal list. He was the recipient of the Careers360 'Outstanding Faculty Researcher Award' 2023, 'Megastar Award' Chitkara Excellence Awards 2023/2024, the Chitkara University Excellence Award 2023 (Publications in Business School Category),

viii **About the Editors**

and in 2021 (February) for highest cited author and publications with highest H-index (Business School Category). He is an active resource person for faculty development programmes, management development programmes, and corporate trainings. He is a member of the thesis review board of a number of universities. He presently reviews for reputable journals such as *Technological Forecasting and Social Change* (Elsevier), *Public Health* (Elsevier) *Benchmarking* (Emerald), *Technology Analysis and Strategic Management* (Taylor and Francis), *International Journal of Consumer Studies* (Wiley), *Journal of Public Affairs* (Wiley), *Routledge Studies in Global Student Mobility*, *International Journal of Emerging Markets* (Emerald), *Sustainability (MDPI), Management Decision* (Emerald), *IIM KSMR* (Sage), etc. He serves on the editorial boards of *Frontiers in Psychology* (SSCI/Scopus indexed), *Open Psychology Journal* (Scopus indexed), *Proceedings on Engineering Sciences* (Scopus indexed), and *Research on Enterprise in Modern Economy (Gdańsk University of Technology, Poland). He is currently guest editing a special issue in International Journal of Information and Management Data Insights (Elsevier).* He also serves on the executive committee of Indian Business School Advisory Council of ETS Global, USA. He is presently on the Jury of the QS Reimagine Education Awards, Abu Dhabi, 2023. He is a Research Fellow at INTI International University, Malaysia, Visiting Professor at Pathumthani University, Thailand, and Adjunct Faculty, IMSAR – MD University, India.

Murali Raman, Professor and Deputy Vice-Chancellor (Academic Development and Strategy), Asia Pacific University of Technology and Innovation, Malaysia, is both a Rhodes Scholar and Fulbright Fellow. His academic credentials include a PhD from SISAT, Claremont, USA; MBA (Imperial College, London); MSc Human Resources (London School of Economics, UK). He was affiliated to Stanford's Technology Venture Programme as a Faculty Fellow. He has published more than 120 papers in international journals, conferences, and book chapters, in management information system-related areas. He is currently the Deputy Vice-Chancellor at Asia Pacific University of Technology and Innovation, Kuala Lumpur, Malaysia.

Birud Sindhav is a Professor of Marketing at the University of Nebraska at Omaha. He has a PhD with a marketing focus from the University of Oklahoma, Norman. His research interests focus on areas of B-to-B relationships, organisational justice, green advertising, social media, grassroots entrepreneurship in emerging economies, and sales function in startups. His work has been published in *Journal of Retailing, Journal of International Marketing, Journal of Marketing Theory and Practice, Journal of Marketing Channels,* and other outlets. He is on the editorial review boards of the *European Journal of Marketing, Journal of Marketing Theory and Practice*, and *Journal of Inter-organizational Relationships.* He is a Senior Research Fellow at the Institute for Collaboration Science at his university. He teaches or has taught digital marketing, social media marketing, marketing in a high technology environment, principles of marketing, marketing

About the Editors **ix**

research, and doing business in China in the MBA and undergraduate programmes. He has also taught in Finland, Austria, Egypt, and India. He is a recipient of the UNO Alumni Outstanding Teaching Award among other awards. He has also provided service and consultation within and outside of the university. Prior to his academic career, he was a marketing executive with Amul, the largest food organisation in India.

About the Contributors

Adeline Sneha J. is a Senior Lecturer in the School of Computing, Asia Pacific University of Technology and Innovation, Technology Park Malaysia, Kuala Lumpur, Malaysia. She received her PhD from the Sathyabama Institute of Science and Technology, Chennai, India. Her research spans several areas of Internet of Things data analytics and machine learning, including precision agriculture, signal processing, image processing, data science, and control engineering. She has delivered several invited or plenary lectures at conferences throughout the world. She has published more than 30 papers in various national/international journals. She has received several important recognitions for her research career. She has also been awarded 'Dr. APJ Abdul Kalam Award for Innovative Research' awarded by the Society for Engineering Education Enrichment, 2021. She received 'Women Leadership Award 2022' from GlantorX.

Siti Intan Nurdiana Wong Abdullah is a Senior Lecturer at the Nottingham Business School, Nottingham Trent University, UK. She completed her PhD degree from Universiti Putra Malaysia in 2020. Her areas of research include sustainable tourism, green consumption behaviour, consumer attitudes, and sustainable consumerism. She is a dedicated educator and researcher with more than 15 years of teaching experience and 5 years of practical industry experience. As part of her current role, she is a member of the School's Marketing and Consumer Studies Research Group and a member of the Chartered Institute of Marketing and Certified Management and Business Educator. She writes and publishes articles, participates in conferences, serves as a reviewer, and editorial member, and has won numerous research grants. She has been actively involved in student recruitment, marketing, international partnerships, curriculum design, mentoring students in work-based learning and event-based learning projects, and consultancy work for small- and medium-sized enterprises. She is passionate about socio-environmental projects and has worked with several non-governmental organisations.

Meenal Arora is a Visiting Faculty Member at Chitkara University, Rajpura, Punjab, with a background in management. She has a PhD, holding UGC NET and MBA qualifications from ICFAI University, Dehradun. With over three years of industrial experience and four years in teaching, she imparts business management education to postgraduates and undergraduates. She has actively participated in national and international conferences and workshops, collaborating with prestigious institutions such as IIM Bodh Gaya and the University of

xii About the Contributors

Bahrain. She serves as a reviewer for international journals, including Emerald Publishing and Scopus-indexed *FIIB Business Review*. Awarded 1st position for the best research paper at the International E-Conference in Advances in Business and Management, she has published two research papers in Scopus-indexed conference proceedings.

Wilfred Blessing was awarded a PhD in Information and Communication Engineering from Anna University, India. He holds 16 years of teaching experience both in Oman and India. He is working on startup awareness for students and government-funded projects. He has won several prizes in national level student projects in Oman. He is skilled in software computing, object-oriented programming, software engineering, artificial intelligence, machine learning, multimedia, information systems, oracle, and so forth. He is interested in industrial collaborations, research activities, research projects, research collaboration with students, professional bodies, authoring articles, content writing, digital marketing research, organising conferences and symposiums, initiating international technical meetups and programming competitions, presenting technical webinars, conducting personality and motivational programme for young students, soft skills training, student counselling, course and curriculum development, content creation, multimedia development, academic committees (quality assurance unit, student development committee, research and consultancy committee, projects committee), editing academic magazines/newsletters (https://www.sct.edu.om/home/index.php/publications), online tools and technologies, and leadership. He has presented keynote addresses and guest lectures to more than 30 universities in Oman and India.

Mohammad Falahat is a Professor at the School of Marketing and Management, Asia Pacific University of Technology and Innovation, Malaysia. Previously, he was Chairperson of the Centre for Entrepreneurial Sustainability and Centre for Sustainable Development and Corporate Social Responsibility in Business at Universiti Tunku Abdul Rahman for 10 years. He received a certificate award for 'Faculty Development in International Entrepreneurship Program' from the University of Colorado Denver, USA, and he is a certified trainer, endorsed by Pembangunan Sumber Manusia Berhad, Malaysia. He has experience in conducting training for postgraduate students, academic staff, and the general public on data analytics, partial least squares structural equation modelling, research methodology, and entrepreneurship. He has secured Fundamental Research Grant Scheme (FRGS) and Trans-disciplinary Research Grant Scheme (TRGS) from the Ministry of Higher Education, and research projects from Private Pension Administrator Malaysia, MASA Policy Development Programme, MCA Belt and Road Centre, and Malaysia Productivity Corporation, to name a few.

Ridhima Goel is a distinguished research scholar at the Institute of Management Studies and Research, Maharshi Dayanand University, Rohtak, India. She brings a unique interdisciplinary perspective to her research with a dual background in an MBA and an MA in English from the same institution.

She has been acknowledged with the Second Best Paper Award in a national seminar at Central University Himachal and has presented her work at national and international conferences. She reviews international journals, including Emerald Publishing and Scopus Indexed, *Global Knowledge Memory and Communication*. Her academic prowess is exemplified by her University Research Fellowship, and she is imparting knowledge as a teacher, instructing postgraduate students in open elective subjects like Fundamentals of Management and Fundamentals of Marketing.

Divya Goswami is an academic and researcher currently serving as a Research Scholar at Chitkara University, Rajpura, Punjab. She holds a master's degree in Commerce and has cleared the national eligibility test in commerce. With a teaching experience spanning over 10.5 years, she has been instrumental in shaping the minds of students of S.A. Jain College, Ambala City. Her teaching portfolio includes both postgraduate and graduate classes, where she has impaired knowledge and guidance to aspiring learners.

Meenu Gupta, Associate Professor, MMDU, Mullana, India. She has published more than 30 national and international papers in refereed and Scopus journals. Four research projects have been applied to different organisations like ICMR, DST, CSR, and others. She has major experiences in the field of accreditation of NBA, NAAC, NIRF, AICTE & UGC. Her patents have been published and applied in the field of Business Management. She is ex. member of many decisional bodies like BOS, RAC, Research Committee, and PhD coordinator. Presently, she is member of Confederation of Indian Industry, Internal Complaint Committee, Treasurer of Maharaja Agrasen Chair, and Associate NCC Officer. She has conducted more than 200 activities for the national unit. She has delivered many sessions on SPSS and Research Methodology in different faculty development programmes (FDPs) and workshops within and outside the university. Her recent session on SPSS delivered in the ICSSR workshop was sponsored by the Ministry of Education of India in December 2023. More than seven FDPs of five days conducted by NITTR have been attended. Many workshops and seminars have been organised for the international business through the Director General of Foreign Trade, Federation of Indian Export Organisation and MSME.

Bernard Lim Jit Heng is a Lecturer at the Tunku Abdul Rahman University of Management and Technology. He is currently taking his PhD study at Universiti Putra Malaysia. His areas of research include financial literacy, financial well-being, and personal finance. He teaches corporate finance, financial market analysis, current issues in finance, and financial management.

Poornima Jirli is a seasoned IT professional with over 15 years of experience in the industry and holds a Doctorate of Business Administration in Strategic Innovation. She has spent her career focussed on driving technological advancements and strategic initiatives within various organisations.

xiv   *About the Contributors*

John Paul Raj V. is an Associate Professor and Associate Dean at Christ University, Banneghatta Road Campus. He has done his PhD in Management from Bharathiar University and an MBA in Human Resources Management. He has over 18 years of experience both in teaching and research. He is basically a motivational trainer and an Organizational Development (OD) consultant. He has conducted over 500 training programmes for corporates as well as educational institutions on team building, interpersonal communication, time management and goal setting, attitude building, leadership retreat, motivation, personality development, kinesics, interview skills, learns to win, group discussion, building professional self, supervisory development programme, workmen development programme, and psychometric test. Some of the well-known clients he had worked with are Nokia, Fenner, Titan, Naga Ltd, Periyar University, and Jegannath Textile. He has published several research papers in Scopus-indexed journals and presented research papers at international conferences.

Isha Kalra, Research Scholar, MMDU, Mullana, India, and Assistant Professor in School of Commerce & Business Management at Geeta University, Panipat, with 13 years of experience in teaching and research, having expertise in the field of marketing. She has published research papers in indexed journals and attended many international and national conferences and faculty development programmes by IIMs and the Institute of National Repute. She has received the Best Teacher Award for the years 2022 and 2023. She has occupied various key positions in her academic career. Currently, she is working as Coordinator BCom. She is an active member of the Ranking Committee of the institution. She has major experiences in the field of accreditation of NAAC, AICTE, UGC. She is a member of many decisional bodies like Academic Council and Board of Studies in Faculty of Commerce and Management at Geeta University, Panipat. She has delivered 80+ motivational sessions and workshops within and outside the University for Faculty and Students.

Ritu Kumari, Research Scholar, Quantum University, Roorkee, Uttarakhand, India. The author published a book chapter titled 'Digital Financial Literacy in India' in the book named *Empowering Financial Literacy: Navigating Education for Wealth: Vol. 1* in November 2023, and the book chapter titled 'Green Frontier: An Introduction to Green Entrepreneurship' in the book *Paradigm Shift Towards Sustainable Business and Management Practices* in December 2023.

Foong Li Law is a Senior Lecturer at the School of Computing, Asia Pacific University of Technology and Innovation, Malaysia. She obtained her PhD in Computer Science with a specialisation in Software Engineering and Requirements Engineering from the University of Malaya in 2019. She is registered as a Professional Technologist with the Malaysia Board of Technologist. Her research interests span a wide range of areas including empirical software engineering, nursing education with a focus on web and mobile development, data analytics, computer vision, and machine learning. Her diverse expertise and interdisciplinary approach contribute to her ability to conduct innovative research and provide valuable insights in these areas.

Wing Son Loh is currently pursuing a part-time PhD (Science) programme at the Lee Kong Chian Faculty of Engineering and Science (LKC FES) at Universiti Tunku Abdul Rahman (UTAR). He holds a Master's degree in Mathematics and an honours degree in Actuarial Science. Additionally, he is also serving as a Lecturer at the Department of Mathematical and Actuarial Sciences for the undergraduate programmes under the LKC FES. Prior to joining UTAR as a Lecturer, he worked as a Full-time Research Assistant. He has successfully secured a project funding from the UTAR Research Fund 2023 Cycle 1 and has published several journal papers as well as conference proceedings.

Yin Xia Loh is an accomplished individual with a strong background in technology management. Having obtained a relevant master's degree in 2022, she currently holds the position of a Lecturer at Southern University College. With a passion for teaching, she actively imparts knowledge to students through IT-related courses, aiming to shape the next generation of talents in the field. With expertise in financial technology and a commitment to fostering growth, she serves as an influential figure in the realm of academia and technological innovation.

Shobana Manigandan is a dedicated scholar with a passion for information technology (IT) and computer science. She completed her Bachelor of Science in Information Technology with First Class Honours, showcasing her commitment to academic excellence. Currently, she is pursuing her Master of Science in Computer Science, embarking on the first year of her postgraduate studies. Her academic journey is marked by a strong foundation in IT and a keen interest in advancing her knowledge and skills in computer science. Her enthusiasm for learning and research is evident in her active participation in academic activities and her continuous pursuit of knowledge.

Ahmad Najmi Amerhaider Nuar is a Senior Lecturer at the Faculty of Computing, Universiti Teknologi Malaysia. Since joining the academic staff in 2023, he has made significant contributions to the university, notably serving as the Head of Marketing and Industry Linkage. His research areas are broad and interdisciplinary, focussing on design science research, computational thinking, intelligent systems, and their practical applications within small to medium-sized enterprises (SMEs) and work system theory. His work aims to bridge the gap between theoretical research and practical implementation, enhancing SME competitiveness and efficiency through innovative technology solutions. Additionally, his interest in work system theory explores the dynamics of work systems within organisations, aiming to improve their effectiveness through better design and alignment of technological and human resources (HR). In recognition of his substantial contributions, he received the Outstanding Faculty Member Award at the MDEC PDTI Outstanding Awards 2023.

xvi   *About the Contributors*

Sathish Pachiyappan is currently serving as Assistant Professor at Christ (Deemed to be University), Bannerghatta Road Campus, Bengaluru. He has done his Doctoral degree from VIT (Deemed to be University), Vellore. He specialised in Finance and Accounting, doing his research in the same area. He has completed MBA from Anna University and BCom from SRM University, Chennai. Currently, as a part of his research work, he has published articles in peer-reviewed journals which includes Scopus-indexed journals, Web of Science-indexed journals, Australian Business Deans Council (ABDC)-listed journals, and EBSCO host journals. Also, he has published book chapters in Elsevier, Emerald, Springer, and IGI Global. He is well versed in handling Python, STATCRAFT, E-Views (Econometrics), and SPSS for financial data analysis in research areas. He is gold medallist and earned first rank in BCom at SRM University, Chennai, and also earned class topper in MBA and 39th rank holder in Anna University.

Nara Srujana Rani, a graduate of BBA Finance and International Business from Christ University, specialised in international business. She graduated in 2023 and dived into a full-time role in sales at an EdTech company and then shifted to a marketing internship at an HR application-based company. With a keen interest in exploring business dynamics, consumer behaviour, digital marketing, and market research, she is eager to delve deeper into these areas and make meaningful contributions to the business world.

S. Brilly Sangeetha has 19 years of experience in teaching and 4 years in research. Her area of research is networks, blockchain technology, artificial intelligence, and data science. She has completed a Postdoctoral Fellowship in Blockchain Technology. She is a successful professional and has trust in student-centred learning with a lot of activities to build them in the right way for the development of the interpersonal skills. She is the editor and reviewer of many international journals including Springer and shared her valuable feedback to the authors. She has published more than 30 international journals. Her passion for writing made her to write technical books and publish many Indian and Australian patents. She also has copyrights to her credit. She is an active member of ISTE (The Indian Society For Technical Education), IEEE, CSI (Computer Society of India), and IE (The Institution of Engineers). She is also a CISCO-certified network associate and has organised many seminars, workshops, and conferences. She has been awarded with 'Best Emerging Principal of the year 2020-21' by Xel Research and 'Best Young Principal of the Year 2020-21' from National Education Brilliance awards. She has held many positions like advisory committee member, technical committee member, and resource person for national, international conferences, workshops, and seminars and shared her valuable insights through her vast experience.

Sasithradevi A., PhD, is currently working as Associate Professor in Vellore Institute of Technology, Chennai, Tamil Nadu, India. She completed her ME in Communication System from Anna University and completed her PhD in the area

About the Contributors **xvii**

of video retrieval from Anna University. She published many papers in reputed journals and conferences. Her research interests include image and video analysis, pattern recognition, machine, and deep learning.

Choon Sen Seah obtained his Doctorate in Information Technology from Universiti Tun Hussein Onn Malaysia and has a keen interest in technology. His research/technical interest and experience encompass data science, digital entrepreneurship, financial technology, precision farming, and information systems. In terms of research output, he has secured around RM550,000 worth of research grants and consultation projects as principal investigator. He has achieved significant accomplishments in his field, including publishing over 20 indexed articles and books, receiving multiple awards, and supervised more than 10 teams in winning awards in international innovation competitions.

Anuja Shukla is working as Associate Professor at Jaipuria Institute of Management, Noida. She has more than 12 years of teaching experience with over 24 paper publications. Her research articles have been published in _International Journal of Information Management_ (A*), _Psychology and Marketing_ (A), _VISION_ (C), and _FIIB_ (ABS 1). She has also won best research paper awards at FMS, Symbiosis, and Amity. Her areas of research interest include eWOM, consumer behaviour, m-commerce, AR/VR, and emerging technologies.

Vinay Pal Singh, Senior Assistant Professor, Quantum University, Roorkee, Uttarakhand, India. The author published a chapter titled 'Big-Data Analytics: A New Paradigm Shift in Micro Finance Industry' in the book _Advances in Data Science and Analytics: Concepts and Paradigms_ in October 2022, and the book chapter titled 'Industry 4.0: Driving the Digital Transformation in Banking Sector' in the book named _Advances in Industry 4.0: Concepts and Applications_ in June 2022. The author published a chapter in the book named _Sustainable Approaches to Poverty Alleviation: Revisiting the Dimensions of Poverty_ in September 2023.

Jagdeep Singla is presently employed as a faculty at the Institute of Management Studies and Research, Maharshi Dayanand University, India. He had also served as a Professor at HPKV Business School, Central University of Himachal Pradesh, Dharamshala. After completing his postgraduation, he has more than 28 years of teaching and industry experience. During his academic career, he has authored several books in different areas such as operations management, operations and supply chain management, brand management, etc., which are formulated as a part of the course curriculum of Maharshi Dayanand University. He has plenty of research papers/articles to his credit, published in national and international journals of repute. He has supervised 11 PhDs. His areas of specialisation are production and operations management, supply chain management, marketing management, HR management, and brand management.

Thavamalini Sivasamy works at the School of Computing, Asia Pacific University of Technology and Innovation, Malaysia. She does research in Software

xviii *About the Contributors*

Engineering and eLearning tools. She is a successful professional and has trust in student-centred learning with a lot of activities to build them in the right way for the development of the interpersonal skills. She is working on interpersonal skill development for students and enabling effective communication, teamwork, empathy, and building positive attitudes among the students.

Chin Ike Tan is a registered Professional Technologist and an appointed examinations and qualifications committee member for Malaysian Board of Technologist. He is also the Founding Chairman for the Game Development Council of Malaysia. He is currently an Associate Professor and the Head of School at the School of Computing, Asia Pacific University of Technology and Innovation, Malaysia. He earned his MSc in Computing from the University of Teesside, UK, and his PhD in Game-Based Learning from Sultan Idris Education University. His research spans various areas of game development including user experience, game mechanics, gamified systems, and game-based learning.

Phuah Kit Teng is currently working as an Associate Professor at Tunku Abdul Rahman University of Management and Technology. She is an experienced academician and researcher with strong skills in research and marketing. Her career goal is to use her skills and knowledge in a leadership position that allows her to be innovative in all aspects. Her research scope is mainly focussed on food-related marketing studies which relate to consumer behaviour. Her areas of study encompass entomophagy, pet food, genetically modified food, Halal-labelled food, Halal poultry, green food, natural functional food, and synthetic functional food. She has authored many articles in various journals and has been the principal researcher and co-researcher of multiple research grants from various institutions. She committed to ongoing professional development and research to ensure innovation in business and marketing.

Saravanan Vellaiyan currently holds the position of Assistant Professor at the School of Business and Management, Christ Deemed to be University, Bengaluru. His expertise lies in the field of Accounting Finance, and he is recognised as a highly qualified academician. He has qualified in UGC-SET professional and completed postgraduate degrees in Management (MBA), and MPhil, and a PhD in Finance from Bharathiar University. His specialised focus within teaching revolves around taxation, encompassing both direct tax and indirect tax. Beyond academia, he actively engages in the industry–academia interface, showcasing his commitment to bridging the gap between theory and practice. His scholarly achievements are evident through his publications in various Scopus-indexed journals, reflecting his dedication to advancing research in his domain. Additionally, he has presented a total of 15 research papers at both international- and national-level conferences, further establishing his prominence in the academic and research community.

Ow Mun Waei is an Assistant Professor at Tunku Abdul Rahman University of Management and Technology (TARUMT). She is an academician and researcher

About the Contributors **xix**

in the field of marketing. Her research interest focusses on consumer behaviour and consumption, examining aspects related to customer loyalty, satisfaction, attitude, perception, and behaviour.

Khoong Tai Wai is a Practitioner-turned-Academician. He has more than 10 years of experience in business development in both the tangible and financial services industries. Currently, he serves as an Assistant Professor at Tunku Abdul Rahman University of Management and Technology. He holds a Chartered Islamic Finance Professional and Registered Financial Planner professional designation. He was appointed to serve as a member of the Certification and CPD Board for the Malaysian Financial Planning Council (MFPC). In addition, he is a MFPC-certified trainer and examiner. His research area focusses on financial inclusion, Islamic finance, and business analytics.

Brian Kee Mun Wong holds a PhD in Tourism Management from the University of Malaya, Kuala Lumpur. He is also a Fellow at the Chartered Institute of Marketing, UK. Currently, as a Professor and the Dean of the Faculty of Business, Design and Arts at Swinburne University of Technology Sarawak Campus, Malaysia, he is actively connecting initiatives between the academics and the industry. His research interest is in the areas of marketing, management, and entrepreneurial mindset.

Preface

In an era marked by unprecedented technological advancements, the retail industry is at the forefront of a transformative journey. *Augmenting Retail Reality, Part A: Blockchain, AR, VR, and the Internet of Things* delves into the dynamic interplay between cutting-edge technologies and the evolving landscape of retail commerce. This book serves as a comprehensive guide for retailers, researchers, students, and technology enthusiasts, exploring how innovations such as the internet of things (IoT), blockchain, robotics, augmented reality (AR), virtual reality (VR), and other emerging technologies are reshaping the retail sector.

The genesis of this book is rooted in the recognition that technology is not merely an auxiliary component but a fundamental driver of change in retail. As the digital revolution continues to accelerate, retailers must navigate a complex and rapidly evolving environment where customer expectations are constantly shifting, and new opportunities for growth are continually emerging. This publication is a response to the urgent need for an in-depth examination of how these technologies are transforming customer experiences, operational efficiencies, and business models within the retail industry.

Our journey begins with an exploration of the IoT's role in linking supply and demand in retail. This foundational chapter sets the stage for understanding how IoT enables a seamless integration of customer touchpoints, thereby enhancing the shopping experience and optimising supply chain operations. The subsequent chapters delve into the transformative power of blockchain and cryptocurrencies, fortifying payment gateway security, and the rise of Industry 4.0 technologies that are driving the future of smart retail.

AR and VR take centre stage as we examine their profound impact on creating immersive shopping environments and enhancing customer engagement. We explore the dynamic relationship between employees and artificial intelligence (AI)-powered service robots, highlighting the collaborative potential and operational efficiencies that these technologies bring to retail settings. Additionally, this book addresses the convergence of IoT and over-the-top platforms, offering insights into how digital content distribution is being revolutionised.

The narrative is enriched by practical examples, success stories, and best practices from industry leaders. Each chapter provides a detailed analysis of current trends, challenges, and opportunities, offering readers a holistic understanding of the technological landscape in retail. By bridging the gap between theoretical insights and real-world applications, this book empowers readers to make informed decisions and drive innovation within their own spheres of influence.

xxii Preface

Augmenting Retail Reality: Blockchain, AR, VR, and the Internet of Things is not just a compilation of technological insights; it is a beacon guiding retailers towards a future where technology and commerce seamlessly merge. As we stand at the cusp of this new era, it is imperative to embrace the possibilities that these technologies offer. This book is dedicated to all those who seek to understand, navigate, and lead in the ever-evolving world of retail technology.

We extend our deepest gratitude to the ***contributors*** whose expertise and insights have made this publication possible. Their dedication to exploring the frontiers of retail technology has been instrumental in shaping the comprehensive and forward-looking narrative presented in these pages. We hope that this book will serve as an invaluable resource, inspiring innovation and fostering a deeper understanding of the transformative potential of technology in retail.

Welcome to the future of retail.

Balraj Verma, *Chitkara Business School, Chitkara University, Punjab, India*
Amit Mittal, *Chitkara Business School, Chitkara University, Punjab, India*
Murali Raman, *Asia Pacific University of Technology
and Innovation, Malaysia*
Birud Sindhav, *University of Nebraska Omaha, USA*

Chapter 1

Linking Supply and Demand in Retail Through the Internet of Things (IoT)

Adeline Sneha J.[a], Sasithradevi A.[b], S. Brilly Sangeetha[c], Wilfred Blessing[d], Shobana Manigandan[e] and Thavamalini Sivasamy[a]

[a] *Asia Pacific University of Technology and Innovation, Malaysia*
[b] *Vellore Institute of Technology, India*
[c] *IES College of Engineering, India*
[d] *University of Technology and Applied Sciences, Ibri, Sultanate of Oman*
[e] *TMG College of Arts and Science, India*

Abstract

The development of Internet of Things (IoT) is revolutionising the retail sector with innovation. With the help of IoT, retailers can now offer shoppers a personalised, interactive shopping experience, making it easier for them to find what they need and discover new products. Consequently, this is generating fresh prospects and propelling the sector's expansion. The distribution chain in retail provides the products and information that enable customers to learn about products through various channels other than the ones they use to buy them. Keeping up with the rapidly changing demand and supply necessitates a sophisticated inventory and supply chain operation, in addition to the integration of all customer touchpoints. Because it enables businesses to rebalance supply and demand, the IoT has the potential to be a key component of channel integration. This chapter offers a strategic framework for classifying IoT initiatives on an opportunity map and differentiating them according to their primary area of impact and value creation. This chapter uses the enabling capabilities of the IoT to support adoption.

Keywords: IoT; retailing; eshop; supply; demand; retail; linking supply and demand

---

Augmenting Retail Reality: Blockchain, AR, VR, and the Internet of Things, Part A, 1–10
Copyright © 2025 by Adeline Sneha J., Sasithradevi A., S. Brilly Sangeetha, Wilfred Blessing, Shobana Manigandan and Thavamalini Sivasamy
Published under exclusive licence by Emerald Publishing Limited
doi:10.1108/978-1-83608-634-520241001

1. Introduction

The IoT has transformed the retail sector, enhancing the overall shopping experience for consumers and merchants alike. Fig. 1.1 represents the several IoT-driven solutions in retail (Elizabeth, 2023). The IoT is significantly reshaping the dynamics of supply and demand. Retailers' business operations and customer interactions have been completely transformed by IoT technologies, characterised by interconnected devices and sensors. The potential for IoT integration to enhance transparency and efficiency in supply chain management has garnered attention. The use of IoT-enabled sensors for real-time tracking and monitoring of goods throughout the supply chain helps minimise stockouts and overstock scenarios, reduces delays, and improves logistics while enabling predictive analytics for inventory management. The potential applications and business implications of blockchain technology often lead to debates. Min (2019) explains how blockchain technology can make supply chains more resilient during periods of heightened risk and uncertainty. The IoT will consist of billions of devices equipped with sensors, actuators, and possibly even voices. This integration allows for the identification, capture, collection, and management of continuous data from billions of connected devices, supporting a range of applications such as corporate, human-driven, modern, and natural monitoring applications (Kaur et al., 2022). The ability of IoT to help businesses adjust supply and demand makes it a key component of channel integration (Felipe et al., 2019; Verma & Tandon, 2022). The findings highlight how retailers can use these data to predict trends, optimise pricing strategies, and generally improve customer satisfaction. Wang et al. (2019)

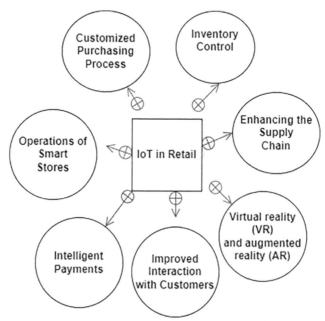

Fig. 1.1. IoT-Driven Solutions in Retail. *Source*: Authors' representation.

examine how physical stores have evolved into smart retail spaces. The study explores how IoT technologies, such as smart mirrors and interactive displays, enhance the immersive and customised shopping experience. This not only affects consumer behaviour but also the overall demand for goods and services. Effective inventory management is crucial for supply chain optimisation. Ensuring the reliability and security of IoT systems in retail is essential. Picot-Coupey et al. (2023) investigate livestreaming shopping as a novel retail concept. As digital technology has changed consumer expectations and behaviour, businesses are being forced to develop creative customisation tactics to meet customers' increasingly individualised needs (Xin et al., 2024). The systematic review on retail and supply chain is explored by Taj et al. (2023).

IoT technologies are changing the way traditional retail paradigms are applied, from supply chain optimisation to demand forecasting and the development of smart retail environments. Table 1.1 depicts the IoT-driven solutions in retail (Onomondo, 2023). To fully realise the potential of IoT in retail and ultimately create more customer-focused and efficient operations, it is imperative to address issues such as security and trust. Businesses hoping to stay competitive and meet customers' ever-changing demands will need to understand and leverage IoT's capabilities.

Table 1.1.   IoT-Driven Solution Shopping Experience.

IoT Driven Solution	Shopping Experience
Customized Purchasing Process	**Customer Insights:** Information about consumer behavior, preferences, and demographics is gathered by Internet of Things devices like beacons and sensors. Retailers can offer tailored promotions, discounts, and suggestions using this data to create individualized shopping experiences.
Inventory Control	**RFID tags and smart shelves:** Retailers can monitor and manage inventory in real-time with the use of RFID tags and real-time by the Internet of Things. This guarantees that popular products are always available and minimizes stockouts and overstock situations.
Enhancing the Supply Chain	**Supply Chain:** IoT devices make it possible to track assets in real-time along the entire supply chain. This enhances the overall efficiency of the supply chain, minimizes delays, and optimizes logistics.
Improved Interaction with Customers	**Interactive Displays:** By offering more product details, enabling virtual try-ons, and promoting an interactive shopping experience, interactive displays and smart mirrors with IoT capabilities can interact with customers in-store.
Intelligent Payments	**Contactless Payments:** The Internet of Things makes contactless payment methods possible, which speeds up and simplifies customer transactions. This includes mobile wallets and NFC (Near Field Communication) technology.

(*Continued*)

4 Adeline Sneha J. et al.

Table 1.1. (*Continued*)

IoT Driven Solution	Shopping Experience
Operations of Smart Stores	**Energy Management:** By regulating lighting, heating, and cooling systems in response to in-store foot traffic and outside variables in real-time, IoT can be used to optimize energy consumption within stores.
	Predictive maintenance is made possible by IoT sensors that track the condition of appliances and HVAC systems, cutting down on downtime.
Virtual reality (VR) and augmented reality (AR)	**Virtual Try-Ons:** Augmented reality (AR) and virtual reality (VR) technologies improve the shopping experience for customers by enabling virtual try-ons of apparel and accessories, which aids in better decision-making.

Source: Authors' compilation.

2. IoT in Retail

Like any other technological breakthrough, the development of a successful IoT strategy must be motivated by the production of economic value. Fig. 1.2 shows the retailing with IoT. This simple structure can assist senior management in creating a good demand and supply chain. Because enabling IoT capabilities are based on the company's current operations, identifying them is simple and boosting the sales. IoT capabilities should be arranged according to their primary impact area, which might be supply, demand, or both (Felipe et al., 2019). Customers can feel secure in their purchasing selections when they are equipped with provenance knowledge, which comprises details regarding the products' origin, production, changes, and custody (Montecchi et al., 2019). With the goal of locating and resolving causes of contamination in the global food supply chain, tracking and authenticating the food chain to comprehend provenance is essential (Galvez et al., 2018). Cycle time and preservation cost optimisation guide supply chain decisions (Goswami & Verma, 2024; Iqbal & Kang, 2024). In the process of achieving sustainable operations, the retail industry has utilised IoT technology extensively. However, this has brought to light a number of operational challenges, including security and privacy. So, a more methodical, in linked domains, theoretical analysis must be carried out (Ma et al., 2022).

IoT devices collect data from the consumer behaviour using the preferences and demographics. Marketing efforts and product help to create a personalised shopping experience. IoT helps the retailers to understand the trends and inventory patterns accordingly. IoT helps to identify the payments and smart cards, to streamline the checkout process. Use of cameras linking them to IoT helps to monitor the customers movements and ensure the high safety to enhance the shopping experiences. Figs. 1.3 and 1.4 show the enhanced focus on consumer behaviour and experiences in the retail (Chawla et al., 2024; Jiang et al., 2024; Zheng et al., 2024).

IoT-Driven Retail: Enhancing Experience 5

Fig. 1.2. Retailing With IoT. *Source*: Authors' representation.

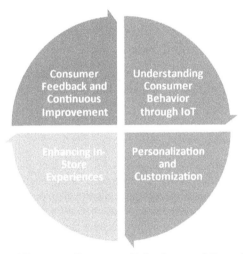

Fig. 1.3. Enhanced Focus on Consumer Behaviour and Experiences in Retail. *Source*: Authors' representation.

Fig. 1.4. IoT Options in Demand Side. *Source*: Authors' representation.

The basic idea is to rank any possible IoT opportunity based on its associated capabilities and value-adding mechanism. Capabilities can be enhanced or enabled; these are two distinct concepts. Although an IoT endeavour may entail some combinations of these capabilities, it will be helpful to treat each one independently. By enabling the firm to do existing tasks more efficiently, an enabling capability creates value. Motion sensors, for instance, can execute traffic counts more effectively than humans, while radio frequency identification (RFID) tags can essentially automate inventory counts. Many multinational companies are working on effective technology for supply chain management. Employee-focused connected platforms are made possible by IoT. Smart glasses are one tool that warehouse employees can utilise to receive continuous instruction, so they spend less time finishing tasks. Furthermore, IoT raises awareness in resource and labour management by gathering data linked to efficiency. Supply chain managers will guarantee that every party engaged in the delivery performs to the best of their abilities because of technology.

3. IoT Options in Demand Side

The disparity between client demand and supply is addressed by an IoT-based demand side management. Demand-side IoT possibilities are primarily divided into three categories as shown in Fig. 1.4.

3.1. Camera Networks

Retailers have embraced these networks for inventory management. Camera networks collect information about conversion rates, length of visits, frequency of visits (sometimes using facial recognition software), patterns of entrances and exits, and interactions between sales representatives and clients. To describe the movement and activity of clients, a daily study is carried out. Typically housed on the cloud, software analytics leverage data that are communicated and saved to enhance store layouts and facilitate effective mobile marketing through interacting with customers through personalised offers displayed on display screens or through 'chatbots'.

3.2. Smartphones

This method offers far less information regarding in-store customer behaviour and the entire shopping experience, although being less expensive than a camera network. Customers are offered Wi-Fi access, and if they accept, the system follows them using a network of wireless access points.

3.3. Smartcards

This is the least expensive method of recording the frequency of client visits and their purchasing preferences when paired with information on the actual transactions made by the consumer. However, the card technology does not record the activity of customers while they are in the store; instead, it can only identify the purchasing habits of customers over time.

4. IoT Options in Supply Side

RFID technology and IoT-enabled smart shelves support real-time inventory tracking. The positive effects on demand fulfilment, decrease stockouts, and helps to enhance process related to inventory. Most clothing businesses need a high device density because they carry anything from thousands to hundreds of products. Therefore, the IoT solution the retailer uses to track every item out for the supply and monitor inventory will depend on the required device density. Passive RFID tags operating at ultra-high frequencies are the most frequently used IoT device for a high-density environment.

5. Enhancing Capabilities in IoT-Based Supply and Demand Linking in Retail

IoT can play a vital role in channel integration because it enables businesses to restore supply and demand equilibrium. Compared to closed systems, connected platforms are quicker and simpler to use. Businesses may make sure that everyone involved in the supply chain lifecycle has access to pertinent data and can quickly resolve issues by implementing a cloud-based IoT system. Additionally, tools for various users (workers, managers, operators, and consumers) on the web and mobile platforms enable them to engage with the insights and utilise the data gathered to create strategies and various scenarios that are pertinent to their jobs and needs.

Like any technology, the production of business value must be the driving force behind the development of a successful IoT strategy. To assist top management in developing such a plan, this chapter offered a basic structure. The overall concept is to classify every potential IoT opportunity according to the capabilities it is associated with and the value it adds. The two types of capacities that are represented to identify are enabling and enhancing.

5.1. Analytics in Supply

Analytics in supply cleverly integrate IoT devices connected via Bluetooth or Wi-Fi. These devices can track their retail environment, offer smooth in-store navigation, and help customers locate requested items. The data collected for supply including item state, sales rate, in-store product placement, availability of goods, stores, and location are gathered via IoT sensors placed in the location.

The following strategies are taken into account for effective linking of supply and demand.

8   Adeline Sneha J. et al.

The supply chains are made ready.

- A gateway device receives the gathered data and processes it before forwarding it to the central IoT, which serves as a central hub for managing and monitoring IoT devices.
- The chosen Azure service is then used to export the data, where strong analytics capabilities are ready to extract insightful information.
- Cloud storage services effectively store structured data, enabling smooth data administration.
- Retail operations may now make well-informed decisions and streamline procedures by using business tools like Power BI, which query the data and produce useful insights.
- Navigation of the supply products is much improved with IoT deployment, enabling quick product searches and building a strong shopping environment with better product choices and store layouts.
- This game-changing strategy transforms how consumers engage with retailers, resulting in a smooth and pleasurable buying experience.

5.2. Beacon-Based Targeted Alerts

Beacons are Bluetooth devices that are used to send out smartphone notifications to prospective suppliers in proximity about special discounts, offers, and events based on the demands.

5.3. Smart Carts

Shopping carts with sensors enable retailers to see customers' flow based on preferences for different categories and subcategories, so opening up new growth potential. Insightful path analysis, trend analysis, and streamlined checkout procedures are made possible by technology. These smart carts can precisely track wheel movements and log the distance travelled within the store thanks to connectivity protocols. The gathered information is safely transferred to a cloud server, where it becomes an invaluable tool for thorough analysis that eventually yields actionable insights. Retailers can successfully accommodate client preferences with this creative strategy, increasing customer loyalty.

5.4. Inference

It is predicted that the number of IoT devices in the world would nearly double from 15.1 billion in 2020 to over 29 billion by 2030 (Lional, 2023) as shown in Fig 1.5. In 2030, the biggest number of IoT devices will be found in China with roughly 8 billion consumer devices. IoT-based technology will therefore help businesses and customers when used in logistics and business.

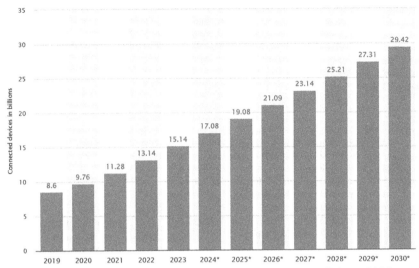

Fig. 1.5. Forecast of IoT-Connected Devices Worldwide (Vailshery, 2023). *Source*: Authors' representation.

6. Discussion

IoT has revolutionised the way businesses interact with their customers in the retail management sector. This work proposes linking retail with demand, which enhances retail performance efficiently and provides customers with unique and customised shopping experiences. By integrating supply chain management and IoT, retailers can gain deeper insights into their products, customers, and demand, enabling them to develop strategies that are more relevant. Understanding the market and segmenting products based on the target audience aids in data collection throughout the product lifecycle. IoT also enables employee-focused connected platforms. For example, warehouse employees can use smart glasses to receive continuous instructions, reducing the time spent on tasks. Additionally, IoT improves awareness in resource and labour management by collecting data related to efficiency. With this technology, supply chain managers can ensure that every party involved in the delivery process performs to the best of their abilities.

References

Felipe, C., & Sadr, R. (2019). The Internet of Things (IoT) in retail: Bridging supply and demand. *Business Horizons, 62*(1), 47–54.

Chawla, U., Verma, B., & Mittal, A. (2024). Resistance to O2O technology platform adoption among small retailers: The influence of visibility and discoverability. *Technology in Society*, *76*(C). DOI: 10.1016/j.techsoc.2024.102482.

Elizabeth, K. (2023). *IoT in retail: Top 5 use cases and real-life examples*. https://www.retailtouchpoints.com/features/executive-viewpoints/iot-in-retail-top-5-use-cases-and-real-life-examples

Galvez, J. F., Mejuto, J. C., & Simal-Gandara, J. (2018). Future challenges on the use of blockchain for food traceability analysis. *TrAC Trends in Analytical Chemistry*, *107*, 222–232.

Goswami, D., & Verma, B. (2024). The intersection of ethics and big data: Addressing ethical concerns in digital age of artificial intelligence. In B. Verma, B. Singla, A. Mittal (Eds.), *Digital technologies, ethics, and decentralization in the digital era* (pp. 269–285). IGI Global.

Iqbal, M. W., & Kang, Y. (2024). Circular economy of food: A secondary supply chain model on food waste management incorporating IoT based technology. *Journal of Cleaner Production*, 140566.

Jiang, L., Loahavilai, P. O., & Udomwong, P. (2024, March). The impact of live streamers' characteristics on female consumers' purchasing behavior in the southeast Asian e-commerce market. In *Proceedings of the 1st international conference on artificial intelligence, communication, IoT, data engineering and security, IACIDS 2023*, 23–25 November 2023, Lavasa, Pune, India.

Kaur, J., Santhoshkumar, N., Nomani, M. Z. M., Sharma, D. K., Maroor, J. P., & Dhiman, V. (2022). Impact of internets of things (IOT) in retail sector. *Materials Today: Proceedings*, *51*, 26–30.

Ma, B. J., Zhang, Y., Liu, S., Jiang, Y., He, Y., & Yan, K. (2022). Operational strategies for IoT-enabled brick-and-mortar retailers in a competitive market. *Computers & Industrial Engineering*, *173*, 108665.

Min, H. (2019). Blockchain technology for enhancing supply chain resilience. *Business Horizons*, *62*(1), 35–45.

Montecchi, M., Plangger, K., & Etter, M. (2019). It's real, trust me. Establishing supply chain provenance using blockchain. *Business Horizons*, *62*(3), 283–293.

Onomondo. (2023). *How IoT in retail is changing the global retail industry*. https://onomondo.com/blog/how-iot-in-retail-is-changing-the-global-retail-industry/

Picot-Coupey, K., Bouragba, Y., Collin Lachaud, I., Gallarza, M. G., & Ouazzani, Y. (2023). Live streaming shopping as a new retail format: Insights from a qualitative study of consumers and retailers. *International Journal of Retail & Distribution Management*, *51*(9/10), 1313–1351.

Taj, S., Imran, A. S., Kastrati, Z., Daudpota, S. M., Memon, R. A., & Ahmed, J. (2023). IoT-based supply chain management: A systematic literature review. *Internet of Things*, *24*, 100982.

Vailshery, L. S. (2023, July 17). *Number of IoT connected devices worldwide 2019-2023, with forecasts to 2030*. STATISTA. https://www.statista.com/statistics/1183457/iot-connected-devices-worldwide/

Verma, B., & Tandon, U. (2022). Modelling barriers to wearable technologies in Indian context: Validating the moderating role of technology literacy. *Global Knowledge, Memory and Communication*, *73*(6/7), 984–1004.

Wang, X., Yuen, K. F., Ma, F., & Wong, Y. D. (2019). The determinants of customers' intention to use smart lockers for last-mile deliveries. *Journal of Retailing and Consumer Services*, *49*, 316–326.

Xin, B., Song, Y., & Xie, L. (2024). Dynamic pricing and service customization strategy for IoT-based smart products. *Technological Forecasting and Social Change*, *199*, 123046.

Zheng, Z., Mao, W., Xing, Y., & Wu, F. (2024). On designing market model and pricing mechanisms for IoT data exchange. *IEEE Transactions on Mobile Computing*.

Chapter 2

Discovering the Wonders of Blockchain: Utilising Bitcoins for Transaction Purpose

Bernard Lim Jit Heng[a], Phuah Kit Teng[b],
Siti Intan Nurdiana Wong Abdullah[c], Ow Mun Waei[b]
and Khoong Tai Wai[b]

[a]*Department of Finance, Faculty of Accountancy, Finance and Business, Tunku Abdul Rahman University of Management and Technology, Malaysia*
[b]*Department of Marketing, Faculty of Accountancy, Finance and Business, Tunku Abdul Rahman University of Management and Technology, Malaysia*
[c]*Marketing Department, Nottingham Business School, Nottingham Trent University, United Kingdom*

Abstract

By market capitalisation, Bitcoin, which debuted in 2009, is the biggest cryptocurrency globally. A decentralised ledger system called blockchain is used in the creation, distribution, trading, and storage of Bitcoin, with the original goal being to address the shortcomings of fiat currency. This chapter highlights potential dangers and legal concerns when Bitcoin interacts with the actual economy and the traditional financial system. Besides, the details also discuss the platform's design principles and attributes for a non-technical readership. When assessing its transactional potential, some recognise its potential for speculation, while others are doubtful of its admirable intent. The write-up also explores the potential of the adoption of cryptocurrencies in Southeast Asia due to the vast adoption of Bitcoins in countries such as Vietnam and the Philippines following the establishment of cryptocurrency technology and e-commerce. In addition, rankings of the cryptocurrency and legal stance from each country in Southeast Asia were exhibited as the solid foundation of cryptocurrencies existent for transaction purposes. The rise of central bank digital currencies (CBDC) and the future directions of Bitcoins were also highlighted in this write-up to spur the debate on whether

---

Augmenting Retail Reality: Blockchain, AR, VR, and the Internet of Things, Part A, 11–42
Copyright © 2025 by Bernard Lim Jit Heng, Phuah Kit Teng, Siti Intan Nurdiana Wong Abdullah, Ow Mun Waei and Khoong Tai Wai
Published under exclusive licence by Emerald Publishing Limited
doi:10.1108/978-1-83608-634-520241003

cryptocurrency remains a fad of sensation or is legalised as the medium of exchange in an ever-growing digital world of commerce.

Keywords: Bitcoins; cryptocurrency; digital payment; digital currency; legal tender; peer-to-peer system

1. Background of Blockchain Technology

The definition of blockchain often adopts an informal tone, tailored to specific use cases and frequently employs marketing terminology to emphasise the properties and security approaches inherent in blockchain (Viriyasitavata & Hoonsonponb, 2019). Various descriptions have emerged, such as portraying blockchain as a public ledger for recording transactions supported by multiple nodes without a central authority, facilitated through a distributed cryptographic protocol (Correia et al., 2011). Another perspective characterises it as a decentralised, replicated, immutable, and tamper-evident log, enabling any party to read data and verify correctness (Bano et al., 2018; Correia et al., 2011), or as a technology using community validation to synchronise ledger content across multiple users (Aste et al., 2017). Other perspectives define it as a distributed ledger containing information about transactions or events, replicated, and shared among network participants (Li et al., 2017), or as a distributed database comprising an ever-expanding, organised records list across multiple server memory devices (Rahman et al., 2020).

In 2008, Nakamoto introduced blockchain as the foundational technology for Bitcoin, creating a decentralised peer-to-peer (P2P) financial transaction system (Nakamoto, 2019). Before the emergence of Bitcoin, traditional financial transactions heavily relied on centralised intermediaries like banks and governments (Hutt, 2018). The core structure of blockchain involves the linkage of blocks through cryptographic hashes, and each node maintains a complete copy of all the blocks (Al-Saqaf & Seidler, 2017; de Leon et al., 2017; Scott et al., 2017). This interconnected design, along with cryptographic features, ensures the virtual immutability and transparency of transaction records (Grewal et al., 2018; Shiva Sai Kumar, 2020).

While blockchain technology initially emerged with Bitcoin applications (Nakamoto, 2008), its current reach extends far beyond cryptocurrencies, showing the potential to disrupt various traditional industries (Scott et al., 2017; White, 2017). Embracing the principle of decentralisation, smart contracts emerge as a crucial blockchain application, enabling automated asset transfers when specific conditions are met, thereby reshaping business models by eliminating the need for intermediaries (Al-Saqaf & Seidler, 2017).

The structure of a blockchain consists of a series of blocks, each comprising data, a hash, and the hash of the previous block. The hash, a unique alphanumeric code, functions as the block's identifier (Moosavi et al., 2021). Typically, common hashes are 256 bits long and are represented in the hexadecimal numeral system for more efficient digit representation (Moosavi et al., 2021). While the decimal system, using numbers 0–9, serves as the standard numerical system, hexadecimal includes these digits along with six additional ones (Moosavi et al., 2021). The hash of the last block is intricately connected to the preceding block, forming the interlinked chain of blocks (Moosavi et al., 2021). The hashing function operates by taking input and generating an unpredictable output through a designated hashing algorithm (Vujicic et al., 2018).

The foundational technology of blockchain has widespread applications across various industries, including banking, trading, insurance, data protection, voting, intellectual property, identity authentication, leasing, and government services (Atzori, 2017; de Meijer, 2016; Liebenau & Elaluf-Calderwood, 2016; Trautman, 2016; Yermack, 2017). Its implications and applications extend to diverse sectors such as financial transactions, manufacturing, logistics, and supply chain management (SCM) (Abeyratne & Monfared, 2016; Pournader et al., 2020; Saberi et al., 2019; Tapscott, 2017; Verma et al., 2024). Blockchain serves as a valuable tool for measuring outcomes and performance in key SCM processes (Gurtu & Johny, 2019). Once input tracking data are recorded on a blockchain ledger, they become immutable, enabling other suppliers in the chain to track shipments, monitor progress, and trace deliveries (Mishra et al., 2018). The elimination of intermediaries enhances auditing efficiency and reduces costs, empowering individual suppliers to conduct real-time checks and balances (Koetsier, 2017). Furthermore, blockchain provides a precise method for measuring product quality during transportation (Gurtu & Johny, 2019). The shipping industry is increasingly embracing blockchain platforms to streamline global supply processes (Gurtu & Johny, 2019). Francisco and Swanson (2018) explored the transparency and traceability that blockchain introduces to SCM, while Saberi et al. (2019) delved into adoption barriers, and Kshetri (2018) considered SCM objectives.

The functionalities of blockchain, encompassing data integrity protection, real-time information sharing, and programmable automatic controls, possess the capacity to revolutionise established ecosystems by obviating the necessity for manual processes and intermediaries (Moosavi et al., 2021). Acknowledged as one of the six megatrends by the World Economic Forum (WEF. 2015), blockchain stands out as a significant innovation in computer technology with the potential to mould the future global landscape (Tapscott, 2017). The key characteristics of blockchain can be succinctly summarised in Table 2.1.

However, the most well-known environmental impact of blockchain technology is related to its energy consumption and potential harm to climate change. To execute related computer calculations in block chaining, a significant amount of computing power and electricity are needed. Expanding the application of blockchain technology may undermine attempts to mitigate climate change since power is still primarily produced from fossil fuels in many parts of the world. Combustible fuel generation continued to account for 67.3% of global gross power production in 2016 (International Energy Agency (IEA), 2019). Hence, a comprehensive evaluation of every mechanism's energy impact and efficiency is still necessary. Further investigations include transitioning to more environmentally friendly energy sources and creating computations that require less energy (Jones, 2017). Restructuring the incentives for blockchain maintenance could potentially help lower Bitcoin's energy usage (de Vries, 2019).

Table 2.1.   Key Characteristics of Blockchain.

Characteristics	Description	Citation
Centralisation and decentralisation	In contrast to traditional centralised systems that depend on trusted intermediaries, blockchain's decentralised structure operates on a network of distributed computers (nodes). This eliminates the necessity for central authorities, thereby reducing the risks associated with a single point of failure.	Aste et al. (2017); Viriyasitavata and Hoonsoponb (2019)
Permissioned and permissionless blockchains	Permissionless (public) blockchain: this model is accessible to all participants, permitting anyone to openly validate transactions. Permissioned (private) blockchain: limited to specific groups, usually within a business or consortium; this model regulates access and validation parameters according to predefined policies.	Buterin (2014); Viriyasitavata and Hoonsoponb (2019)
Transparency and immutability	Blockchain guarantees transparency by granting all network participants access to a detailed transaction history. The use of cryptographic hashes to link blocks ensures immutability, making the ledger resistant to unauthorised modifications. This inherent feature facilitates auditability, allowing for the verification and traceability of records.	Aste et al. (2017)
Validity and security	In blockchain systems, transactions undergo validation by multiple nodes, making falsification easily detectable. The system's structure incorporates proposers, acceptors, and learners, employing cryptographic techniques, public/private keys, and consensus algorithms (such as PoW or PoS) to ensure transaction security and validation.	Aste et al. (2017); Viriyasitavata and Hoonsoponb (2019); Correia et al. (2011)
Anonymity and identity	In public blockchains, users can maintain untied identities, providing a degree of privacy and avoiding exposure.In private and permissioned blockchains, governed by known entities, identity verification is required for participation. This approach strikes a balance between privacy and regulatory compliance.	Viriyasitavata and Hoonsoponb (2019); Yeow et al. (2018)

Source: Summary of key characteristics of blockchain from various sources compiled by authors on 30 December 2023.

Concerns regarding electronic waste (e-waste) are also raised by blockchain, as they are by other new Information Communication Technologies (ICT)-based technologies. Each Bitcoin transaction generates 135 g of e-waste, which is more than a Visa transaction (de Vries, 2019). However, there is still a lack of analysis about blockchain's effects on sustainability and the environment. This especially applies to energy usage. More accurate data on blockchain energy use are needed, both now and in the future. This calls for more exacting approaches and different scenarios. At the local, national, and international levels, thorough monitoring and sustainability assessments are necessary.

Blockchain networks are commonly classified into three main types: public or open blockchain, private blockchain, and consortium/federated blockchain (Buterin, 2014). In private blockchains, ledgers are shared and validated by a pre-defined group of nodes, with an emphasis on permission-based access, where the owner holds the highest authority to control access to authorised nodes (Jirgensons & Kapenieks, 2018; Zaidan et al., 2015). The system requires initiation or validation for nodes seeking participation, and authorised nodes are responsible for consensus maintenance (Radanović & Likić, 2018). Private blockchains find suitability in closed systems where all nodes are fully trusted, often deployed for applications like voting, SCM, digital identity management, and asset ownership (Paul et al., 2021).

Public blockchains offer access to all participants and uphold a distributed ledger with permissionless validation through consensus mechanisms (Paul et al., 2021; Viriyasitavata & Hoonsoponb, 2019). There are no access restrictions, allowing anyone to read and write to the network. Examples of public blockchain technologies include Bitcoin, Ethereum, and Litecoin, employing proof of work (PoW) and proof of stake (PoS) consensus algorithms (Cong et al., 2019; Viriyasitavata & Hoonsoponb, 2019).

Consortium/federated/permissioned blockchains represent a hybrid model that blends aspects of both private and public blockchains, incorporating multiple carefully selected parties (Paul et al., 2021; Viriyasitavata & Hoonsoponb, 2019). Permissioned blockchains, tailored for semi-closed systems with a limited number of enterprises typically organised in consortiums, emphasise controlled access (Viriyasitavata & Hoonsoponb, 2019). Hybrid blockchains, engaging with both centralised and decentralised systems, exhibit features like integrity, transparency, and security, although they are not entirely open (Omar et al., 2021; Yang et al., 2017). In federated blockchains, a collective of organisations or companies jointly oversees the network, eliminating the dominance of a single organisation (Khan et al., 2019). This federated or consortium blockchain model empowers participating organisations with complete authority to implement necessary changes for network smoothness (Sajana et al., 2018). Data openness levels vary, typically involving access controls defined by the consortium to manage participant access and information within blockchains (Viriyasitavata & Hoonsoponb, 2019). Despite not being fully open, these systems offer partial decentralisation benefits, providing a degree of fault tolerance in the face of potentially malicious nodes. Examples of permissioned blockchain implementations include Hyperledger Fabric, Ripple, and Stellar (Viriyasitavata & Hoonsoponb, 2019).

16 Bernard Lim Jit Heng et al.

Despite their distinctions, various blockchain types share fundamental benefits offered by the technology. These include functioning on a P2P network to achieve decentralisation, ensuring ledger integrity through consensus mechanisms that involve multiple nodes and maintaining data immutability even when dealing with faulty or malicious nodes (Jayachandran, 2017).

Blockchain platforms exhibit variations in consensus mechanisms, governance models, scalability, and specific use cases. The selection of a blockchain platform is dictated by the requirements of a project or application. Furthermore, the ever-evolving nature of the blockchain landscape sees the continual development of new platforms and updates, actively shaping the trajectory of blockchain technology. Table 2.2 provides a detailed overview of the distinctions among various blockchain platforms. Table 2.3 illustrates some examples of the blockchain's application in organisations. Table 2.4 identifies the blockchain's limitations and suggests possible solutions to improve the blockchain network.

Table 2.2.   Blockchain Platforms.

No.	Blockchain Platforms	Application
1.	Bitcoin	The pioneering decentralised cryptocurrency utilises a PoW consensus mechanism. In its P2P network, transactions are verified by nodes through cryptography and recorded in a decentralised public ledger called a blockchain, all without centralised oversight.
2.	Ethereum	A decentralised blockchain equipped with smart contract capabilities. Currently, in the process of shifting from PoW to PoS under Ethereum 2.0, it operates as a versatile blockchain supporting smart contracts and decentralised applications (DApps). Ether serves as the native cryptocurrency of the platform, ranking second only to Bitcoin in market capitalisation among cryptocurrencies.
3.	Dogecoin	As an open-source P2P cryptocurrency employing blockchain technology, it operates within a highly secure decentralised system for storing information. This system functions as a public ledger and is upheld by a network of computers known as nodes.
4.	Binance smart chain (BSC)	Utilising proof of stake authority (PoSA) as its consensus mechanism, this platform serves as a smart contract platform that is interoperable with the Binance exchange.
5.	PandacakeSwap (CAKE)	A decentralised cryptocurrency exchange recognised for its low fees and rapid transaction processing. It allows individuals with a cryptocurrency wallet to easily swap tokens or engage in staking, wherein users allow the exchange to utilise their tokens in return for earning rewards.

(Continued)

Table 2.2. (*Continued*)

No.	Blockchain Platforms	Application
6.	Ripple (XRP)	Employs the ripple protocol consensus algorithm (RPCA) to facilitate real-time gross settlement systems, currency exchange, and networks for remittances.
7.	Cardano	Adopts the Ouroboros PoS consensus mechanism, positioning itself as a smart contract platform with a specific focus on scalability, sustainability, and interoperability.
8.	Polkadot	With its nominated proof-of-stake (NPoS) consensus mechanism, this platform aims to facilitate the trust-free transfer of messages, various types of data, assets, and value across different blockchains. It achieves transactional scalability by distributing transactions across multiple parallel blockchains.
9.	Tezos	One of the original PoS smart contract Layer 1 platforms. It distinguishes itself as a self-upgradable, energy-efficient, security-focused, and seamlessly upgradable blockchain.
10.	Stellar	A decentralised, public blockchain that empowers developers with tools to create experiences resembling cash rather than traditional cryptocurrency. This network boasts superior speed, affordability, and energy efficiency compared to many other blockchain-based systems.
11.	Hyperledger Fabric	A framework for blockchain implementation designed as a basis for developing applications or solutions, featuring a modular architecture. This serves as a permissioned blockchain framework commonly employed in the creation of enterprise solutions, with prevalent use in sectors such as supply chain and finance.
12.	Chainlink	Leverage decentralised Oracle networks with a well-established history of high availability, reliability, and data accuracy. These services facilitate the connection of existing systems to both public and private blockchains, enabling secure cross-chain communication. Additionally, Chainlink supports developers across major blockchains by offering comprehensive documentation, hands-on tutorials, and in-depth workshops.
13.	Corda	Provides a permissioned ledger, asset modelling capabilities, and a multi-party workflow engine, all integrated into a flexible solution specifically designed for businesses, particularly those in finance and trade finance.

Source: Blockchain Platform Compiled By Authors on 30 December 2023.

Table 2.3.   Blockchain's Application in the Organisations.

Case No.	Types of Industry	Organisations' Name	Description	Source
1	Art	Artory	Artory company employed the Ethereum blockchain to provide digital certificates for artwork and other collectibles.	Pu and Lam (2023)
2	Healthcare	AmalMedik Clinic	AmalMedik Clinic employed the cHEART Hyperledger Fabric blockchain-based application to allow its patients to book appointments, access their medical records, and also allow doctors to access patients' medical records for more accurate diagnoses.	Ali (2020)
3	SCM	RoadLaunch	RoadLaunch has developed Factr, a digital wallet incorporated with the company's RoadLaunch Intelligent Digital Logistics platform which allows freight carriers, shippers, and finance partners to perform simplified transactions and make better decision-making based on digital documents and transaction history.	'Top 7 …' (2023)
4	SCM	Deloitte	Deloitte employed Hyperledger in their supply chain tracking system, to track the medical products across different stages and actors in the clinical supply chain. Besides that, Deloitte also uses blockchain and the Internet of Things for shipment tracking and management of biological samples during clinical trials.	Henry et al. (2024)
5	Manufacturing	De Beers	De Beers uses the Tracr blockchain platform to create a diamond certificate which consists of valuable information such as key attributes, and transaction history from mining, cutting, and polishing.	Pu and Lam (2023)

6.	Airline	Singapore Airlines	Singapore Airlines launched the KrisPay reward system which was developed in collaboration with KPMG Digital Village and Microsoft. KrisPay has now upgraded to Kris + which creates a comprehensive and updated lifestyle and payment system which offers customer personalisation based on location and interest.	Ledger Insights. (2020)
7.	Education	Universiti Tunku Abdul Rahman (UTAR)	UTAR issues the UTAR Blockchain Certificate (which was developed in the collaborative effort of UTAR and Silverlake Symmetry and Technology Research Sdn Bhd) to graduates to ensure a highly secured, easily verifiable, and accessible database of digital certificates to all parties concerned, especially employers and industry partners, the collaborative effort of UTAR and Silverlake Symmetry and Technology Research Sdn Bhd.	'Blockchain technology …' (2019)
8.	Nestlé	Food	Nestlé employed the IBM Food Trust blockchain platform to enable coffee buyers to trace the selected edition of Zoégas coffee back to its different origins.	Pollock (2020)
9.	Averspace	Real Estate	Averspace employed the Ethereum blockchain to create and sign digital rental contracts anywhere in the world.	Susan. (2018)
10.	Foton and Energy Web	Renewable Energy	Foton builds the renewable energy marketplace using the Energy Web Decentralised Operating System (EW-DOS), a blockchain-plus suite of middleware, toolkits, and other digital solutions which allows tracking, verification, certification, and trading the international renewable energy certificates (I-RECs).	Kurnaz (2020)

Source: Blockchain application from various sources which was compiled by authors on 30 December 2023.

20   Bernard Lim Jit Heng et al.

Table 2.4.   Blockchain's Limitations and Possible Solutions.

No.	Limitation	Possible Solutions	Source
1.	Scalability issue restricts transactions to roughly 10 transactions per second, while other regular payment systems such as VISA or Paypal can handle thousands of transactions per second.	Layer 1 solutions improved the scalability issue by adding/ modifying the fundamental blockchain attributes, while Layer 2 protocols which use unconventional approaches were able to improve the transaction processing rates, periods, and fees by minimising the use of underlying slow and costly blockchains.	Gangwal et al. (2023)
2.	Energy consumption issues such as the PoW mechanism consume massive power which indirectly impacts the environment by emitting about 90.2 metric tonnes of carbon dioxide equivalent (MtCO2e) annually.	The PoS mechanism does not require substantial computing power and extensive energy consumption.	Khan et al. (2020)
3.	Regulatory compliance issues occurred due to the decentralised nature which makes it challenging to ascertain the legal status of converting transactions in different countries. Cryptocurrencies are subject to varying rules and regulations across different jurisdictions.	A global collaboration among different countries can contribute to the development of standardised regulations, reducing legal disparities across various jurisdictions.	Saleh (2024)
4.	Privacy issues occur as transaction information will be forever visible on the blockchain. When an individual obtains anyone's address, all the past and future activities can be analysed.	Implementing the zero-knowledge proofs can strengthen confidentiality by not revealing the entire transaction history by allowing users to generate proof of membership in a custom association set.	Buterin et al. (2024)
5.	Interoperability issues obstruct users from transferring digital assets or sharing data with other users.	Cross-chain technology facilitates the exchange of information and assets by extending the functionality of blockchain systems and connecting the blockchain island.	Yuan et al. (2023)

Source: Blockchain's limitations and solution from various sources compiled by authors on 30 December 2023.

2. Utilisation of Bitcoins

The fusion of Bitcoin and blockchain technology has become a focal point of scholarly inquiry, attracting extensive research attention. Bitcoin, first conceptualised by the enigmatic figure Satoshi Nakamoto in 2008, introduces a novel decentralised digital currency. Its operational foundation lies in blockchain technology, a distributed ledger system characterised by its transparency, immutability, and cryptographic security features. Blockchain technology was first introduced in 1991 by Stuart Haber and W. Scott Stornetta in their paper 'How to Timestamp a Digital Document' (Gupta, 2017). As for Bitcoin, the blockchain technology is used to record all transactions made with the currency. Each transaction is verified by a network of computers and added to the blockchain, which is a public ledger of all Bitcoin transactions. This ensures that all transactions are secure, transparent, and tamper-proof. Numerous academic studies delve into the technical intricacies of blockchain, emphasising its role in revolutionising traditional financial transactions (Yano et al., 2020; Venkatesan et al., 2017; Weerawarna et al., 2023; Zhang et al., 2022). Scholars highlighted its capacity to enhance security, eliminate the need for intermediaries, and prevent fraudulent activities such as double-spending (Kaplan, 2021, Lee & Wei, 2016).

Besides, the decentralised nature of blockchain has spurred investigations into its broader socio-economic implications, with past researchers examining its potential to disrupt conventional financial systems and promote financial inclusion (Chen & Bellavitis, 2020; Schuetz & Venkatesh, 2020). As the cryptocurrency landscape matures, researchers have extended their focus beyond the technical aspects of Bitcoin and blockchain to explore their wider implications. Studies investigated the legal and regulatory challenges associated with the decentralised nature of Bitcoin and blockchain (Fauzi et al., 2020; Parveen & Alajmi, 2019). Furthermore, scholars analyse the transformative potential of Bitcoin and blockchain in diverse sectors, such as SCM (Min, 2019), healthcare (Wiener & Boyd, 2022), and agrifood (Tripoli & Schmidhuber, 2018).

The term 'DeFi' (decentralised finance) encompasses a wide range of financial services and products aimed at modernising traditional systems through blockchain technology. DeFi offerings cover various service categories including custodial services, payments, know your customer (KYC) and identity verification, infrastructure, exchanges and liquidity, investing, derivatives, prediction markets, marketplaces, insurance, stablecoins, and credit and liquidity (OECD, 2022). While DeFi protocols have made significant advancements in areas like crypto-assets trading, lending, and staking, challenges such as high fees and regulatory compliance persist, particularly in payment services. Stablecoins like Dai play a key role in facilitating DeFi activities, but the sustainability of high yields offered by some protocols remains uncertain (CoinMarketCap. 2022). Regulatory clarity and interoperability are critical for the widespread adoption of DeFi solutions, especially those involving fiat-backed digital tokens.

In addition to financial services, blockchain protocols enable various Web 3 applications, expanding the scope of DeFi. Leading DeFi wallet providers are exploring connections to Metaverse properties and non-fungible token (NFT) collections, representing diverse assets including financial securities and quasi-financial assets like Environmental, Social, and Governance (ESG) credits. The tokenisation of traditionally illiquid assets presents a promising frontier for DeFi, offering opportunities such as 'smart mortgages' and fractional ownership of real assets (Dentons, 2022). Regulatory considerations and market maturity will play a significant role in the evolution and adoption of DeFi solutions.

NFTs, emerging from smart contracts, require these contracts for operation (Mohanta et al., 2018). Smart contracts, as self-executing computer programmes, operate independently once created, ensuring tamper-proof digital agreements (Ali & Bagui, 2021). In contrast to traditional cryptocurrencies, NFTs represent ownership of unique assets, making them easily distinguishable (Borri et al., 2022). Each NFT is cryptographically unique, representing a specific item on the blockchain (Valeonti et al., 2021). Vitalik Buterin's vision to broaden blockchain utility beyond finance influenced the emergence of NFTs (Buterin, 2013).

NFTs and cryptocurrencies coexist within the blockchain ecosystem, with NFTs adhering to the ERC-721 standard (Wang & Nixon, 2021). These standards ensure NFTs' permanence and functionality (Ali & Bagui, 2021). In the gaming industry, NFTs have gained prominence for in-game collectables and microtransactions (Park et al., 2022). Games can be categorised as classic or blockchain based, with NFTs integrated differently (Manzoor et al., 2020). In classic games like Ubisoft's Ghost Recon Breakpoint, NFTs facilitate cosmetic changes and real-money conversion (Chen, 2020; Heilbuth, 2022). Resale transactions benefit users and developers, while blockchain ensures asset persistence and user ownership (Rehman et al., 2021).

Recent technological advancements have disrupted SCM, with blockchain emerging as a promising solution beyond its original association with Bitcoin (Marsal-Llacuna, 2018). Blockchain's distributed data structure facilitates transparent, cost-effective transactions, enhancing SCM by digitising assets and ensuring universal access to information (Laaper, 2017). This technology addresses the complexities of modern supply chains, offering benefits such as improved traceability, reduced losses, optimised costs, and enhanced compliance (Koh et al., 2019; Oberoi et al., 2024). Moreover, blockchain builds trust through transparency, mitigates risks, and strengthens business reputation (Ganeriwalla, 2018). Its implementation simplifies data exchange, promoting agility, speed, and trust within supply chain processes (Schrauf, 2022).

Traceability is crucial in modern SCM, with businesses aiming to improve transparency and efficiency (Laaper, 2017). Blockchain technology streamlines workflows by enabling P2P transactions without the need for central authority validation, enhancing efficiency, credibility, and safety (Morley, 2020). In sectors like food and pharmaceuticals, where robust storage and shipping are vital, blockchain holds significant promise. For instance, Walmart launched a blockchain ledger in collaboration with Tsinghua University, IBM, and JD to track pork in China's supply chain (Sristy, 2021). This initiative contributes to a streamlined and secure food ecosystem, reinforcing Walmart's commitment to food safety. Walmart's partnerships with companies like Nestlé, Dole, and Unilever further demonstrate its dedication to enhancing traceability (Sristy, 2021). Notably, in 2019, Walmart utilised blockchain to achieve end-to-end traceability for shrimp sourced from Andhra Pradesh, India (Sristy, 2021). By leveraging blockchain technology, data can be securely stored, creating a tamper-proof history of the supply chain accessible to all participants. This integration ensures transparency in the food supply chain, crucial in combating food adulteration globally.

The distribution of Bitcoins is characterised by a few key features. First, the issuance of new Bitcoins follows a predetermined and diminishing schedule, with a maximum supply capped at 21 million coins (Meynkhard, 2019). This scarcity is embedded in the Bitcoin protocol to mimic the scarcity of precious metals like gold, providing a deflationary aspect to the cryptocurrency. In terms of initial distribution, Bitcoins are created through a process called mining, where miners compete to solve complex mathematical problems and validate transactions on the blockchain (Altman et al., 2020). This results in the creation of new Bitcoins as a reward. Over time, the mining reward decreases through a process known as the halving, occurring approximately every four years, until the maximum supply is reached (Meynkhard, 2019).

The distribution of Bitcoins is also influenced by market dynamics, as individuals acquire Bitcoins through various means, including purchasing on exchanges, receiving them as payment, or participating in initial coin offerings (ICOs) or token sales. However, a notable aspect of Bitcoin's distribution is the existence of large wallets held by early adopters and miners, often referred to as whales (Heraguemi et al., 2021). This concentration of wealth raises concerns about the potential impact of a small number of entities on the broader Bitcoin market. While Bitcoin aims to provide a decentralised and inclusive financial system, there are ongoing discussions that centre around the need for a more equitable distribution of Bitcoins to ensure the resilience and fairness of the cryptocurrency ecosystem (Sai et al., 2021).

Amid the optimism surrounding these technologies, critical examinations also consider scalability issues, environmental concerns linked to the energy-intensive mining process, and the evolving regulatory landscape (Gulli, 2020). Bitcoin mining has faced criticism for its environmental impact due to the high energy consumption associated with proof-of-work (PoW) mining (Roeck & Drennen, 2022). The Bitcoin market is a dynamic and evolving landscape that attracts both investors and traders. Bitcoin's market capitalisation currently fluctuates in the range of $10–$20 billion, serving as a payment method for millions of individuals, and notably contributing to the expanding remittances market (Gupta, 2017). Investors view Bitcoin as a long-term store of value and a potential hedge against traditional economic uncertainties. Traders engage in activities such as buying and selling Bitcoins based on market trends, technical analysis, and news events. In addition, cryptocurrency exchanges serve as platforms for trading, offering various tools and features to facilitate transactions. The 24/7 nature of the Bitcoin market, coupled with its liquidity, attracts a diverse range of traders, including day traders, swing traders, and algorithmic traders (Hasan et al., 2022).

Nonetheless, risk management is a critical aspect of both investing and trading in the Bitcoin market due to its price volatility (Almeida & Gonçalves, 2022).

Regulatory developments, market sentiment, and macroeconomic factors can significantly influence Bitcoin prices. Additionally, technological advancements and shifts in public perception impact the market's overall dynamics (Guo, 2022). As the cryptocurrency ecosystem continues to mature, investors and traders alike navigate the challenges and opportunities presented by the Bitcoin market, contributing to its ongoing integration into the broader financial landscape.

To overcome some of these challenges, regulations have been introduced but Bitcoin regulations vary significantly across different jurisdictions, reflecting the decentralised and global nature of the cryptocurrency (Zwitter & Hazenberg, 2020). The legal status of Bitcoin varies, with some countries such as El Salvador recognising it as legal tender, while others classify it as a commodity or digital asset (Gorjón, 2021). Moreover, certain jurisdictions have imposed bans or restrictions on the use of Bitcoin (Chen & Liu, 2022). Many countries focus on consumer protection in their regulations, implementing measures to prevent fraud, ensure transparency, and secure users' funds on cryptocurrency exchanges (Howells, 2020). Anti-money laundering (AML) and KYC compliance are common requirements, aiming to prevent illicit activities such as money laundering and terrorist financing (Khisamova, 2020). Noteworthy, international cooperation has become increasingly important in the regulation of Bitcoin due to its borderless nature, with initiatives like the Financial Action Task Force (FATF) working to establish global standards and combat money laundering (Kapsis, 2023).

Besides the regulatory issues revolving around Bitcoin, the price volatility of Bitcoin is a defining characteristic of its market behaviour, marked by rapid and significant fluctuations over short periods. This volatility presents both opportunities and risks for investors and traders engaging with the cryptocurrency. One contributing factor is market speculation, where the limited supply and perceived store of value of Bitcoin led to speculative trading, amplifying market volatility (Lee et al., 2020). Market sentiment, influenced by news, social media, and overall perception, plays a substantial role in shaping Bitcoin prices (Kyriazis et al., 2023). Positive or negative developments, regulatory announcements, and macroeconomic trends can trigger swift and pronounced market responses. For instance, positive regulatory changes can boost confidence, while regulatory uncertainties or crackdowns may lead to market selloffs (Sapkota, 2022). While the price volatility of Bitcoin presents trading opportunities, it also poses various challenges for risk management.

3. Potential and Challenges of Bitcoins for Transactional Purposes

Bitcoin is the most popular cryptocurrency in the world (Abid et al., 2023). Bitcoin has some advantages over fiat money or physical currency. Bitcoin uses a direct decentralised P2P online payment system to exchange value between the buyer and the seller directly, which bypasses the need for a formal centralised financial institution such as a bank (Naheem, 2018). In contrast, fiat money can be controlled by the centralised bank of a particular country. Due to the nature of blockchain technology, Bitcoin transactions are relatively cheaper and faster as compared to conventional banking transfer services, especially international transfer services. Besides that, Bitcoin does not rely on a debt system and is less subject to inflation risk due to its limited supply of 21 million units (Wang & Hausken, 2024). However, fiat money is subjected to inflation whereby the monetary authorities can print money at any time especially during a financial crisis or virus outbreak (Abid et al., 2023).

Due to the various opportunities of Bitcoin, it continually undergoes development and improvement for transactional purposes to enhance scalability, speed, accuracy, and cost issues (Yuneline, 2019). The development of Lightning Network allows Bitcoin users to make payments outside the blockchain to reduce the congestion in the Bitcoin blockchain. This development can expedite the payment system to settle transactions faster. The Lightning Network protocol relies on segregated witness (SegWit) which is one of the Bitcoin major upgrades. SegWit changes the Bitcoin transaction format which enhances the blockchain storage efficiency to potentially store up to four times as many transactions as before and reduces the mining fees (Divakaruni & Zimmerman, 2023). Besides that, Taproot is another significant enhancement to the Bitcoin protocol. Taproot aimed to improve the platform's privacy and efficiency and execute more complex smart contracts (Reuters, 2021).

Despite the advantages and opportunities of Bitcoin, there are some challenges of Bitcoin. First, anonymity in Bitcoin is questionable as it can be misused for illegal activities. Criminals can perform transactions which conceal their real identity to avoid being tracked by the authorities (Dostov & Shust, 2014). Second, Bitcoin is highly volatile as the value is determined by market value, and it is not backed by any centralised authorities (Khan & Hakami, 2022; Yuneline, 2019). Third, Bitcoin transactions are open to speculation which is based on a zero-sum game. Investors can earn high profits or lose terribly (Yuneline, 2019). Fourth, Bitcoin transactions are irreversible; therefore, there is no safety net (Khan & Hakami, 2022).

There is a mixture of public perceptions across different countries. Based on the state of Crypto in Singapore Report 2021, a total of 76.2% of potential Singaporean investors suggested that it is a good price to enter the cryptocurrency market. The other positive comments are such as cryptocurrency has better protection, attractive promotion, higher interest yield farming, friends and family are investing, and it is a new token listing on the exchanges. In contrast, 68.6% of the non-crypto Singaporean investors cited that they lack knowledge and understanding towards cryptocurrency. The other negative comments are the volatility of the markets, the assets being too risky, and the lack of regulatory oversight and investor protection (Gemini, 2021). Besides that, Luno (2017) reported that 48.8% of Malaysian investors trusted Bitcoin and viewed Bitcoin as an investment tool, while 19.7% of Malaysian investors do not trust Bitcoin. About 51.4% of Malaysian investors think Bitcoin is the future of money. In addition, Tangwattanarat (2017) found that Thai investors have a positive attitude and perception towards cryptocurrencies. She found that majority of the Thai investors prefer market volatility and depend on less creditability sources such as positive news on social media and referral persons to make investment decisions but rarely consider reliable sources in their evaluation stage. On the other hand, As-Salafiyah et al. (2023) discovered that Indonesian investors are more sceptical towards the adoption of cryptocurrencies in Indonesia with more dominated negative sentiments over positive sentiments.

Lastly, based on the public perception above, the most important feature to attract more investors should be the security of Bitcoin. Security is the backbone of the stable and flawless working of Bitcoin.

The PoW blockchain protocol was first introduced to establish consensus in a permission-less setting and to prevent Sybil attacks through a computational cryptographic puzzle-solving using the Hash function (Lasla et al., 2022). However, PoW-powered Bitcoin mining consumes massive power with the usage emitting about 90.2 metric tonnes of carbon dioxide equivalent (MtCO2e) annually as more and more computational power is added to the mining system process (de Vries, 2021; Lasla et al., 2022). This excessive energy elevates the cost of potential attacks on the blockchain network. King and Nadal (2012) then introduced the proof-of-stake (PoS) to overcome the energy consumption issue. Within this PoS network, the reliable validators are selected based on the highest possession of coins along with the most prolonged age of possession. Therefore, PoS does not require substantial computing power because it does not have competition between miners. Besides that, PoS does not need extensive electricity consumption such as the use of dedicated hardware for the validation process; therefore, there is no additional electronic waste (Khan et al., 2020). Furthermore, PoS can easily scale up to handle large transaction volumes without affecting environmental impact (Wendl et al., 2023).

Despite that Bitcoin operates through crypto technology with full integrity and a secured decentralised chain of blocks, which provides security against computer hackers, blockchain is still alterable when members of controlling parties agree on it (Verma & Sheel, 2021). Team (2023) reported that crypto hackers have stolen the highest sum of value in 2022, which is $3.8 billion. Therefore, Bitcoin should improve its robustness of security standards to enhance the confidence of the investors.

4. The Adoption of Cryptocurrency in Southeast Asia

Crypto entrepreneurs and high-growth firms are clustering in Southeast Asia, a diversified region with a growing population and increasing affluence. Recent research by venture investment firm White Star Capital indicated that more than 600 crypto or blockchain startups are already headquartered in Southeast Asia. Venture capital funding in the region has been on the rise recently, with a lot of it going to crypto, blockchain, and Web3 firms. These sectors have raised about $1 billion so far in 2022 and are expected to exceed $1.45 billion (Liao, 2022). One of the main contributors for Southeast Asia to be targeted for cryptocurrency is due to its expanding economies. E-commerce has played a crucial role in driving growth in the region and has made a substantial impact on its digital economy, which is projected to exceed $1 trillion ($1.3 trillion) by 2030. This can be seen from the rapid urbanisation, an exponentially expanding number of new internet users and strong government support for digitalisation. In addition, a new phenomenon is set to catalyse the maturation of the region's digital economy: Web3 – known as the decentralised web – which has its foundation in blockchain technology (Issa, 2023).

Southeast Asia's thriving economy has also reaped significant benefits from blockchain technology, opening access for a more equal, transparent, and rewarding digital economy. Creators can sell their work directly to their target audience in P2P marketplaces, boosting their revenue streams and retaining a larger portion of their earnings. Blockchain also enables each transaction to be logged on the on-chain data, allowing ownership and authenticity to be verified, reducing the possibility of unauthorised reproduction of the creator's original works for profit. Countries like Thailand and Vietnam have reached massive numbers of transactions based on crypto transactions and such an upsurge in transactions due to remittance and value perseverance (Loh, 2022).

Countries like Vietnam, Indonesia, and the Philippines rank top among other countries in cryptocurrency adoption due to the potential of cryptocurrencies like Bitcoins for cheaper cost of remittances, support for investment means, and general acceptance of cryptocurrency for value preservation (Kapron, 2023a). Furthermore, because citizens in these countries tend to speculate on new assets, make additional money, and communicate digitally with others, play-to-earn games have gained significant traction contributing to the growth of cryptocurrency. While other developing countries are progressing in adopting cryptocurrencies, Zubir et al. (2020) revealed that most Malaysians continued to choose traditional online payment methods such as PayPal, credit cards, and Touch 'n Go eWallet over cryptocurrency. This resulted in the low adoption of cryptocurrency in Malaysia as compared to other countries in Southeast Asia. As for Singapore and other countries, the risks for holding money in the form of cryptocurrency remain high due to its fluctuation in value and most of them have a high preference for stable currency (Kapron, 2023b).

According to Sonksen (2021), only Singapore and the Philippines allowed cryptocurrencies to be used as legal tender, while other countries like Malaysia, Indonesia, Thailand, Vietnam, Laos, and Brunei restricted the use of cryptocurrency as legal tender for transactions. Cambodia and Myanmar remained ambiguous on their legal stance for individuals but restricted their financial institutions from trading cryptocurrencies. Furthermore, most emerging countries in Asia are planning for their own central bank digital currency (CBDC), and this may pose a significant threat to cryptocurrency as legal tender for e-commerce (Finance Magnates, 2023). The introduction of CBDCs may affect the value and demand for cryptocurrencies, causing changes in market patterns and swings in the payment method.

5. Future Direction and Trends for Bitcoins

Since its establishment, Bitcoin has experienced dynamic evolution, ranging from internal restructure protocol to external market acceptance. Some of the developments in the key area are notable and attract interest from various parties. Such development revolves around aspects that include protocol upgrading, regulation, market trends, technology advancements, as well as community and development activity. The Bitcoin protocol is the set of rules and specifications that govern the functioning network. The public ledger stores all transactions and defines how transactions are verified, confirmed, and recorded on the blockchain (Bazzanella & Gangemi, 2023; Loporchio et al., 2023). Besides, the protocol also outlines the rules for the new Bitcoin's creation through the mining process. The key components of protocol consist of blockchain, consensus mechanism, mining, halving, wallets, decentralisation, and transaction validation (Bazzanella & Gangemi, 2023; Essaid et al., 2023). The latest development is looking to strengthen this position for future usage.

Specifically, the technology advancements related to Bitcoin involve SegWit, lightning network, taproot upgrade and Schnorr signatures, CoinJoin and coin-mixing services, bulletproofs, hardware wallets, and privacy-focused wallets. The SegWit is a protocol upgrade that separates transaction signature data from transaction data, allowing for more efficient use of block space (Kedziora et al., 2023). It addresses the malleability issue and enables the implementation of further upgrades. Besides, the lightning network acts as a second-layer scaling solution designed to enable faster and cheaper transactions (Dasaklis & Malamas, 2023; Sahoo et al., 2023). It allows users to create off-chain payment channels, reducing the load on the main blockchain (Basu et al., 2023). The lightning network has been gaining traction, with ongoing developments and increased adoption.

The taproot upgrade introduces improvements to Bitcoin's scripting language, enhancing privacy and expanding smart contract capabilities (Casas et al., 2021). It makes complex transactions appear as simple ones on the blockchain, improving efficiency and reducing transaction fees (Azouvi & Vukolić, 2022; Basu et al., 2023). Along with the taproot upgrade, the Schnorr signatures offer a more efficient and compact way of representing multiple signatures in a transaction (Yang et al., 2022). This contributes to reducing the overall size of transactions and improving scalability. Privacy-focused technologies such as CoinJoin allow users to combine their transactions with others, thus making it more challenging to trace the origin and destination of Bitcoins (Chan et al., 2021). Various coin-mixing services also aim to enhance transaction privacy (Sun et al., 2022). The bulletproof cryptographic method enables reduction of the size of confidential transactions, which are transactions that hide the transaction amount (Holub & O'Connor, 2018; Li et al., 2020). By reducing the size of these transactions, bulletproofs contribute to improved scalability and lower transaction fees. Hardware wallet technology advancement enhances the security of private keys. These wallets provide a secure environment for key management, protecting users from various types of attacks (Holmes & Buchanan, 2023). Aligned with the wallets, the privacy-focused wallet was designed specifically to enhance user privacy by implementing features (Perry, 2022).

There are several platforms for Bitcoin trading, and among the prevalent platforms include Coinbase, Binance, Kraken, and Bitstamp (Table 2.5). Each of the platforms showcases its own expertise services areas; however, posts are similar in a few areas such as security measures and regulatory compliance.

Table 2.5. Comparison of Selected Trading Platforms for Bitcoin.

	Coinbase	Binance	Kraken	Bitstamp
Founded	June 2012 by Brian Armstrong and Fred Ehrsam	July 2017 by Changpeng Zhao	2011 by Jesse Powell	August 2011 by Nejc Kodrič and Damijan Merlak
Officially launched	October 2012	July 2017	September 2013	2011
Services and features	Cryptocurrency exchange, wallet services, professional trading platform, user-friendly interface, availability in numerous countries, Coinbase pro, security measures, educational resources, Coinbase card, custodial and non-custodial services, regulatory compliance, listing of cryptocurrencies	Cryptocurrency exchange, Binance futures, Binance coin, launchpad, user base and global reach, BSC, security measures, educational resources, community and social features, token listings, Binance academy, margin trading, regulatory compliance	Cryptocurrency exchange, futures trading, margin trading, staking, user base and global reach, security measures, cryptocurrency pairs, regulatory compliance, Kraken pro, OTC (over-the-counter) trading, and security audits, Kraken security labs	Cryptocurrency exchange, fiat trading pairs, bitcoin-euro trading, user base and global reach, security measures, regulatory compliance, partnerships with financial institutions, Bitstamp pro, mobile app, cryptocurrency pairs, liquidity, stability and reliability

Source: Comparison of different trading platforms for Bitcoins by authors on 30 December 2023.

The implementation of cryptocurrency is still in the infant stage, and more aspects need to be considered. For discussion purposes, the recommendation of the future implementation is to be categorised into introduction, growth, and maturity implementation stages (Fig. 2.1). The introduction stage intends to strengthen the cryptocurrency position, the growth stage establishes more integration, and maturity involves mass market adoption. However, the actual progression will depend on various factors such as technological advancements, regulatory changes, and market dynamics.

During the introduction stage, there is a need to continue the development of blockchain technology and cryptocurrencies by exploration of new consensus mechanisms and scalability solutions (Kumar et al., 2023). Besides, there is a need for global authorities to work on establishing clear regulatory frameworks for cryptocurrencies, whereby collaboration creates a conducive environment between the industry and regulators, and then the need for continuous entry of institutional investors into the cryptocurrency space to develop financial products and services related to cryptocurrencies.

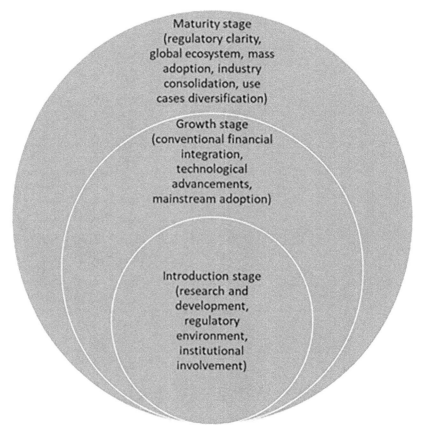

Fig. 2.1. Cryptocurrency Implementation Stages. *Source*: Own work.

The growth stage enhances the integration with conventional finance systems, which involves large-scale blockchain projects and smart contract platform development. There is a need for ongoing blockchain technology improvements to address scalability, security, and interoperability. In addition, the adoption by mainstream platforms such as businesses and merchants will eventually extend the DeFi platform usage (Banaeian et al., 2023; Wang et al., 2023).

Finally, the maturity stage embarks regulatory frameworks establishment to oversee the industry and provide legal clarity and consumer protection (Kshetri, 2023; Shaikh et al., 2024). Besides, to increased cross-border usage of cryptocurrencies, a well-established global ecosystem with interoperability between various blockchain networks are required (Azouvi & Vukolić, 2022; Basu et al., 2023). This stage encompasses wide public acceptance of cryptocurrencies, whereby integration of digital currencies is being issued by central banks together with decentralised cryptocurrencies. In addition, the B2B (Business-to-business) will signify industry maturity which leads to the consolidation of a more stable market, and the establishment of dominant players and industry standards. Finally, cryptocurrencies will be widely utilised in various sectors such as supply chain and healthcare which requires identity verification for safety purpose (Habib et al., 2022; Anane-Simon, & Atiku, 2023; Menon & Jain, 2024).

The presence of cryptocurrencies poses potential challenges to conventional financial institutions' practices and subsequently impacts the financial industry from various dimensions. First, the decentralisation and disintermediation effect. Cryptocurrencies operate on decentralised networks, whereby eliminating the need for middle platforms such as financial intermediaries (Babin et al., 2023). This could challenge the conventional financial institution model and reduce the reliance on the centralised platform concept. This potential to compete with fiat currencies subsequently challenges the central bank's regulation over currency issuance and monetary policy (Arora et al., 2023).

Besides, it expands the financial inclusion segment, which provides an opportunity for individuals without access to conventional banking services to global financial system participation (Catalini et al., 2022; Chung et al., 2023). This challenges conventional financial institutions to adapt to the changing demographics and needs. In terms of market segment, cryptocurrencies may appeal to a younger demographic segment that prefers digital assets and decentralised services. In addition, the rise of the institutional business-to-business (B2B) market with the interest in cryptocurrencies has led to challenges related to custody and secure management of digital assets (Hyland-Wood et al., 2020). Conventional financial institutions are challenged to explore ways to offer cryptocurrency custody services.

In terms of fee structure, cryptocurrencies provide fast and relatively low-cost across global border transactions (Catalini et al., 2022). As compared with conventional financial institutions with slower and more expensive global transaction processes, it typically incurs specific trading hours. However, cryptocurrency markets operate anytime and, in every way, providing users with continuous access to trading timeframes. The accessibility and availability of cryptocurrencies can attract individuals seeking more flexibility. Conventional financial institutions may need to adapt their services to meet the changing preferences of the market needs. Furthermore, with the cryptocurrencies regulatory landscape still evolving, this post-uncertainty regarding regulations can create challenges for conventional financial institutions to match that need to adapt their compliance and risk management processes (Volosovych et al., 2023).

While blockchain technology underlying cryptocurrencies is considered secure, the broader cryptocurrency ecosystem faces challenges related to hacking, fraud, and theft. Thus, conventional financial institutions need to adapt security measures to mitigate these risks. In addition to blockchain, the rise of DeFi projects built challenges conventional financial institutions' business models, such as services of lending, borrowing, and trading without conventional intermediaries' platforms. Furthermore, blockchain technology is driving innovation in the financial sector, whereby conventional financial institutions may face challenges in keeping pace with these technological advancements.

Overall, blockchain is transitioning from publicity to practical business and government solutions. Blockchain has developed rapidly from its beginnings by enabling Bitcoin to be a general-purpose technology being applied across industries. However, key challenges focused on scalability, interoperability, sustainability, and regulation were still in discussion.

First, scalability constitutes a major challenge. Bitcoin processes 3–7 transactions per second and Ethereum manages 10–15, as compared with conventional Visa's capacity of 24,000 transactions per second. Such limitations caused network congestion and prohibitive transaction fees. For example, during the 2021 NFT launch Clay Nation inundated Ethereum with over 174,000 transactions from a drop of 10,000 NFTs, spiking fees above $1,000 and severely retarding the network. In addition, the proposed scaling mechanisms remain underdeveloped. This includes an on-chain optimisation approach such as sharding pursued by Ethereum 2.0, off-chain solution state channels adopted by Perun, and Layer 2 protocols deployed on Ethereum Polygon rollup.

Second, energy sustainability concerns are rising on PoW (Proof of Work) of cryptocurrencies as statistics showed that Bitcoin mining alone consumes on average 91 TWh annually, which is equivalent to Finland's national electricity usage. In China particularly, substantial mining still employs non-renewable energy sources such as coal, which represented over 75% of Bitcoin mining preceding its 2021-year prohibition. There are debates around Bitcoin's carbon footprint; however, China still depends heavily on coal-fired power. While renewable energy-mining initiatives are expanding, critics contend that this represents a huge environmental impact concerning Bitcoin's transaction processing capabilities.

Third, interoperability concerns between discrete blockchains and ecosystems, especially enabling seamless asset and data transfers, for instance, between Ethereum and Solana, or even among Ethereum's Layer 2 platforms, is currently encumbered. Such fragmentation restricts synergies across crypto networks. Emerging solutions including Polkadot, Cosmos, and LayerZero enable greater interoperability; however, practical implementations are still limited.

Fourth, ambiguous regulations continue to plunge the crypto space into uncertainty, as illustrated by the FTX exchange 2022 downfall. FTX corporation inclined with minimal regulatory supervision, enabling questionable practices, subsequently faces collapse. Besides, India threatened outright prohibition of private cryptocurrencies in 2021 preceding its decision to tax crypto assets, thus creating an anxiety feeling among investors. Such volatile policy led to undermining confidence in cryptocurrencies. Thus, it is a call to consider global regulations that could conversely promote sustainable innovation.

In future, the approach to how the technology navigates these hurdles will determine its role in revolutionising finance, data integrity, and transparency. Thus, targeted technical and regulatory solutions concentrating on scalability, sustainability, interoperability, and governance concerns will be integral for cryptocurrencies to actualise mainstream adoption, stability, and their potentially disruptive capabilities across finance and technology.

In conclusion, the digital industry for Bitcoins is still in the developing stage and faces challenges, including regulatory scrutiny, price volatility, and scalability issues. The relationship between cryptocurrencies and conventional financial institutions is complex and evolving, with some institutions exploring methods to coexist and integrate the cryptocurrency market.

References

Abeyratne, S., & Monfared, R. (2016). Blockchain-ready manufacturing supply chain using distributed ledger. *International Journal of Research in Engineering and Technology*, *5*(9), 1–10. https://doi.org/10.15623/ijret.2016.0509001

Abid, I., Bouri, E, Galariotis, E., Guesmi, K., & Mzoughi, H. (2023). Bitcoin vs. fiat currencies: Insights from extreme dependence and risk spillover analysis with financial markets. *International Review of Financial Analysis*, *90*, 102806. https://doi.org/10.1016/j.irfa.2023.102806

Ali, M., & Bagui, S. (2021). Introduction to NFTs: The future of digital collectibles. *International Journal of Advanced Computer Science and Applications*, *12*(10), 50–56. https://doi.org/10.14569/IJACSA.2021.0121007

Ali, N. (2020). *Blockchain – Exploring its potential for Malaysian healthcare*. Asian Hospital & Healthcare Management. https://www.mhtc.org.my/2020/06/18/blockchain-exploring-its-potential-for-malaysian-healthcare/

Al-Saqaf, W., & Seidler, N. (2017). Blockchain technology for social impact: Opportunities and challenges ahead. *Journal of Cyber Policy*, *2*(3), 338–354.

Altman, E., Menasché, D., Reiffers-Masson, A., Datar, M., Dhamal, S., Touati, C., & El-Azouzi, R. (2020). Blockchain competition between miners: A game theoretic perspective. *Frontiers in Blockchain*, *2*, 26.

Anane-Simon, R., & Atiku, S. O. (2023). Future of public sector enterprises in the metaverse. In *Multidisciplinary approaches in AI, creativity, innovation, and green collaboration* (pp. 167–188). IGI Global. https://doi.org/10.4018/978-1-6684-6366-6.ch009

Arora, B., Giri, J. N., & Sachdeva, K. (2023). Barriers and potential of blockchain technology in FinTech. In *Revolutionizing financial services and markets through FinTech and blockchain* (pp. 183–206). IGI Global. https://doi.org/10.4018/978-1-6684-8624-5.ch012

As-Salafiyah, A., Huda, N., & Sakinah, S. (2023). Cryptocurrency in Indonesia: A sentiment analysis. *European Journal of Islamic Finance*, *10*(3), 1–8. https://doi.org/10.13135/2421-2172/5985

Aste, T., Tasca, P., & Di Matteo, T. (2017). Blockchain technologies: Foreseeable impact on industry and society. *IEEE Computer*, *50*(9), 18–28.

34 Bernard Lim Jit Heng et al.

Atzori, M. (2017). Blockchain technology and decentralized governance: Is the state still necessary? *Journal of Governance and Regulation, 6*(1), 45–62. https://doi.org/10.22495/jgr_v6_i1_p5

Azouvi, S., & Vukolić, M. (2022). Pikachu: Securing PoS blockchains from long-range attacks by checkpointing into bitcoin PoW using taproot. In *Consensus day 2022 – Proceedings of the 2022 ACM workshop on developments in consensus, co-located with CCS 2022* (pp. 63–65). ACM Digital Library. https://doi.org/10.1145/3560829.3563563

Babin, R., Smith, D., & Shah, H. (2023). Central bank digital currency: Advising the financial services industry. *Journal of Information Technology Teaching Cases, 13*(2), 145–153. https://doi.org/10.1177/20438869221116901

Banaeian, F. S., Imani, R. A., & Rajabzadeh, A. M. (2023). Blockchain and its derived technologies shape the future generation of digital businesses: A focus on decentralized finance and the Metaverse. *Data Science and Management, 6*(3), 183–197. https://doi.org/10.1016/j.dsm.2023.06.002

Bano, S., Sonnino, A., Al-Bassam, M., Azouvi, S., McCorry, P., Meiklejohn, S., & Danezis, G. (2018). Consensus in the age of blockchains. https://arxiv.org/pdf/1711.03936.pdf

Basu, S., Easley, D., O'Hara, M., & Sirer, E. G. (2023). StableFees: A predictable fee market for cryptocurrencies. *Management Science, 69*(11), 6508–6524. https://doi.org/10.1287/MNSC.2023.4735

Bazzanella, D., & Gangemi, A. (2023). Bitcoin: A new proof-of-work system with reduced variance. *Financial Innovation, 9*(1), Art. No. 91. https://doi.org/10.1186/s40854-023-00505-2

Blockchain technology and QR codes for UTAR certificates. (2019). University Tunku Abdul Rahman. https://news.utar.edu.my/news/2019/Nov/06/02/02.html

Borri, N., Liu, Y., & Tsyvinski, A. (2022). *The economics of non-fungible tokens.* https://doi.org/10.2139/ssrn.4052045

Buterin, V. (2013). *A next-generation smart contract & decentralized application platform.* Ethereum White Paper. https://blockchainlab.com/pdf/Ethereum_white_paper-a_next_generation_smart_contract_and_decentralized_application_platform-vitalik-buterin.pdf

Buterin, V. (2014). *A next-generation smart contract and decentralized application platform.* White Paper.

Buterin, V., Illum, J., Nadler, M., Schär, F., & Soleimani, A. (2024). Blockchain privacy and regulatory compliance: Towards a practical equilibrium. *Blockchain: Research and Applications, 5*, 100176. https://doi.org/10.1016/j.bcra.2023.100176

Casas, P., Romiti, M., Holzer, P., Mariem, S. B., Donnet, B., & Haslhofer, B. (2021). Where is the light(ning) in the taproot dawn? Unveiling the bitcoin lightning (IP) network. In *2021 IEEE 10th international conference on cloud networking* (pp. 87–90). IEEE. https://doi.org/10.1109/CloudNet53349.2021.9657121

Catalini, C., De Gortari, A., & Shah, N. (2022). Some simple economics of stablecoins. *Annual Review of Financial Economics, 14*, 117–135. https://doi.org/10.1146/annual-financial-111621-101151

Chan, W. K., Chin, J. J., & Goh, V. T. (2021). Simple and scalable blockchain with privacy. *Journal of Information Security and Applications, 58*, Art. No. 102700. https://doi.org/10.1016/j.jisa.2020.102700

Chen, C., & Liu, L. (2022). How effective is China's cryptocurrency trading ban? *Finance Research Letters, 46*, 102429.

Chen, J. T. (2020). Blockchain and the feature of game development. In J. C. Hung, N. Y. Yen, & J.-W. Chang (Eds.), *Frontier computing* (Vol. 551, pp. 1797–1802). Springer. https://doi.org/10.1007/978-981-15-3250-4_239

Chen, Y., & Bellavitis, C. (2020). Blockchain disruption and decentralized finance: The rise of decentralized business models. *Journal of Business Venturing Insights, 13*, e00151.

Chung, S., Kim, K., Lee, C. H., & Oh, W. (2023). Interdependence between online peer-to-peer lending and cryptocurrency markets and its effects on financial inclusion. *Production and Operations Management, 32*(6), 1939–1957. https://doi.org/10.1111/poms.13950

CoinMarketCap. (2022). *Top stablecoin tokens by market capitalization.* https://coinmarketcap.com

Cong, L. W., & He, Z. (2019). Blockchain disruption and smart contracts. *The Review of Financial Studies, 32*(5), 1754–1797.

Correia, M., Veronese, G. S., Neves, N. F., & Verissimo, P. (2011). Byzantine consensus in asynchronous message-passing systems: A survey. *International Journal of Critical Computer-Based Systems, 2*(2), 141–161.

Dasaklis, T. K., & Malamas, V. (2023). A review of the lightning network's evolution: Unraveling its present state and the emergence of disruptive digital business modes. *Journal of Theoretical and Applied Electronic Commerce Research, 18*(3), 1338–1364. https://doi.org/10.3390/jtaer18030068

de Leon, D. C., Stalick, A. Q., Jillepalli, A. A., Haney, M. A., & Sheldon, F. T. (2017). Blockchain: Properties and misconceptions. *Asia Pacific Journal of Innovation and Entrepreneurship, 11*(3), 286–300.

de Meijer, C. R. W. (2016), The UK and blockchain technology: A balanced approach. *Journal of Payments Strategy & Systems, 9*(4), 220–229.

Dentons. (2022, September 26). *The tokenization of real estate: An introduction to fractional real estate investment.* Dentons. https://www.dentons.com/en/insights/articles/2022/september/6/the-tokenization-of-real-estate

de Vries, A. (2019). Renewable energy will not solve bitcoin's sustainability problem. *Joule, 3*(4), 893–898. www.sciencedirect.com/science/article/abs/pii/S254243511930087X

de Vries, A. (2021). Bitcoin boom: What rising prices mean for the network's energy consumption. *Joule, 5,* 509–513.

Divakaruni, A., & Zimmerman, P. (2023). The lightning network: Turning Bitcoin into money. Federal Reserve Bank of Cleveland, Working Paper No. 22–19. https://doi.org/10.26509/frbc-wp-202219

Dostov, V., & Shust, P. (2014). Cryptocurrencies: An unconventional challenge to the AML/CFT regulators? *Journal of Financial Crime, 21*(3), 249–263. https://doi.org/10.1108/JFC-06-2013-0043

Essaid, M., Lee, C., & Ju, H. (2023). Characterizing the Bitcoin network topology with Node-Probe. *International Journal of Network Management, 33*(6), art. No. e2230. https://doi.org/10.1002/nem.2230

Fauzi, M. A., Paiman, N., & Othman, Z. (2020). Bitcoin and cryptocurrency: Challenges, opportunities and future works. *The Journal of Asian Finance, Economics and Business (JAFEB), 7*(8), 695–704.

Finance Magnates. (2023, March 8). *The rise of central bank digital currencies (CBDCs): Impacts on the crypto market.* https://www.financemagnates.com/cryptocurrency/coins/the-rise-of-central-bank-digital-currencies-cbdcs-impacts-on-the-crypto-market/

Francisco, K., & Swanson, D. (2018). The supply chain has no clothes: Technology adoption of blockchain for supply chain transparency. *Logistics, 2*(1), 2. https://doi.org/10.3390/logistics2010002

Ganeriwalla, A. C. (2018). *Does your supply chain need a blockchain?* Boston Consulting Group. https://www.bcg.com/publications/2018/does-your-supply-chain-need-blockchain

Gangwal, A., Gangavalli, H. R., & Thirupathi, A., (2023). A survey of Layer-two blockchain protocols. *Journal of Network and Computer Applications, 209,* 103539. https://doi.org/10.1016/j.jnca.2022.103539

Gemini. (2021). *The state of crypto in Singapore: An independent study to find out what people think about cryptocurrency.* Retrieved January 4, 2024, from https://www.gemini.com/gemini-2021-state-of-crypto-sg.pdf

36   Bernard Lim Jit Heng et al.

Grewal, D., Motyka, S., & Levy, M. (2018). The evolution and future of retailing and retailing education. *Journal of Marketing Education, 40*(1), 85–93.

Gulli, A. (2020). (Un) sustainability of Bitcoin mining. *Rutgers Computer and Technology Law Journal, 46*, 95.

Guo, Z. Y. (2022). Risk management of Bitcoin futures with GARCH models. *Finance Research Letters, 45*, 102197.

Gupta, V. (2017). *A brief history of blockchain.* https://hbr.org/2017/02/a-brief-history-of-blockchain

Gurtu, A., & Johny, J. (2019). The potential of blockchain technology in supply chain management: A literature review. *International Journal of Physical Distribution & Logistics Management, 49*(9), 881–900. https://doi.org/10.1108/IJPDLM-11-2018-0371

Habib, G., Sharma, S., Ibrahim, S., Ahmad, I., Qureshi, S., & Ishfaq, M. (2022). Blockchain technology: Benefits, challenges, applications, and integration of blockchain technology with cloud computing. *Future Internet, 14*(11), art. No. 341. https://doi.org/10.3390/fi14110341

Hasan, M., Naeem, M. A., Arif, M., Shahzad, S. J. H., & Vo, X. V. (2022). Liquidity connectedness in the cryptocurrency market. *Financial innovation, 8*, 1–25.

Heilbuth, H. (2022, May 19). *NFTs explained, their role in the future of gaming, and why people hate them.* Gamesradar. https://www.gamesradar.com/nft-explained/

Henry, W., Chen, E., Kathawate, R., & Coulter, J. (2024). *Using blockchain to drive supply chain transparency.* Deloitte. https://www2.deloitte.com/us/en/pages/operations/articles/blockchain-supply-chain-innovation.html

Heraguemi, K., Kadri, H., & Zabi, A. (2021). Whale optimization algorithm for solving association rule mining issues. *International Journal of Computing and Digital Systems, 10*(1), 333–342.

Holmes, A., & Buchanan, W. J. (2023). A framework for live host-based Bitcoin wallet forensics and triage. *Forensic Science International: Digital Investigation, 44*, art. No. 301486. https://doi.org/10.1016/j.fsidi.2022.301486

Holub, A., & O'Connor, J. (2018). COINHOARDER: Tracking a Ukrainian Bitcoin phishing ring DNS style. *eCrime Researchers Summit, eCrime*, 1–5. https://doi.org/10.1109/ECRIME.2018.8376207

Howells, G. (2020). Protecting consumer protection values in the fourth industrial revolution. Journal of *Consumer Policy, 43*(1), 145–175.

Hutt, R. (2018). *All you need to know about blockchain, explained simply.* World Economic Forum. https://www.weforum.org/agenda/2016/06/blockchain-explained-simply/

Hyland-Wood, D., Robinson, P., Johnson, S., Hare, C., Henderson, B., Lewicki, C., & Saltini, R. (2020). Blockchain properties for near-planetary, interplanetary, and metaplanetary space domains. *Journal of Aerospace Information Systems, 17*(10), 554 – 561. https://doi.org/10.2514/1.I010833

International Energy Agency (IEA). (2019). *Commentary: Bitcoin energy use – Mined the gap.* International Energy Agency. www.iea.org/newsroom/news/2019/july/bitcoin-energy-use-mined-the-gap.html

Issa, O. A. (2023, August 29). *Unleashing Southeast Asia's true Web3 potential with cloud-based blockchain technology.* The Edge Singapore. https://www.theedgesingapore.com/digitaledge/focus/unleashing-southeast-asias-true-web3-potential-cloud-based-blockchain-technology

Jayachandran, P. (2017). *The difference between public and private blockchain.* Retrieved February 5, 2018, from https://www.ibm.com/blogs/blockchain/2017/05/the-difference-between-public-and-private-blockchain/

Jirgensons, M., & Kapenieks, J. (2018). Blockchain and the future of digital learning credential assessment and management. *Journal of Teacher Education for Sustainability, 20*(1), 145–156.

Blockchain and Bitcoins   37

Jones, B. (2017, December 18). *The hidden cost of Bitcoin? It may be making you money, but it's hurting our planet*. Futurism, Earth and Energy. https://futurism.com/hidden-cost-bitcoin-our-environment

Kaplan, A. (2021). Cryptocurrency and corruption: Auditing with blockchain. In T. Aksoy, & U. Hacioglu (Ed.), *Auditing ecosystem and strategic accounting in the digital era: Global approaches and new opportunities* (pp. 325–338). Springer International Publishing.

Kapron, Z. (2023a, May 14). *Why emerging Southeast Asia is crypto friendly*. Forbes. https://www.forbes.com/sites/digital-assets/2023/05/14/why-emerging-southeast-asia-is-crypto-friendly/?sh=134f608f545b

Kapron, Z. (2023b, Dec 14). *Stablecoins gain traction in Asia, but challenges remain*. Forbes. https://www.forbes.com/sites/digital-assets/2023/12/14/stablecoins-gain-traction-in-asia-but-challenges-remain/?sh=65fa5f5d5c12

Kapsis, I. (2023). Crypto-assets and criminality: A critical review focusing on money laundering and terrorism financing. In D. Jasinski, A. Phillips, E. Johnston (Eds.), *Organised Crime, Financial Crime, and Criminal Justice* (pp. 122–141). Routledge.

Kedziora, M., Pieprzka, D., Jozwiak, I., Liu, Y., & Song, H. (2023). Analysis of segregated witness implementation for increasing efficiency and security of the Bitcoin crypto-currency. *Journal of Information and Telecommunication, 7*(1), 44–55. https://doi.org/10.1080/24751839.2022.2122301

Khan, A. G., Zahid, A. H., Hussain, M., Farooq, M., Riaz, U., & Alam, T. M. (2019). A journey of WEB and Blockchain towards Industry 4.0: An Overview. In *2019 International conference on innovative computing (ICIC)*, Lahore, Pakistan (pp. 1–7). https://doi.org/10.1109/ICIC48496.2019.8966700

Khan, F. A., Asif, M., Ahmad, A., Alharbi, M., & Aljuaid, H. (2020). Blockchain technology, improvement suggestions, security challenges on the smart grid and its application in healthcare for sustainable development. *Sustainable Cities and Society, 55*, 102018. https://doi.org/10.1016/j.scs.2020.102018

Khan, R., & Hakami, T. A. (2022). Cryptocurrency: Usability perspective versus volatility threat. *Journal of Money and Business, 2*(1), 16–28. https://doi.org/10.1108/JMB-11-2021-0051

Khisamova, Z. I. (2020). Concept of digital currencies of central banks: Main risks in observing the requirements of aml ('anti-money laundering') and KYC ('know your client'). *Actual Problems of Economics and Law, 508*, 508–515.

King, S., & Nadal, S. (2012). Ppcoin: Peer-to-peer crypto-currency with proof-of-stake. *Self-published Paper, 19*(1).

Koetsier, J. (2017). *Blockchain beyond bitcoin: How blockchain will transform business in 3 to 5 years*. www.inc.com/john-koetsier/how-blockchain-will-transform-business-in-3-to-5-years.html

Koh, L., Orzes, G., & Jia, F. (2019). The fourth industrial revolution (Industry 4.0): Technologies disruption on operations and supply chain management. *International Journal of Operations & Production Management, 39*(6/7/8), 817–828. https://doi.org/10.1108/IJOPM-08-2019-788

Kshetri, N. (2018). Blockchain's roles in meeting key supply chain management objectives. *International Journal of Information Management, 39*, 80–89. https://doi.org/10.1016/j.ijinfomgt.2017.12.005

Kshetri, N. (2023). The nature and sources of international variation in formal institutions related to initial coin offerings: Preliminary findings and a research agenda. *Financial Innovation, 9*(1), Art. No. 9. https://doi.org/10.1186/s40854-022-00405-x

Kumar, P., Özen, E., & Vurur S. (2023). Adoption of blockchain technology in the financial sector. *Contemporary Studies of Risks in Emerging Technology, Part A*, 271–288. https://doi.org/10.1108/978-1-80455-562-020231018

Kurnaz, E. (2020). *Foton and Energy Web launched a blockchain-based I-REC marketplace in Turkey*. Energy Web. https://medium.com/energy-web-insights/foton-and-energy-web-launch-blockchain-based-i-rec-marketplace-in-turkey-e2847db835f

Kyriazis, N., Papadamou, S., Tzeremes, P., & Corbet, S. (2023). The differential influence of social media sentiment on cryptocurrency returns and volatility during COVID-19. *The Quarterly Review of Economics and Finance*, *89*, 307–317.

Laaper, S. A. (2017). *Using blockchain to drive supply chain transparency: Future trends in the supply chain*. Deloitte. https://www2.deloitte.com/us/en/pages/operations/articles/blockchain-supply-chain-innovation.html

Lasla, N., Al-Sahan, L., Abdallah, M., & Younis, M. (2022). Green-PoW: An energy-efficient blockchain Proof-of-Work consensus algorithm. *Computer Networks*, *214*, 109118.

Ledger Insights. (2020). *Singapore Airlines extends its blockchain-based reward digital wallet*. Ledger Insights. https://www.ledgerinsights.com/singapore-airlines-extends-its-blockchain-based-reward-digital-wallet/

Lee, A. D., Li, M., & Zheng, H. (2020). Bitcoin: Speculative asset or innovative technology? *Journal of International Financial Markets, Institutions and Money*, *67*, 101209.

Lee, V., & Wei, H. (2016, June). Exploratory simulation models for fraudulent detection in the Bitcoin system. In W. Xie, C. Hu, & W. Chen (Eds.), *2016 IEEE 11th conference on industrial electronics and applications (ICIEA)* (pp. 1972–1977). IEEE.

Li, W., Andreina, S., Bohli, J.-M., & Karame, G. (2017). Securing proof-of-stake blockchain protocols. In: *Data privacy management, cryptocurrencies and blockchain technology: ESORICS, 2017 international workshops, DPM, 2017 and CBT 2017* (297–315). September 14–15, 2017. Springer, Cham.

Li, X., Xu, C., & Zhao, Q. (2020). Shellproof: More efficient zero-knowledge proofs for confidential transactions in the blockchain. In *IEEE international conference on blockchain and cryptocurrency* (Art. No. 9169437). https://doi.org/10.1109/ICBC48266.2020.9169437

Liao, R. (2022, June 14). *In Southeast Asia, a booming crypto scene*. TechCrunch. https://techcrunch.com/2022/06/14/crypto-southast-asia-2022/

Liebenau, J., & Elaluf-Calderwood, S. (2016). *Blockchain innovation beyond bitcoin and banking*. https://ssrn.com/abstract=2749890

Loh, D. (2022, September 21). *Thailand and Vietnam emerge as ASEAN crypto trading hot spots*. Nikkei Asia. https://asia.nikkei.com/Spotlight/Cryptocurrencies/Thailand-and-Vietnam-emerge-as-ASEAN-crypto-trading-hot-spots

Loporchio, M., Bernasconi, A., Di Francesco Maesa, D., & Ricci L. (2023). Is Bitcoin gathering dust? An analysis of low-amount Bitcoin transactions. *Applied Network Science*, *8*(1), Art. No. 34. https://doi.org/10.1007/s41109-023-00557-4

Luno, T. (2017). *How Malaysians use Bitcoin*. Luno. https://discover.luno.com/malaysians-use-bitcoin/

Manzoor, A., Samarin, M., Mason, D., & Ylianttila, M. (2020). Scavenger hunt: Utilization of blockchain and IoT for a location-based game. *IEEE Access*, *8*, 204863–204879. https://doi.org/10.1109/ACCESS.2020.3037182

Marsal-Llacuna, M. L. (2018). Future living framework: Is blockchain the next enabling network? *Technological Forecasting and Social Change*, *128*, 226–234. https://doi.org/10.1016/j.techfore.2017.12.005

Menon, S., & Jain, K. (2024). Blockchain technology for transparency in agri-food supply chain: Use cases, limitations, and future directions. *IEEE Transactions on Engineering Management*, *71*, 106–120. https://doi.org/10.1109/TEM.2021.3110903

Meynkhard, A. (2019). Fair market value of bitcoin: Halving effect. *Investment Management & Financial Innovations*, *16*(4), 72.

Min, H. (2019). Blockchain technology for enhancing supply chain resilience. *Business Horizons*, *62*(1), 35–45.

Mishra, D., Gunasekaran, A., Papadopoulos, T., & Childe, S. J. (2018). Big data and supply chain management: A review and bibliometric analysis. *Annals of Operations Research, 270*(1), 313–336. https://doi.org/10.1007/s10479-016-2236-y

Mohanta, B. K., Panda, S. S. & Jena, D. (2018). An overview of smart contract and use cases in Blockchain Technology. In *Proceeding of the 2018 9th International Conference on Computing, Communication and Networking Technologies (ICCCNT)* (pp. 1–4). IEEE, Bengaluru, India. doi: 10.1109/ICCCNT.2018.8494045.

Moosavi, J., Naeni., L. M., Fathollahi-Fard, A. M., & Fiore, U. (2021). Blockchain in supply chain management: A review, bibliometric, and network analysis. *Environmental Science and Pollution Research*. https://doi.org/10.1007/s11356-021-13094-3

Morley, M. (2020, February 12). *Top 5 use cases of Blockchain in the supply chain in 2021*. Open Text. https://blogs.opentext.com/blockchain-in-the-supply-chain/

Naheem, M. A. (2018). Regulating virtual currencies – The challenges of applying fiat currency laws to digital technology services. *Journal of Financial Crime, 25*(2), 562–575. https://doi.org/10.1108/JFC-08-2016-0055

Nakamoto, S. (2008). *Bitcoin: A peer-to-peer electronic cash system*. www.bitcoin.org/bitcoin.pdf

Nakamoto, S. (2019). *Bitcoin: A peer-to-peer electronic cash system*. Manubot.

Oberoi, S., Arora, S., Verma, B., & Roy, K. K. (2024). What do we know about artificial intelligence and blockchain technology integration in the healthcare industry? In B. Verma, B. Singla, & A. Mittal (Eds.), *Driving decentralization and disruption with digital technologies* (pp. 124–138). IGI Global.

OECD. (2022, January 19). *Why decentralised finance (DeFi) matters and the policy implications*. OECD. https://www.oecd.org/daf/fin/financial-markets/Why-Decentralised-Finance-DeFi-Matters-and-the-Policy-Implications.pdf

Omar, I. A., Jayaraman, R., Salah, K., Yaqoob, I., & Ellahham, S. (2021). Applications of blockchain technology in clinical trials: Review and open challenges. *Arabian Journal for Science and Engineering, 46*(4), 3001–3015.

Park, A., Kietzmann, J., Pitt, L., & Dabirian, A. (2022). The evolution of nonfungible tokens: Complexity and novelty of NFT use-cases. *IT Professional, 24*(1), 9–14. https://doi.org/10.1109/MITP.2021.3136055

Parveen, R., & Alajmi, A. (2019). An overview of Bitcoin's legal and technical challenges. *Journal of Legal, Ethical and Regulatory Issues, 22*, 1.

Paul, P., Aithal, P. S., Saavedra, R., & Ghosh, S. (2021). Blockchain technology and its types – A short review. *International Journal of Applied Science and Engineering (IJASE), 9*(2), 189–200. https://ssrn.com/abstract=4050933

Perry, T. S. (2022). A bitcoin wallet for the masses: Square simplified credit-card transactions. Now it wants to build cryptocurrency hardware. *IEEE Spectrum, 59*(1), 42–43. https://doi.org/10.1109/MSPEC.2022.9676357

Pollock, D. (2020). *Nestlé expands use of IBM food trust blockchain to its Zoégas coffee brand*. Forbes. https://www.forbes.com/sites/darrynpollock/2020/04/15/nestl-expands-use-of-ibm-food-trust-blockchain-to-its-zogas-coffee-brand/?sh=434d48a41684

Pournader, M., Shi, Y., Seuring, S., & Koh, S. L. (2020). Blockchain applications in supply chains, transport and logistics: A systematic review of the literature. *International Journal of Production Research, 58*(7), 2063–2081.

Pu, S., & Lam, J. S. L. (2023). The benefits of blockchain for digital certificates: A multiple case study analysis. *Technology in Society, 72*, 102176. https://doi.org/10.1016/j.techsoc.2022.102176

Radanović, I., & Likić, R. (2018). Opportunities for the use of blockchain technology in medicine. *Applied Health Economics and Health Policy, 16*(5), 583–590.

Rahman, A., Jahidul, I., Khan, S,I., Kabir, S., Pritom, A. I., & Karim, R. (2020). BlockSDotCloud: Enhancing security of cloud storage through blockchain-based SDN in IoT network. In *2020 2nd International conference on sustainable technologies for*

40 Bernard Lim Jit Heng et al.

Industry 4.0 (STI) (pp. 1–6). https://www.researchgate.net/publication/350935758_Block-SDoTCloud_Enhancing_Security_of_Cloud_Storage_through_Blockchain-based_SDN_in_IoT_Network

Rehman, W., Zainab, H. E., Imran, J., & Bawany, N. Z. (2021). NFTs: Applications and challenges. In *Proceedings of the 22nd international Arab conference on information technology (ACIT)*. https://doi.org/10.1109/ACIT53391.2021.9677260 https://www.researchgate.net/publication/357900561_NFTs_Applications_and_Challenges

Reuters, G. C. (2021, November 16). Bitcoin goes through a major upgrade. Here is what it means. *The Economic Times.* https://economictimes.indiatimes.com/jobs/c-suite/navigating-excellence-

Roeck, M., & Drennen, T. (2022). Life cycle assessment of behind-the-meter Bitcoin mining at US power plant. The *International Journal of Life Cycle Assessment, 27*(3), 355–365.

Saberi, S., Kouhizadeh, M., Sarkis, J., & Shen, L. (2019). Blockchain technology and its relationships to sustainable supply chain management. *International Journal of Production Research, 57*(7), 2117–2135. https://doi.org/10.1080/00207543.2018.1533261

Sahoo, S. S., Hosmane, M. M., & Chaurasiya, V. K. (2023). A secure payment channel rebalancing model for layer-2 blockchain. *Internet of Things (Netherlands), 22*, Art. No. 100822. https://doi.org/10.1016/j.iot.2023.100822

Sai, A. R., Buckley, J., & Le Gear, A. (2021). Characterizing wealth inequality in cryptocurrencies. *Frontiers in Blockchain, 4*, 38.

Sajana, P., Sindhu, M., & Sethumadhavan, M. (2018). On blockchain applications: Hyperledger fabric and Ethereum. *International Journal of Pure and Applied Mathematics, 118*(18), 2965–2970.

Saleh, A. M. S. (2024). Blockchain for secure and decentralized artificial intelligence in cybersecurity: A comprehensive review. *Blockchain: Research and Applications.* https://doi.org/10.1016/j.bcra.2024.100193

Sapkota, N. (2022). News-based sentiment and bitcoin volatility. *International Review of Financial Analysis, 82*, 102183.

Schrauf, S. (2022). *Blockchain in the supply chain: How to exploit the potential of blockchain technology.* PWC. https://www.pwc.de/en/strategy-organisation-processes-systems/blockchain-in-the-supply-chain.html

Schuetz, S., & Venkatesh, V. (2020). Blockchain, adoption, and financial inclusion in India: Research opportunities. *International Journal of Information Management, 52*, 101936.

Scott, B., Loonam, J., & Kumar, V. (2017). Exploring the rise of blockchain technology: Towards distributed collaborative organizations. *Strategic Change, 26*(5), 423–428.

Shaikh, M. Z., Dixit, N., Manjunatha, D., Chaudhary, A., & Khubalkar, D. (2024). Applications of blockchain technology and cryptocurrencies: Current practice and future trends. *International Journal of Intelligent Systems and Applications in Engineering, 12*(4s), 30–40. https://ijisae.org/index.php/IJISAE/article/view/3749

Shiva Sai Kumar, B. (2020). *WTF is Hashing in Blockchains?* Hackernoon. Retrieved from https://hackernoon.com/wtf-is-hashing-in-blockchains-z6f836i1

Sonksen, C. (2021). Cryptocurrency regulations in ASEAN, East Asia, & America: To regulate or not to regulate. *Washington University Global Studies Law Review, 20*(1), 171–200.

Sristy, A. (2021). *Blockchain in the food supply chain – What does the future look like?* Walmart Inc. https://tech.walmart.com/content/walmart-global-tech/en_us/news/articles/blockchain-in-the-food-supply-chain.html

Sun, X., Yang, T., & Hu, B. (2022). Bitcoin coin mixing detection method with a high recall. *Applied Intelligence, 52*(1), 780–793. https://doi.org/10.1007/s10489-021-02453-9

Susan. (2018). *Averspace and frasers property Singapore launches project to digitalize leasing transactions.* Techsauce. https://techsauce.co/news/averspace-and-frasers-property-singapore-launches-project-to-digitalize-leasing-transactions

Tangwattanarat, N. (2017). *A study of the perception of Thai cryptocurrency investors towards the digital currency market.* Master's thesis, Thammasat University. https://ethesisarchive.library.tu.ac.th/thesis/2017/TU_2017_5902040251_8421_6783.pdf

Tapscott, D. (2017). How will blockchain change banking? How won't it? *Huffington Post.* www.huffingtonpost.com/don-tapscott/how-will-blockchain-chang_b_9998348.html

Team, C. (2023, February 1). *2022 Biggest year ever for crypto hacking with $3.8 billion stolen, primarily from defi protocols and by north Korea-linked attackers.* Chainalysis. https://www.chainalysis.com/blog/2022-biggest-year-ever-for-crypto-hacking/

Top 7 leading companies in the blockchain supply chain industry. (2023). Emergenresearch. https://www.emergenresearch.com/blog/top-7-leading-companies-in-the-blockchain-supply-chain-industry

Trautman, L. J. (2016). *Is disruptive blockchain technology the future of financial services? The consumer finance law quarterly report.* https://ssrn.com/abstract=2786186

Tripoli, M., & Schmidhuber, J. (2018). *Emerging opportunities for the application of blockchain in the agri-food industry.* Food and Agriculture Organization of the United Nations and International Centre for Trade and Sustainable Development (ICTSD).

Valeonti, F., Bikakis, A., Terras, M., Speed, C., Hudson-Smith, A., & Chalkias, K. (2021). Crypto collectibles, museum funding and OpenGLAM: Challenges, opportunities and the potential of non-fungible tokens (NFTs). *Applied Sciences, 11*(21), 9931. https://doi.org/10.3390/app11219931

Venkatesan, S., Srinivasan, S., & Kumar, S. S. (2017). Blockchain technology in finance. *IEEE Xplore, 1,* 1–6.

Verma, B., Singla, B., & Mittal, A. (Eds.). (2024). *Digital technologies, ethics, and decentralization in the digital era.* IGI Global.

Verma, S., & Sheel, A. (2021). Blockchain for government organizations: Past, present and future. *Journal of Global Operations and Strategic Sourcing, 15*(3), 406–430. https://doi.org/10.1108/JGOSS-08-2021-0063

Viriyasitavata, W., & Hoonsoponb, D. (2019). Blockchain characteristics and consensus in modern business processes. *Journal of Industrial Information Integration, 13,* 32–39.

Volosovych, S., Sholoiko, A., & Shevchenko, L. (2023). Cryptocurrency market transformation during the pandemic covid-19. *Financial and Credit Activity: Problems of Theory and Practice, 1*(48), 114–126. https://doi.org/10.55643/fcaptp.1.48.2023.3949

Vujicic, D., Jagodic, D., & Randic, S. (2018). Blockchain technology, bitcoin, and Ethereum: A brief overview. In *2018 17th International Symposium INFOTEH-JAHORINA (INFOTEH)* (pp. 1–6). https://doi.org/10.1109/INFOTEH.2018.8345547

Wang, G., & Hausken, K. (2024). Hard money and fiat money in an inflationary world. *Research in International Business and Finance, 67,* 102115. https://doi.org/10.1016/j.ribaf.2023.102115

Wang, G., & Nixon, M. (2021). Tokenization on blockchain. In *Proceedings of the 14th IEEE/ACM international conference on utility and cloud computing companion* (pp. 1–9). https://doi.org/10.1145/3492323.3495577 https://www.researchgate.net/publication/356406963_SoK_Tokenization_on_Blockchain

Wang, L., Cheng, H., Zheng, Z., Yang, A., & Xu, M. (2023). Temporal transaction information-aware Ponzi scheme detection for Ethereum smart contracts. *Engineering Applications of Artificial Intelligence, 126,* Art. No. 107022. https://doi.org/10.1016/j.engappai.2023.107022

Weerawarna, R., Miah, S. J., & Shao, X. (2023). Emerging advances of blockchain technology in finance: A content analysis. *Personal and Ubiquitous Computing, 27,* 1495–1508.

WEF. (2015). Deep shift: Technology tipping points and societal impact. www.weforum.org/reports/deep-shift-technology-tipping-points-and-societal-impact/

Wendl, M., Doan, M. H., & Sassen, R. (2023). The environmental impact of cryptocurrencies using proof of work and proof of stake consensus algorithms: A systematic review.

Journal of Environmental Management, 326, 116530. https://doi.org/10.1016/j.jenvman.2022.116530

White, G. R. T. (2017). Future applications of blockchain in business and management: A Delphi study. *Strategic Change, 26*(5), 439–451.

Wiener, J. G., & Boyd, C. J. (2022). Cryptocurrency in surgery – Current adoption and future direction. *The American Journal of Surgery, 223*(4), 825–826.

Yang, X. M., Li, X., Wu, H. Q., & Zhao, K. Y. (2017). The application model and challenges of blockchain technology in education. *Modern Distance Education Research, 2,* 34–45.

Yano, M., Dai, C., Masuda, K. and Kishimoto, Y (2020). *Blockchain and cryptocurrency – building a high quality marketplace for crypto data.* Springer. https://link.springer.com/book/10.1007/978-981-15-3376-1

Yang, X., Liu, M., Au, M. H., Luo, X., & Ye, Q. (2022). Efficient verifiably encrypted ECDSA-like signatures and their applications. *IEEE Transactions on Information Forensics and Security, 17,* 1573–1582. https://doi.org/10.1109/TIFS.2022.3165978

Yeow, K., Gani, A., Ahmad, R. W., Rodrigues, J. J. P. C., & Ko, K. (2018). Decentralized consensus for edge-centric internet of things: A review, taxonomy, and research issues. *IEEE Access, 6,* 1513–1524.

Yermack, D. (2017). Corporate governance and blockchains. *Review of Finance, 21*(1), 7–31. https://doi.org/10.1093/rof/rfw074

Yuan, H., Fei, S., & Yan, Z. (2023). Technologies of blockchain interoperability: A survey. *Digital Communications and Networks.* https://doi.org/10.1016/j.dcan.2023.07.008

Yuneline, M. H. (2019). Analysis of cryptocurrency's characteristics in four perspectives. *Journal of Asian Business and Economic Studies, 26*(2), 206–219. https://doi.org/10.1108/JABES-12-2018-0107

Zaidan, B. B., Haiqi, A., Zaidan, A. A., Abdulnabi, M., Kiah, M. M., & Muzamel, H. (2015). A security framework for nationwide health information exchange based on telehealth strategy. *Journal of Medical Systems, 39*(5), 51.

Zhang, Y., Li, Y., & Wang, Y. (2022). Blockchain and digital finance. *Financial Innovation, 8*(1), 1–10.

Zubir, A. S., Awi, N. A., Ali, A., Mokhlis, S., & Sulong, F. (2020). Doing business using cryptocurrency in Malaysia. *International Journal of Management and Humanities (IJMH), 4*(9). https://doi.org/10.35940/ijmh.I0899.054920

Zwitter, A., & Hazenberg, J. (2020). Decentralized network governance: Blockchain technology and the future of regulation. *Frontiers in Blockchain, 3,* 12.

Chapter 3

Guardians of Trust: Fortifying Payment Gateway Security for Digital Prosperity

Choon Sen Seah[a], Yin Xia Loh[b], Mohammad Falahat[c], Wing Son Loh[d] and Ahmad Najmi Amerhaider Nuar[a]

[a]*Faculty of Computing, Universiti Teknologi Malaysia, Johor, Malaysia*
[b]*Faculty of Engineering and Information Technology, Southern University College, Johor, Malaysia*
[c]*School of Marketing and Management, Asia Pacific University of Technology and Innovation (APU), Malaysia*
[d]*Lee Kong Chian Faculty of Engineering and Science, Universiti Tunku Abdul Rahman, Selangor, Malaysia*

Abstract

The exponential rise of digital payments has underscored the critical importance of digital payment security, particularly in payment gateway systems. This chapter delves into the vulnerabilities within these systems and proposes a comprehensive security enhancement framework to address them. Recent security breaches, such as those at SONY and Ontario's birth registry, have emphasised the urgent need for improved protective measures. The proposed framework integrates advanced technologies like data encryption, next-generation firewalls (NGFWs), unified threat management (UTM), network traffic analysis, and multi-factor authentication (MFA). It aims not only to defend against current cyber threats but also to remain adaptable to future vulnerabilities, ensuring the integrity, confidentiality, and availability of transactional data. Moreover, aligning with regulatory standards such as the Payment Card Industry Data Security Standard (PCI DSS) and the General Data Protection Regulation (GDPR) is crucial for building trust and ensuring security in the digital transaction ecosystem. This chapter also highlights the importance of balancing security measures with user experience and advocates for

---

Augmenting Retail Reality: Blockchain, AR, VR, and the Internet of Things, Part A, 43–58
Copyright © 2025 by Choon Sen Seah, Yin Xia Loh, Mohammad Falahat, Wing Son Loh and Ahmad Najmi Amerhaider Nuar
Published under exclusive licence by Emerald Publishing Limited
doi:10.1108/978-1-83608-634-520241006

user education and user-centric security solutions. Emerging technologies like artificial intelligence (AI) and blockchain are proposed for real-time fraud detection and maintaining immutable transaction records, offering innovative solutions to contemporary security challenges. Empirical analysis supports the efficacy of the proposed framework, showing improvements in data loss prevention, user satisfaction, and fraud mitigation. This framework, termed 'Guardians of Trust', represents a paradigm shift in payment gateway security, providing a scalable and forward-looking model that balances robust security protocols with user experience and compliance considerations. This chapter contributes significantly to the academic discourse on digital payment security.

Keywords: Cybersecurity; security framework; payment security; security standard; emerging technologies; payment gateway system; digital payment threats

Introduction

Digital payments have experienced exponential growth in recent years, revolutionising the way we conduct transactions (Choong et al., 2023). Digital payments, characterised by their speed and convenience, have become a fundamental element of commerce, profoundly transforming the transactional landscape (Semerikova, 2020). In this dynamic environment, payment gateways stand as crucial intermediaries, safeguarding the flow of funds with sophisticated security measures (Barbereau & Bodó, 2023). Yet, recent breaches have shed light on the vulnerabilities inherent in these systems, raising legitimate concerns regarding the confidentiality and integrity of sensitive financial data (Osita et al., 2022). This growth has also brought about significant security challenges for payment gateway systems. The increasing number of incidents involving data breaches highlights the vulnerabilities inherent in current payment gateways, raising concerns about unauthorised access and fraudulent activities.

Case studies from the past year reveal a spectrum of security incidents that have rattled consumer confidence. Notable among these was the breach at SONY, where a ransomware group exploited system vulnerabilities to extract sensitive data, including build logs and Java files (Saleem & Naveed, 2020). Similarly, Ontario's birth registry suffered a data breach due to a well-known vulnerability in the MOVEit file transfer tool, compromising the data of millions (Borden, 2023). The magnitude of these breaches indicates a critical need for enhanced security protocols and continuous vigilance in digital payment systems (Low et al., 2022).

In the face of such challenges, businesses and payment gateways have been prompted to adopt multifaceted security measures. The Secure Sockets Layer and Transport Layer Security (SSL/TLS) encryption protocols have become the bedrock of data transmission security, alongside tokenisation techniques that render stolen payment information useless to fraudsters (Tyagi, 2023). Furthermore, the integration of MFA, employing a combination of knowledge, possession, and inherence-based validation, has fortified defences against unauthorised access.

The urgency for such enhanced security is underscored by vulnerabilities in emerging payment technologies and platforms. Weak server-side controls, insufficient customer education on fraud tactics, and unsecured remote access in the wake of a shift towards remote work are some of the factors exacerbating the risk of cyberattacks (Loh et al., 2023a). Indeed, PwC India highlights the diversity of threats ranging from identity theft and phishing to more sophisticated web skimming and social engineering tactics that capitalise on human error and trust (George et al., 2024).

In response to the evolving threat landscape, this chapter aims to address a pivotal research question: 'How can payment gateway systems be substantially reinforced to instil user confidence and effectively thwart unauthorised access and fraudulent activities?' To address this, a comprehensive approach is needed to strengthen the defences of payment gateway systems. A multifaceted security enhancement framework that encompasses advanced data encryption technologies, NGFWs, UTM, network traffic analysis tools, and MFA is proposed. These components work cohesively to fortify payment gateway security and mitigate emerging threats.

With the strategic implementation of this security framework, we can expect a transformative shift in the payment gateway landscape. Our objective is to establish a fortified digital payment environment where security and user confidence are paramount, aligning seamlessly with the customer journey and providing peace of mind in an increasingly digital world.

Literature Review

The digital era has witnessed a surge in online transactions, driven by the convenience of payment gateway systems (Seah et al., 2022). However, this convenience has also made them attractive targets for cybercriminals. Recent high-profile data breaches have brought to light the pressing need for enhanced payment gateway security (Taherdoost, 2023). These incidents have highlighted the vulnerabilities that exist within current systems, necessitating a proactive approach to fortify their defences (Chatterji et al., 2023; Kumar et al., 2023). To address the evolving landscape of cyber threats, organisations are turning to innovative security technologies. Among these technologies, advanced data encryption has emerged as a fundamental pillar of payment gateway security. Encryption technologies such as VeraCrypt (Spero et al., 2019) and Checkmarx (Otieno, 2023) offer robust data protection by replacing outdated encryption standards. These modern encryption methods ensure the confidentiality and integrity of sensitive payment data, reducing the risk of potential breaches (Josyula et al., 2024). Latest security methodologies were studied to highlight the empowerment and strength of it.

Next-Generation Security Measures

NGFWs have gained prominence in fortifying network security (Ahmadi, 2023a). NGFWs provide real-time monitoring and filtering of network traffic, proactively blocking emerging threats. By directly connecting with the underlying biometric hardware and securely handling the biometric authentication process, the Application Programming Interface (API) prioritises security. This design adheres to biometric security best practices by protecting user privacy and building confidence in the authentication system (Habibu et al., 2021). Their integration enhances the security posture of payment gateway systems by safeguarding against various attack vectors (Muhammad et al., 2022).

UTM

UTM systems consolidate multiple security features into a single platform (Rajkumar & Arunakranth, 2023). These features encompass functions such as intrusion detection, anti-virus, and content filtering. UTM's unified approach provides comprehensive protection and streamlines security management.

Network Traffic Analysis Tools

Network traffic analysis tools, such as Wireshark, have proven invaluable in fortifying security through robust network traffic analysis (Vasani et al., 2023). Security professional teams consistently employ Wireshark to scrutinise data packets, ensuring the identification and investigation of any unusual or suspicious patterns that could signal a potential security threat. Wireshark's configuration for capturing and analysing payment transactions, along with the establishment of baseline patterns, empowers security teams to efficiently discern anomalous activities (Ozkan-Ozay et al., 2024).

MFA

MFA is a pivotal component of modern security frameworks. By requiring users to provide multiple forms of identity before granting access, MFA substantially reduces the vulnerability to credential-based attacks (Ahmad et al., 2023). It introduces an additional layer of security that needs a second form of identification to guarantee that only the right persons have access to the user's data, resources, and apps (Loh et al., 2024; Verma et al., 2024). MFA typically involves combining two or more of the following factors: something the user knows (knowledge-based), something the user has (possession-based), and something the user is (biometric-based) (Karim et al., 2024). In the context of payment gateway security, implementing MFA fortifies user verification processes, significantly reducing the risk of unauthorised breaches (Sinigaglia et al., 2020).

Regulatory and Compliance Aspects

In the realm of payment gateway security, adherence to regulatory and compliance frameworks is non-negotiable. The regulatory framework is critical in shaping the security postures of organisations and instilling trust in digital transactions. It uncovers the pivotal role of regulatory standards such as the PCI DSS and the GDPR in fortifying payment systems.

PCI DSS is an established set of security standards designed to ensure all entities that process, store, or transmit credit card information uphold security measures that protect cardholder data (Lessa & Gebrehawariat, 2023). This standard is vital for preventing card fraud through increased controls around data and its exposure to compromise. The compliance with PCI DSS involves stringent requirements like maintaining a secure network, protecting cardholder data, implementing strong access control measures, and regularly monitoring and testing networks (Belmabrouk, 2023).

GDPR, on the other hand, is a comprehensive data protection regulation that imposes obligations onto organisations anywhere, so long as they target or collect data related to people in the European Union (EU) (Bharti & Aryal, 2023). It emphasises the principles of transparency, fairness, and accountability, mandating the protection of personal data through adequate security measures, including the protection against unauthorised or unlawful processing and against accidental loss, destruction, or damage using appropriate technical or organisational measures.

User Experience and Adoption Challenges

The evolution of digital payment systems is not without its challenges, particularly when considering the balance between enhancing security measures and maintaining a seamless user experience. This section explores the potential impact of heightened security on user experience and identifies the key challenges in user adoption of advanced payment systems.

The integration of stringent security measures, while essential for safeguarding sensitive financial information, can inadvertently complicate the user experience (Olweny, 2024). Measures such as MFA, though critical for security, may introduce additional steps in the transaction process, potentially leading to user frustration and transaction abandonment. Similarly, complex password requirements and security protocols, while necessary, can deter users from completing transactions if perceived as too cumbersome (Aslan et al., 2023). This section examines the fine line between securing digital payments and ensuring a frictionless user experience, highlighting the importance of designing user-centric security solutions that minimise inconvenience while maximising protection.

The adoption of advanced payment systems is often hindered by a lack of user awareness and understanding of the benefits and operation of these systems (Kayode-Ajala, 2023). Users accustomed to traditional payment methods may be resistant to change, particularly if they perceive new technologies as overly complicated or unnecessary. Additionally, concerns about privacy and data security can further impact user willingness to transition to digital payment methods (Rahardja et al., 2023). By addressing these user experience and adoption challenges, digital payment providers can ensure that security enhancements do not impede but rather facilitate the broader acceptance and use of digital payment systems. This approach not only enhances the security of transactions but also promotes a more inclusive digital economy by catering to the diverse needs and preferences of users.

Methodology

This chapter implemented, integrated, and utilised different security methodologies in a complete payment system. The proposed framework (Fig. 3.1) is presented with the combination of customer journeys. It highlighted the needs and capabilities of different security assessments to be enforced in a digital payment system. Table 3.1 presented the comparative security assessment between the usual conventional security system and the proposed enhanced security system, Guardians of Trust.

Implementation of Advanced Data Encryption

The adoption of advanced data encryption technologies, including VeraCrypt and Checkmarx, replaces outdated encryption standards. This measure ensures data confidentiality and integrity by employing robust encryption methods.

Integration of NGFWs

NGFWs are introduced to the payment gateway ecosystem, providing real-time monitoring and filtering of incoming and outgoing traffic to proactively block emerging threats. Their integration enhances the security posture by safeguarding against various attack vectors. The selection of NGFWs will be based on their ability to safeguard against various attack vectors. Configuration will focus on real-time threat detection and blocking capabilities.

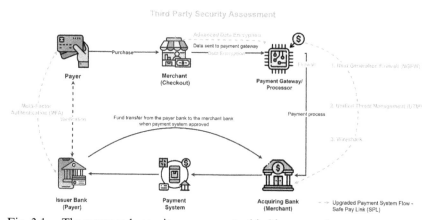

Fig. 3.1. The proposed security assessment added in a complete payment system (developed for this study)

Table 3.1. Comparative Between Conventional Security System and Proposed Security System (Developed for This Study).

System Aspect	Conventional Security System	Guardians of Trust
Data encryption	**Weak cryptographic implementation**: Uses an outdated algorithm which is vulnerable and susceptible to brute-force attacks	**Third-party security assessment**: Uses the VeraCrypt as encryption tool to secure data on storage devices. Checkmarx is used to provide actionable results and recommendations, facilitating secure coding practices.
Firewall	**Proxy firewall vulnerabilities**: This results in the risk of data breaches when accessing secured information, application compatibility issues that could result in security gaps, performance bottlenecks impacting transaction processing, and configuration challenges along with a reliance on professional setup.	**NGFW**: Uses the deep packet inspection (DPI), intrusion prevention system (IPS), and threat intelligence integration. **UTM**: Used as anti-virus and anti-malware measures and prevents data loss. **Wireshark tool**: Used to analyse the real-time transaction information.
Verification	**Absent of supplementary verification**: Only uses the knowledge-based authentication (KBA), which causes vulnerability that makes hacking easier.	**MFA**: Uses possession-based, biometric-based, and notification-based authentication for the approval for a transaction.

UTM Integration

UTM is integrated into the payment gateway system, consolidating various security features into a single platform. These features encompass functions like intrusion detection, anti-virus, and content filtering, providing comprehensive protection and streamlining security management. It will be seamlessly integrated into the payment gateway system to provide a unified and streamlined security platform.

Utilisation of Network Traffic Analysis Tools

Network traffic analysis tools, exemplified by Wireshark, are employed for a granular examination of network traffic. This enables the rapid identification and response to anomalous activities, enhancing the system's resilience against sophisticated attacks.

Implementation of MFA

MFA is implemented to fortify user verification processes, substantially reducing the vulnerability to credential-based attacks. It introduces an additional layer of security by requiring users to provide multiple forms of identity before granting access. This additional layer of security will significantly enhance user verification.

Balancing Security With User Convenience

In addressing the long-term challenge of fortifying payment gateway systems against cyber threats, this methodology section outlines strategies aimed at achieving an equilibrium between heightened security measures and maintaining user convenience. A pivotal aspect of this approach includes the implementation of user-friendly MFA mechanisms, such as adaptive authentication, alongside comprehensive user education and awareness programmes to facilitate the seamless adoption of these measures (Ahmad et al., 2023).

Adaptive Authentication

Adaptive authentication stands as a cornerstone strategy in this methodology, offering a dynamic solution that tailors the authentication process to the associated risk profile of each transaction (Adeyemo & Obafemi, 2024). This approach leverages a variety of contextual factors, including user location, device recognition, and the transaction's behavioural patterns, to assess risk and adjust the authentication requirements accordingly. For low-risk scenarios, users might experience streamlined authentication processes, whereas high-risk transactions prompt for more rigorous verification methods. This flexibility not only enhances security but also optimises user experience by minimising unnecessary authentication steps for transactions deemed low risk.

User Education and Awareness

Recognising that technological solutions alone cannot fully address the complexities of cybersecurity, this methodology places a significant emphasis on user education and awareness initiatives. These programmes are designed to inform users about the importance of security measures, the functionality of adaptive authentication, and best practices for safeguarding their personal and financial information (Goswami & Verma, 2024; Olaniyi et al., 2023). By fostering a culture of security awareness, users become more adept at recognising potential threats and more receptive to using advanced security features, thereby reducing resistance to new security protocols. Beyond adaptive authentication and user education, this methodology incorporates several complementary strategies to further balance security and user convenience. These include the following:

Biometric Authentication: Utilising biometrics, such as fingerprint scans or facial recognition, offers a seamless authentication experience that combines high security with user convenience (Yeh et al., 2024). Biometrics provide a quick and user-friendly method for verifying identity, significantly reducing the perceived burden of security measures.

Single Sign-On (SSO): Implementing SSO capabilities can reduce the frequency with which users must authenticate across different services and platforms, enhancing convenience without compromising security.

Transparent Communication: Maintaining open channels of communication regarding the purpose and operation of security measures reassures users of their necessity and effectiveness. Transparency about data handling and privacy protections further bolsters user trust and acceptance.

Feedback Mechanisms: Incorporating user feedback into the continuous improvement of security measures ensures that the user experience is consistently evaluated and optimised. This feedback loop can identify pain points in the authentication process, allowing for adjustments that enhance both security and convenience.

Integration With Emerging Technologies

In an era where digital payment systems are increasingly targeted by sophisticated cyber threats, integrating emerging technologies such as AI and blockchain presents a strategic advantage (Loh et al., 2023b). This subsection delves into how these technologies can be harnessed to bolster payment gateway security, enhance real-time fraud detection, and ensure the integrity of transaction records without detracting from the user experience.

The deployment of AI and machine learning algorithms stands at the forefront of this strategy, offering unparalleled capabilities in real-time fraud detection and behavioural analysis (Ling et al., 2024). These technologies analyse vast amounts of transaction data to identify patterns and anomalies indicative of fraudulent activity. By learning from historical fraud data and continuously updating its models, AI can adapt to new threats more efficiently than static, rule-based systems (Hassan et al., 2023). An illustrative example of this application is seen in the financial sector, where companies like Mastercard have integrated AI-driven systems to analyse transaction risk in real time, significantly reducing false positives and enhancing customer satisfaction by minimising unnecessary transaction declines (Kaswan et al., 2023). For instance, the use of machine learning for dynamic risk scoring enables more accurate fraud predictions based on current transaction contexts rather than relying solely on historical data.

Blockchain technology offers a transformative approach to securing transaction records and enhancing the integrity of payment systems (Asante Boakye et al., 2023). By creating decentralised, immutable ledgers for recording transactions, blockchain makes it virtually impossible for fraudsters to alter transaction data. This characteristic not only aids in preventing fraud but also provides a transparent audit trail that can be invaluable in dispute resolution. An example of blockchain's potential in payment gateways is demonstrated by IBM's Blockchain World Wire, which facilitates cross-border payments with enhanced security and reduced settlement times, showcasing the technology's ability to secure transactions and improve user experiences simultaneously (Kayani, 2023).

52 *Choon Sen Seah et al.*

Additionally, blockchain's role in securing digital identities underscores its potential to mitigate identity theft, a prevalent issue in digital transactions.

A case study worth noting involves the use of AI by PayPal to analyse billions of transactions (Ahmadi, 2023b). By employing advanced machine learning algorithms, PayPal has been able to identify and mitigate fraudulent transactions with greater accuracy and speed, showcasing the practical application and benefits of AI in real-world payment systems.

In short, the methodology presented combines the integration of AI and blockchain technologies with a balanced approach to security implementation within payment gateway systems, representing a forward-thinking strategy that enhances security and fraud prevention capabilities. These cutting-edge technologies not only fortify defences against evolving cyber threats but also ensure the security and integrity of transactions, improving the overall user experience. By integrating adaptive authentication, prioritising user education, and employing additional user-centric strategies, this approach not only aims to meet the stringent demands of the digital age but also enhances security frameworks while ensuring a positive and seamless user experience. This comprehensive strategy underscores the importance of addressing the dual objectives of robust security and user convenience, enabling payment gateways to achieve a higher standard of security.

These security enhancements are pilot tested in a controlled environment, with empirical findings used to assess their impact on data loss prevention, user satisfaction, and fraud mitigation within the fortified payment gateway system. The results of these experiments are analysed and discussed in the following section.

Result and Discussion

The implementation of multilayered security measures in Guardians of Trust resulted in significant improvements across key metrics. Fig. 3.2 presented the details of the result.

Data Loss Prevention: It achieved a data loss prevention percentage of 98%, representing a substantial improvement over the old system's 70%. This reflected the heightened resilience against potential data breaches.

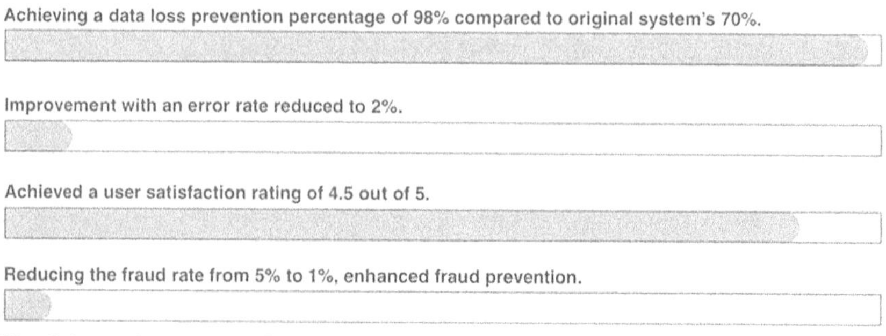

Achieving a data loss prevention percentage of 98% compared to original system's 70%.

Improvement with an error rate reduced to 2%.

Achieved a user satisfaction rating of 4.5 out of 5.

Reducing the fraud rate from 5% to 1%, enhanced fraud prevention.

Fig. 3.2.   The Result of Key Metrics Run in Closed Environment (Developed for This Study).

User Satisfaction: The introduction of MFA improved user satisfaction significantly, raising the rating from a modest 3 out of 5 in the old system to an impressive 4.5 out of 5. Users' increased confidence and contentment with the system demonstrated the positive impact of enhanced security measures on the user experience.

Fraud Mitigation: The deployed advanced fraud detection algorithms and MFA, leading to a substantial reduction in the fraud rate to 1%. In contrast, the conventional security system struggled with a historical fraud rate of 5%. This underscored the effectiveness in safeguarding users and the payment system from fraudulent activities.

The proposed security enhancement framework outlined in this chapter is designed to not only align with the regulatory requirements but to exceed them, thereby offering a more robust protection scheme for payment gateways. The integration of advanced encryption standards surpasses the basic encryption requisites of PCI DSS, fortifying data integrity and confidentiality. Additionally, the deployment of NGFWs and UTM systems extend beyond traditional network monitoring, providing proactive threat detection and response mechanisms, a prerequisite for both PCI DSS and GDPR compliance.

Network traffic analysis tools and MFA further underscore the commitment to exceed the regulatory mandates. The granular scrutiny of network traffic surpasses PCI DSS requirements for regular monitoring and testing, enabling the identification of anomalies that could signify a breach. MFA goes beyond GDPR's call for secure processing by adding layers of user verification, significantly minimising the risk of unauthorised data access.

Non-compliance with regulations like PCI DSS and GDPR not only attracts hefty fines but also exposes businesses to litigation risks. For instance, GDPR violations can result in penalties of up to 4% of annual global turnover or €20 million (whichever is greater), while PCI DSS non-compliance could lead to fines ranging from $5,000 to $100,000 per month until compliance is achieved (Besenyő & Kovács, 2023). Beyond fines, there are legal consequences such as class-action lawsuits from affected individuals, especially in cases of significant data breaches.

A security breach or non-compliance can severely damage an organisation's reputation, leading to a long-lasting impact on consumer trust. Trust is a fundamental component of customer loyalty and retention; hence, its erosion can have dire consequences for business sustainability (Paschalidou et al., 2023). In light of this, the framework's proactive approach to security could be presented as a mechanism to build and maintain consumer trust, highlighting cases where companies recovered from breaches through prompt and transparent action, thus regaining customer confidence.

Enhancing the security of payment gateway systems requires a multifaceted approach, blending technical measures with human and procedural strategies. This enhanced discussion delves into the essential role of training and awareness programmes, as well as the challenges associated with costs, complexity, and potential user resistance, particularly concerning MFA. These considerations are crucial for achieving a holistic security posture that not only defends against cyber threats but also fosters a culture of security mindfulness among users and stakeholders.

The human element plays a critical role in the cybersecurity ecosystem. Despite the sophistication of security technologies, the system's overall effectiveness can be significantly undermined by human error or negligence. Training and awareness programmes are therefore paramount. Such initiatives should aim to educate employees and users about the latest cyber threats, the importance of adhering to security protocols, and the role each individual plays in maintaining the system's integrity. For instance, regular training sessions on recognising phishing attempts can drastically reduce the likelihood of successful email-based attacks. Similarly, awareness programmes highlighting the importance of secure password practices can reinforce the system's first line of defence.

Implementing robust security measures like MFA introduces additional considerations regarding costs, system complexity, and potential resistance from users. While MFA significantly enhances security by requiring multiple verification factors, its deployment and maintenance can be costly and complex, particularly for small- to medium-sized enterprises (SMEs) with limited information technology (IT) resources. The complexity of managing an MFA system can also introduce challenges in ensuring system compatibility and user accessibility.

Furthermore, user resistance to MFA cannot be overlooked. The additional steps required for authentication, while crucial for security, can be perceived as inconvenient, leading to frustration or non-compliance among users. Addressing this challenge requires a delicate balance between security and user convenience. Strategies such as adaptive authentication, which adjusts authentication requirements based on the transaction's risk profile, can mitigate user resistance by streamlining the authentication process for low-risk activities.

To navigate these challenges, organisations should consider the total cost of ownership (TCO) of security measures, taking into account not just the initial deployment costs but also ongoing maintenance and user support. Additionally, involving users in the design and implementation phases can help identify potential friction points and adjust the approach to enhance user acceptance.

The overall security posture underwent a transformative shift with the multi-layered security approach, addressing inherent vulnerabilities present in the conventional security system. The comprehensive security features ensured a secure payment environment, fostering trust among users and stakeholders alike. It represented not just a technological upgrade but a fundamental improvement in the health and security of the payment gateway system.

Conclusion

Guardians of Trust that combines advanced data encryption, NGFWs, UTM integration, network traffic analysis tools, and MFA aims to bolster the security of the payment gateway system. The empirical findings generated from controlled experiments will serve as a basis for informed decision-making, further refinement of security strategies, and the establishment of a fortified payment gateway system that ensures data security and user confidence while addressing evolving threats. The proposed framework integrates seamlessly with the customer journey, prioritising both security and user experience.

Achieving a holistic security posture for payment gateways necessitates a comprehensive approach that integrates technical security measures with human and procedural elements. By investing in training and awareness programmes, carefully considering the implications of implementing complex security solutions like MFA, and striving for a balance between security and convenience, organisations can enhance their defence mechanisms against cyber threats while maintaining user trust and compliance.

The proposed framework not only aligns with the foundational aspects of PCI DSS and GDPR but enhances the security protocols to offer a forward-looking, comprehensive payment gateway security model. This commitment to exceed the basic requirements reflects an acknowledgement of the evolving cyber threat landscape and an earnest effort to safeguard consumer data in the digital payment ecosystem.

In summary, Guardians of Trust successfully addresses vulnerabilities in the payment gateway system, employing advanced security measures to enhance data encryption, firewall capabilities, and user authentication. The transition results in a transformative shift in the overall security posture, fostering trust among users and stakeholders.

References

Adeyemo, K., & Obafemi, F. J. (2024). A survey on the role of technological innovation in Nigerian deposit money bank fraud prevention. *South Asian Journal of Social Studies and Economics*, *21*(3), 133–150.

Ahmad, M. O., Tripathi, G., Siddiqui, F., Alam, M. A., Ahad, M. A., Akhtar, M. M., & Casalino, G. (2023). BAuth-ZKP – A blockchain-based multi-factor authentication mechanism for securing smart cities. *Sensors*, *23*(5), 2757.

Ahmadi, S. (2023a). Next generation AI-based firewalls: A comparative study. *International Journal of Computer (IJC)*, *49*(1), 245–262.

Ahmadi, S. (2023b). Open AI and its impact on fraud detection in financial industry. *Journal of Knowledge Learning and Science Technology*, *2*(3), 263–281. ISSN 2959–6386.

Asante Boakye, E., Zhao, H., & Ahia, B. N. K. (2023). Blockchain technology prospects in transforming Ghana's economy: A phenomenon-based approach. *Information Technology for Development*, *29*(2–3), 348–377.

Aslan, Ö., Aktuğ, S. S., Ozkan-Okay, M., Yilmaz, A. A., & Akin, E. (2023). A comprehensive review of cyber security vulnerabilities, threats, attacks, and solutions. *Electronics*, *12*(6), 1333.

Barbereau, T., & Bodó, B. (2023). Beyond financial regulation of crypto-asset wallet software: In search of secondary liability. *Computer Law & Security Review*, *49*, 105829.

Belmabrouk, K. (2023). Cyber criminals and data privacy measures. In N. Mateus-Coelho & M. Cruz-Cunha (Eds.), Contemporary challenges for cyber security and data privacy (pp. 198–226). IGI Global. https://doi.org/10.4018/979-8-3693-1528-6.ch011

Besenyő, J., & Kovács, A. M. (2023). Healthcare cybersecurity threat context and mitigation opportunities. *Security Science Journal*, *4*(1), 83–101.

Bharti, S. S., & Aryal, S. K. (2023). The right to privacy and an implication of the EU general data protection regulation (GDPR) in Europe: Challenges to the companies. *Journal of Contemporary European Studies*, *31*(4), 1391–1402.

Borden, R. (2023). *How does the maximus 8-K filing fit with the new sec rules?* Mondaq Business Briefing, NA-NA.

Chatterji, N., Manohar, S., & Verma, B. (2023). Assessing the influence of graduate characteristics on employer satisfaction: A multi-dimensional analysis. *The Open Psychology Journal, 16*(1), 1–11.

Choong, Y. O., Seow, A. N., Low, M. P., Ismail, N. H., Choong, C. K., & Seah, C. S. (2023). Delving the impact of adaptability and government support in small-and medium-sized enterprises business resilience: The mediating role of information technology capability. *Journal of Contingencies and Crisis Management, 31*(4), 928–940.

George, A. S., Baskar, T., & Srikaanth, P. B. (2024). Cyber threats to critical infrastructure: Assessing vulnerabilities across key sectors. *Partners Universal International Innovation Journal, 2*(1), 51–75.

Goswami, D., & Verma, B. (2024). The intersection of ethics and big data: Addressing ethical concerns in digital age of artificial intelligence. In B. Verma, B. Singla, & A. Mittal (Eds.) *Digital technologies, ethics, and decentralization in the digital era* (pp. 269–285). IGI Global.

Habibu, T., Luhanga, E. T., & Sam, A. E. (2021). A study of users' compliance and satisfied utilization of biometric application system. *Information Security Journal: A Global Perspective, 30*(3), 125–138.

Hassan, M., Aziz, L. A. R., & Andriansyah, Y. (2023). The role artificial intelligence in modern banking: An exploration of AI-driven approaches for enhanced fraud prevention, risk management, and regulatory compliance. *Reviews of Contemporary Business Analytics, 6*(1), 110–132.

Josyula, H. P., Reddi, L. T., Parate, S., & Rajagopal, A. (2024). A review on security and privacy considerations in programmable payments. *International Journal of Intelligent Systems and Applications in Engineering, 12*(9s), 256–263.

Karim, N., Kanaker, H., Abdulraheem, W., Ghaith, M., Alhroob, E., & Alali, A. (2024). Choosing the right MFA method for online systems: A comparative analysis. International *Journal of Data and Network Science, 8*(1), 201–212.

Kaswan, K. S., Dhatterwal, J. S., Kumar, N., & Lal, S. (2023). Artificial intelligence for financial services. In S. Grima, K. Sood, & E. Özen (Eds.), *Contemporary studies of risks in emerging technology, part A* (pp. 71–92). Emerald Publishing Limited.

Kayani, U. N. (2023). Exploring prospects of blockchain and fintech: Using SLR approach. *Journal of Science and Technology Policy Management.*

Kayode-Ajala, O. (2023). Applications of cyber threat intelligence (CTI) in financial institutions and challenges in its adoption. *Applied Research in Artificial Intelligence and Cloud Computing, 6*(8), 1–21.

Kumar, S., Gupta, U., Singh, A. K., & Singh, A. K. (2023). Artificial intelligence: Revolutionizing cyber security in the digital era. *Journal of Computers, Mechanical and Management, 2*(3), 31–42.

Lessa, L., & Gebrehawariat, D. (2023). Effectiveness of banking card security in the Ethiopian financial sector: PCI-DSS security standard as a lens. *International Journal of Industrial Engineering and Operations Management, 5*(2), 135–147.

Ling, C. L., Waheeda, J. F., Sen, S. C., Xia, L. Y., Amerhaider, N. A. N., & Wah, H. K. (2024). E-payment security mechanisms on Lazada: The case of Malaysian and Thai. *Procedia Computer Science, 234*, 1340–1347.

Loh, W. S., Ling, L., Chin, R. J., Lai, S. H., Loo, K. K., & Seah, C. S. (2024). A comparative analysis of missing data imputation techniques on sedimentation data. *Ain Shams Engineering Journal, 15*(16), 102717.

Loh, Y. X., Chin, W. Y., Seah, C. S., Lee, S. Z., Jalaludin, F. W., & Leong, S. K. (2023b). The implementation of blockchain technology in Malaysia and Singapore financial industry. In L. Sun (Ed.), *2023 16th international symposium on computational intelligence and design (ISCID)* (pp. 131–134). IEEE.

Loh, Y. X., Nuar, A. N. B. A., Huspin, S. H. B., & Seah, C. S. (2023a). Risk assessment method for scams detection among micro enterprises: A design science research approach. In L. Sun (Ed.), *2023 16th international symposium on computational intelligence and design (ISCID)* (pp. 143–146). IEEE.

Low, M. P., Seah, C. S., Cham, T. H., & Teoh, S. H. (2022). Digitalization adoption for digital economy: An examination of Malaysian small medium-sized enterprises through the technology–organization–environment framework. *Business Process Management Journal, 28*(7), 1473–1494.

Muhammad, T., Munir, M. T., Munir, M. Z., & Zafar, M. W. (2022). Integrative cybersecurity: Merging Zero Trust, layered defense, and global standards for a resilient digital future. *International Journal of Computer Science and Technology, 6*(4), 99–135.

Olaniyi, O. O., Okunleye, O. J., Olabanji, S. O., & Asonze, C. U. (2023). IoT security in the era of ubiquitous computing: A multidisciplinary approach to addressing vulnerabilities and promoting resilience. *Asian Journal of Research in Computer Science, 16*(4) , 1–18.

Olweny, F. (2024). Navigating the nexus of security and privacy in modern financial technologies. *GSC Advanced Research and Reviews, 18*(2), 167–197.

Osita, G. C., Chisom, C. D., Okoronkwo, M. C., Esther, U. N., & Vanessa, N. C. (2022). Application of emerging technologies in mitigation of e-commerce security challenges. *CCU Journal of Science, 2*, 2734–3766.

Otieno, M., Odera, D., & Ounza, J. E. (2023). Theory and practice in secure software development lifecycle: A comprehensive survey. *World Journal of Advanced Research and Reviews, 18*(3), 53–78.

Ozkan-Ozay, M., Akin, E., Aslan, Ö., Kosunalp, S., Iliev, T., Stoyanov, I., & Beloev, I. (2024). *A comprehensive survey: Evaluating the efficiency of artificial intelligence and machine learning techniques on cyber security solutions.* IEEE Access.

Paschalidou, K., Tsitskari, E., Alexandris, K., Karagiorgos, T., & Filippou, D. (2023). Segmenting fitness center customers: Leveraging perceived ethicality for enhanced loyalty, trust, and word-of-mouth communication. *Sustainability, 15*(22), 16131.

Rahardja, U., Sigalingging, C. T., Putra, P. O. H., Nizar Hidayanto, A., & Phusavat, K. (2023). The impact of mobile payment application design and performance attributes on consumer emotions and continuance intention. *Sage Open, 13*(1), 21582440231151919.

Rajkumar, B., & Arunakranthi, G. (2023, February). Evolution for a secured path using NexGen firewalls. In R. Nayak (Ed.), *2022 OPJU international technology conference on emerging technologies for sustainable development (OTCON)* (pp. 1–6). IEEE.

Saleem, M., & Naveed, M. (2020). Sok: Anatomy of data breaches. *Proceedings on Privacy Enhancing Technologies, 4*, 153–174.

Seah, C. S., Loh, Y. X., Wong, Y. S., Jalaludin, F. W., & Loh, L. H. (2022, April). The influence of COVID-19 pandemic on Malaysian e-commerce landscape: The case of Shopee and Lazada. In S. Liu (Eds.), *Proceedings of the 6th international conference on e-commerce, e-business and e-government* (pp. 17–23). Association for Computing Machinery (ACM).

Semerikova, E. (2020). Payment instruments choice of Russian consumers: Reasons and pain points. *Journal of Enterprising Communities: People and Places in the Global Economy, 14*(1), 22–41.

Sinigaglia, F., Carbone, R., Costa, G., & Zannone, N. (2020). A survey on multi-factor authentication for online banking in the wild. *Computers & Security, 95*, 101745.

Spero, E., Stojmenović, M., & Biddle, R. (2019). Helping users secure their data by supporting mental models of VeraCrypt. In C. Stephanidis (Ed.), *HCI international 2019-posters: 21st international conference, HCII 2019*, Orlando, FL, USA, July 26–31, Proceedings, Part I 21 (pp. 211–218). Springer International Publishing.

Taherdoost, H. (2023). E-business security and control. In H. Taherdoost (Ed.), *E-business essentials: Building a successful online enterprise* (pp. 105–135). Springer Nature Switzerland.

Tyagi, A. K. (Ed.). (2023). *Privacy preservation and secured data storage in cloud computing.* IGI Global.

Vasani, V., Bairwa, A. K., Joshi, S., Pljonkin, A., Kaur, M., & Amoon, M. (2023). Comprehensive analysis of advanced techniques and vital tools for detecting malware intrusion. *Electronics, 12*(20), 4299.

Verma, B., Singla, B., & Mittal, A. (Eds.). (2024). *Digital technologies, ethics, and decentralization in the digital era.* IGI Global.

Yeh, J. Y., Seah, C. S., Loh, Y. X., Low, M. P., Nuar, A. N. A., & Jalaludin, F. W. (2024). Exploring the actual implementation of e-wallet application in Malaysia. *Baghdad Science Journal, 21*(2(SI)), 600–608.

Chapter 4

Industry 4.0 Technologies: Managing the Future of Smart Retail

Ritu Kumari and Vinay Pal Singh

Quantum University, Roorkee, Uttarakhand

Abstract

The retail industry is undergoing a significant digital revolution. Emerging technologies are changing the way shoppers interact with companies and shops, causing a significant upheaval in the business. The primary purpose of the research is to recognise the concept of retail along with its service applications and novel technologies that will drive the future around the world. Retailers must keep up with the latest technological advancements to remain competitive as the supply chain grows more intricate and consumers become more astute, tech-savvy, and gadget-literate about using multiple channels. The analysis indicates technologies including artificial intelligence (AI), smart labelling, beacons, augmented reality (AR), virtual reality (VR), drone deliveries, and Internet of Things (IoT) have emerged as future trends. It has been found that retailers need to have strong digital relationships to engage and interact with consumers as well as to mould and influence experiences. They can create connections to assist customers in making decisions that are beneficial to them. India's retail industry is well-positioned to prosper in the dynamic market environment by adopting innovation and transformation and also centred on omnichannel tactics, which offer customers a seamless experience by giving them a comprehensive, single glance at each retail business from the comfort of their home or place of business. The application of literary works to explain the notion of Industry 4.0 in the retail sector while recognising and comprehending pertinent technological developments. This chapter establishes the groundwork for upcoming research on technologies that will eventually be utilised in retail management.

Keywords: Retail technology; retail sector; innovation; Industry 4.0; artificial intelligence; internet of thing (IoT)

Augmenting Retail Reality: Blockchain, AR, VR, and the Internet of Things, Part A, 59–82
Copyright © 2025 by Ritu Kumari and Vinay Pal Singh
Published under exclusive licence by Emerald Publishing Limited
doi:10.1108/978-1-83608-634-520241009

1. Introduction

The retail sector is undergoing a significant digital revolution (Von Briel, 2018; Xu et al., 2018; Zhang & Hänninen, 2022). It is proactively embracing innovation. Retailers are being forced to think strategically about how to best position themselves in this dynamic retail sector to thrive. Retailing was undergoing a significant change before COVID-19, driven by advances in technology (Grewal et al., 2017). These changes had an impact on an extensive variety of activities, including in-store tactics, back-end processes (such as logistics or storage facilities), communication (such as sites and networking platforms), and merchandise promotion and display. Although offerings like streaming services, food subscription services, etc. are not novel, still technology has played a major role in their expansion throughout the pandemic. The front-end services that influence the retail interface with customers and the back-end technology that supports retail operations have benefited from the increased use of AI, VR, and big data along mobile applications (Grewal et al., 2021). The largest merchants in the entire world have already committed billions of dollars to technologies (Yarkova, 2018). Retailers serve as the final link in the supply chain that generates revenue for producers and clients (Ivanova, 2020).

Developing efficient retail processes for consumers, staff, merchants, and providers requires a strong technological foundation. Nearly every retailer has stepped up its technological efforts to better assist consumers in the rapidly evolving retail industry. Expanding on this idea, Shankar et al. (2021) investigate the motivations for and results of employing fresh retail technology in a variety of contexts. Consequently, they provide forecasts regarding the potential effects of these technologies' adoption on consumer spending, fulfilment, and commitment. The associated benefits for performance results such as enhanced delivery business processes, income, market share, and shareholder value are also taken into account.

Encouragement to utilise a range of technologies including smartphones as well as portable scanners is an instance that technology is increasing retail earnings. As evidence, studies have revealed that customers who use cell phones while shopping often become sidetracked and end up making larger purchases (Grewal et al., 2018). In a similar vein, customers who use handheld scanners focus more on the product and probably approach it, which encourages them to make larger purchases (Grewal & Roggeveen, 2020). Even though they encompass an extensive variety of technologies, many modern retail technologies fall under the category of AI. AI is a potent tool that can use the enormous amounts of consumer data that are readily available in a variety of formats (such as grocery, pharmacy, and logistics) to guide retail actions. Some believe AI will take centre stage in the retail sector because of the knowledge and insights it can offer merchants (Chui et al., 2018). Taking note of this, Guha et al. (2021) concentrate on the growing relevance of AI technologies in retail, pointing out the variety of AI-based solutions that are becoming available.

Individuals with rapid availability of data would be more knowledgeable as well as make greater investments compared to those utilising outdated data, given the sudden shifts in buying trends that occurred on a weekly or daily basis. Tech is assisting retailers as well as brands to stay up with the dramatic alterations in buyer behaviour. One example of this is the use of mobile global positioning system (GPS) tracking providing traffic reports in stores (Anantharaman et al., 2023; Chawla et al., 2024; Doolittle & McMillan, 2020). Because of how embedded this technology has ingrained in the everyday lives of individuals, customers have access to a multitude of options in the current multichannel environment. Certain consumer demographics would rather make purchases through mobile apps, but they would also rather pick them up in person from a physical store. Some people conduct their research through digital platforms but make their actual purchases in physical stores (Nakano & Kondo, 2018; Oberoi et al., 2024; Souiden et al., 2019).

1.1 Objectives of the Study

We will try to bridge this knowledge gap about how technologies affect retailing in this chapter. The notion of retail technology is first explained, along with various industry issues. In the section that follows, we go over a recent development in the retail sector of India. We then go on to describe the reasons behind and effects of technology adoption by consumers, workers, sellers, and retailers. We talk about the technologies that will shape retail in the next part. Our analysis of how technology is changing retailing comes to a close, and we also suggest some directions for further research in this area.

2. Background

2.1 Understanding Retail Technology

All electronic applications and developments that assist retailers in managing and improving their business operations are collectively referred to as retail technology. Retail technology instances involve computerised inventory control, shelf surveillance, cashier-less payment process, and AR. Retail media channels experienced significant growth these days, and over the subsequent five years, they are expected to grow at a rate of 25% annually. Retailers can easily provide clients with personalised adverts on their web pages and mobile applications with this kind of retail technology. Consumers benefit from a seamless buying experience that lets them make lists, find novel offerings, and take delight in discounts and incentives. Inside their enclosed environment, retailers gain an initial understanding of consumer habits. Issues over inflation, problems with supply chains, and a weak economy will still be present in 2023, which will affect consumer behaviour and mindsets. Customer loyalty is still shaky as shoppers look for ease and price reductions to get through the rough patch (Turner, 2023). Retail electronic commerce platforms will keep equipping organisations with tools throughout hard times, such as

- The purchasing process becomes more complicated, and cross-channel purchase is commonplace.
- Customers want brands to recognise and accommodate their preferences.

62　*Ritu Kumari and Vinay Pal Singh*

- Digital discounts, incentives, and promos will keep influencing consumer preference and loyalty.
- Retailers who maintain internal retail technology are better off as a result of consolidation in the industry.

There are some impediments to retail technology, which include the adoption of digital transactions that are hindered by a lack of financial awareness, which relies on technology to empower people with financial tools. This lack of technology in stores affects coworkers' performance, leading to backlogs in tasks and hindering their ability to meet scheduled deliveries (Winn, 2023). India's small retailers face funding issues to invest in infrastructure for online payments. Consumers prefer debit and credit cards, but Indian banks hinder the use of electronic wallets provided by private businesses on their bank websites. This can be due to the inability to connect to payment platforms or limitations on accessing bank accounts. Regulators must confront banks for rent-seeking practices (Singhraul & Garwal, 2018).

2.2 Problems Faced By the Industry in Retail

In total, 72% of entrepreneurs find it challenging to run a firm because of the economic obstacles and ineffective internal processes faced by retail companies. Regular health checks and fresh initiatives might assist in surviving difficult times by addressing internal inefficiencies. Thus, we will talk about the issues that retailers are currently facing.

2.2.1 Inefficient Inventory Control in Retail

Since inventory is a retailer's largest investment, it is the subject of most retail issues and solutions. Ineffective inventory management techniques can drain your resources, lead to inefficient stores, and cause you to lose your competitive advantage. Furthermore, you risk suffering large financial losses if you don't restock on time or don't sell as quickly as you anticipated. According to a McKinsey survey, 32% of companies attributed inventory inconsistencies, such as inaccurate forecasting and fluctuating demand, to their supply chain problems. According to a separate study, between 70% and 90% of instances of shortages are caused by inefficient replenishing techniques. If strategic management is not used to address these problems, your retail business will probably suffer.

2.2.2 Insufficient Effectiveness in Gathering and Evaluating Data

Managing inventory, advertising and promotion, demand fulfilment, and customer service are all important aspects of running a retail firm. Solid, trustworthy data are necessary for planning in these domains. Without a single source of truth, prejudiced, gut-driven decisions are frequently made in organisations. Since you don't have anything else to rely on, it's simpler and more usual (over 58% of poll respondents) to 'trust your instincts'. However, this has consequences. For example, you can think you're profitable even if one of your channels isn't working well if you don't know how much money your physical stores and internet platforms bring in. This lack of information may also contribute to misguided decisions like constantly stockpiling underperforming products.

2.2.3 Ignoring Issues With Cash Flow

Since 82% of small businesses fail and attribute their failure to inadequate management of cash flows, there is a possibility that some short-term problems with cash flow will result in a long-term shortage in operating capital. In addition, short-term cash flow issues can lead to an accumulation of delinquent bills and invoices that are filled with interest and penalties; more severe, this violation of the contract may result in legal action that will permanently harm the company.

2.2.4 Not Placing the Needs of the Consumer First

Retailers who don't ask for or respond to client input risk creating sour ties with them. Your company survives only because of its customers. Unsatisfactory customer service and broken promises can turn off potential clients and damage the reputation of your business. This is probably because 62% of previous customers agreed to tell others about their bad experiences, some of whom could be potential customers. The majority of these clients will vent their annoyance on social media. And nobody knows how far it will spread once it reaches social media. Vlogs on TikTok featuring the hashtag #badcustomerservice have received over 73 million views.

2.3 Current Trends of the Retail Industry in India

Propelled by changes in customer behaviour, developing marketplace dynamics, and technology improvements, the retailing sector within India has experienced a tremendous metamorphosis throughout the years. India's retail industry is positioned for an exciting future since it is one of the world's biggest and most rapidly developing retail marketplaces. We will look at the major developments and patterns influencing the Indian retail sector in this part (Saluja, 2023).

2.3.1 E-Retail and E-Commerce

The retail scene in India has completely changed due to the rise in electronic commerce. Online retailing has experienced a rapid expansion due to a rise in tech-savvy customers and improved internet access. The omnichannel buying experience, which seamlessly combines physical as well as internet channels, is the way that retail across the nation will also develop in the future (Kumar & Ayodeji, 2020).

2.3.2 Electronic and Cashless Transactions

The payment environment has changed as a result of the quick uptake of electronic payment methods like contactless debit or credit cards, UPI as well as mobile money wallets. By providing a variety of payment methods to clients, retail stores are taking advantage of the government's drive towards an internet-based economy, or 'Digital India,' by streamlining payments along with minimising the need for dealing with money. Due to their ease and usability, cashless transactions have become increasingly popular (Madhukar, 2018).

2.3.3 Hyperlocal Stores and Last-Mile Transportation

Urban areas are seeing a rise in the use of hyperlocal retail designs, which let businesses swiftly deliver goods to specified areas. Further last-mile delivery optimisation using cutting-edge logistics technologies like drones and driverless cars is a feature of the Indian retail sector. Considering the rising demands from consumers for dependable and quick service would need increasing efficiency of delivery.

2.3.4 Ethical and Eco-Friendly Retail

India's customer base is becoming more ethical and environmentally sensitive. Demand for socially conscious as well as ecologically friendly items has been raised in the retail sector. Retailers should embrace green practices to match the preferences of customers and build a favourable perception of the brand. Examples of these practices include green packaging (Koch et al., 2022), green energy sources, and fair-trade alliances.

3. Classifications of Technologies Influencing Retail

Technology is the practical application of science to produce faster, more effective, and affordable outputs. Retailing is being impacted by various technologies, affecting both the demand and supply sides. Advances in technology lead to digital services like e-commerce, suggestions, and AI-powered customer choice aid. These technologies also help merchants develop support and payment competencies, such as computerised customer service, electronic payment services, and telemedicine offerings. Delivery capabilities like online ordering and offline pickup are also being impacted. Robots, such as warehouse robots and scanning drones, are helping humans in the supply chain. Technological innovations are sometimes replacing people, redefining their roles in the supply chain (Shankar et al., 2021). We can group these innovations according to stakeholder categories in the context of retailing in the following.

3.1 Technologies Focused on Consumers

Consumers use these technological advances, which retailers support, to improve their interactions with goods, brands, or offerings. Smartphones, gadgets, smart speakers, VR, AR, mixed reality systems, chatbots to communicate, smart mirrors, and technologies for payment are a few examples. According to studies and practical experience in consumer marketing, technological advances can play a significant part in a shopper's trip through the purchase process (Lee et al., 2017). Numerous in-store technologies that interact with customers are among the many that merchants have put into place (Grewal et al., 2019).

The Future of Smart Retail   65

3.2 Technologies Focused on Employees

Technology innovations like smartphones, price scanning devices, RFID, IoT, AR, and smart mirrors are influencing the connection between employees and consumers. Automated mirrors can affect both clients and staff simultaneously, making it crucial to differentiate between synchronous and asynchronous coproduction in these technologies. This helps in completing responsibilities and activities effectively.

3.3 Technologies Focused on Suppliers

Manufacturers that provide goods to merchants employ these kinds of technologies. IoT, settlement, RFID, and blockchain technologies are a few instances. The supply chain's efficiency, control of inventory, and supplier–retailer agreements may all be enhanced by blockchain technology which is an accessible, dispersed, verifiable, and irreversible ledger.

Technology in retailing can be categorised into Non-Info –technology and information technology (IT) categories. The focus is on information-related technology, which may need integration with IT-based technologies. Non-IT-based advancements include biotechnology-based healthcare technologies for pharmacy stores, retail clinics, wellness centres, and fitness centres. Technological categorisations can be domain specific or cross-domain, with some innovations applicable to various retail fields. IT abilities are categorised and examined by (Setia et al., 2017) either internally or externally throughout the supply and demand sides. While certain technologies might be created internally, others might be outsourced. Table 4.1 shows the summary of classifications of retail technologies.

4. New Technology That Will Drive the Future of Retail

As the international retail sector shifts to smooth new retail, Pricewaterhouse-Coopers and Kantar (2020) forecast that novel, smaller outlets will appear. However, new retail might use cloud-based computing as well as analysis of large amounts of data to produce goods and services with value-added. Retailers may anticipate customer demands and make product recommendations based on their choices with the aid of cutting-edge technological solutions. Suppliers can also benefit from optimising logistics, shipping, and stock management. So, Fig. 4.1 shows some technological trends in the retail sector around the world.

The retail sector is becoming more and more dependent on technology, and the future of the sector appears to be full of promising developments. Emerging technologies are changing the way shoppers interact with companies and shop, causing a significant upheaval in the business. Thanks to technology, companies can now easily offer their items and services to clients, giving them the flexibility to purchase whenever and wherever they choose. Retailers are using technology to interact with consumers in fresh and creative ways. Examples of this include the use of AR, VR, and AI-powered customised solutions (Jose, 2023).

Table 4.1. Summary of Categorisation of Retail Technologies.

Categorisation	Tech. Types	Summary
By stakeholder	*Focused at consumers* *Focused at employees* *Focused at suppliers*	VR, AR, and mixed reality systems, IoT, technologies for payments, smart speakers and chatbots, mobile phones. Success depends on creating value for consumers and facilitating retailers. Smartphones, IoT, price scanning devices, handheld scanners, RFID, and automated mirrors. Technology that needs staff members to interface with consumers needs to be handled with greater caution. Payment, blockchain, IoT, and RFID technology. The secret to handling such advancements is regulating inventory, minimising friction, and enhancing the resiliency and efficiency of the supply chain.
By relevance to IT	*IT oriented* *Non- IT oriented*	Emerging retail technologies could need to integrate with the extensive ecosystem of IT-based technology. The secret to success is to invest in relocation and upgrading. Certain biotech-based healthcare technologies apply to pharmacy stores, retail clinics, wellness, and health centres. Ensuring the security and confidentiality of shoppers is crucial for efficiently operating technologies.
By origin source or domain spanning	*A single vs several domains* *Internal as compared to external* *Comparing inside-out vs spanning vs outside-in*	Certain retail technological advancements like mobile payment systems can be used in a variety of retail classifications, whereas others like magic mirrors for attire are category specific.

		Retailers may benefit from technology that has already been implemented in other fields.
		It's possible that certain technologies are outsourced and others can be internal. Although they are costly, in-house technology has the potential to give an advantage over competitors.
		Retailers can embrace new technologies at the insistence of suppliers.
		Retailers can influence suppliers to use new technology.
Through newness	*Radical vs incremental*	More recent iterations like 5G telecommunications, represent gradual advancements, although novel approaches like wireless batteries may be deemed revolutionary.
		When adopting radical technology, retailers must prepare for increased work, expenditures, and handling of change.

Source: Author's compilation.

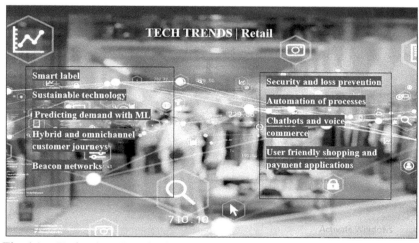

Fig. 4.1. Technology Trends. *Source*: Created by author.

4.1 New Retail Service Applications

4.1.1 VR Applications

Nowadays, we gaze at screens a lot all of the time. We now rely heavily on computers, cell phones, and televisions for a variety of activities, including social networking use, movie watching, and obtaining most of our news. Using a headset with a screen of some kind that projects a virtual environment, VR transports us to a simulated world. Additionally, these types of headsets feature a technique known as head tracking, which enables one to physically move one's head to view the surroundings. Individuals will see a 360-degree perspective of the virtual world as the display moves in the direction you choose. Currently, headsets come in two main categories. The first kind of headgear incorporates a screen. These gadgets link to computer systems and need a reasonably strong system to function properly. They operate well and have excellent visuals; however, they are also rather pricey. VR in retail settings has been shown to boost sales and customer satisfaction while also increasing financial gains and supporting marketing campaigns. Following their realisation of VR's advantages for the retail sector, retailers began using the technology in their operations in a variety of ways.

V-Commerce as a Distinct Field of E-Commerce – E-commerce has gained popularity in the business sector, with retailers utilising VR to sell products online, leading to the creation of V-commerce. The ability to interact with products has helped solve issues like empty carts, reducing the need for shoppers to leave their carts empty.

Virtual Consultations With Consumers – VR facilitates tighter relationships between a brand and its customers. Adding to the great customer experience is the ability for customers to take a virtual trip to the business. Companies can provide customers the chance to interact with them and ask questions in a way that mimics speaking with a consultant in-store.

In-store VR – People often picture themselves using a product they like as soon as they see it in the store. With the help of a VR headset, they can view and use the product beyond their wildest dreams. For example, clients can view how to make smoothies in a blender in VR after placing their VR headsets in the kitchen products and gadgets store.

Staff Training – Customers and employees alike gain from the VR retail industry's improved training. Using VR technology, workers can practise for future employment by experiencing possible scenarios, working through challenging problems, interacting with consumers, and learning about products. Continuous training is necessary as the product line grows without becoming burdensome.

VR has been used by Alibaba, Volvo, Mastercard, and Toms for marketing. Alibaba launched a promotion for digitally generated storefronts that let users browse, select products, view details and costs, and add these to their shopping baskets. Toms displayed a promotional movie for shoes provided to children in Peruvia using VR goggles. Using Google Cardboard, Volvo attracted the attention of rival automakers with their Volvo Reality app. Swarovski's jewellery company and Mastercard marketed home décor.

4.1.2 AR Applications

AR is built on a camera that can record data from the real world and merge information from virtual and real elements into a single perception. Thus, sound, richness of media, location-based information, and item simulation all add to the experience value, and AR lets users engage with virtual goods. Early studies on AR in physical retail settings using interactive displays expected that people would interact with this steerable advance, stimulating information about goods, advertisements, and locations, hence emphasising the technology's hedonistic and utilitarian features. Due to the widespread usage of personal mobile devices like tablet computers and smartphones which enable users to buy through AR apps and so improve experience and happiness, AR applications have since gained popularity. AR thus can enhance shoppers' perception of products, boost involvement, and improve their opinions of their shopping experiences, all of which should have a beneficial impact on consumers' perceptions of retailers and brands. Thus, consumer behaviour may be impacted. In addition, the shopping experience in tech-mediated retailing is improved by customers' sense of freedom and control. Fig. 4.2 also shows the difference between AR and VR. Numerous uses of AR are mentioned as follows:

Colour Matching – By placing the product over a photograph, AR can assist clients in matching the colours of paint and makeup options, making it simpler for them to view the colour of the item in real or on a screen. This is precisely what the Dulux Visualiser app does; it makes it simpler than ever for customers to select the ideal wall colour for their houses.

Digital Fitting Rooms – Online customers face a particular set of difficulties while purchasing clothing. It might be challenging for a customer to imagine how a piece of clothing would appear on their own distinct body after viewing a product photo. Virtual or digital fitting rooms have been tested by companies and

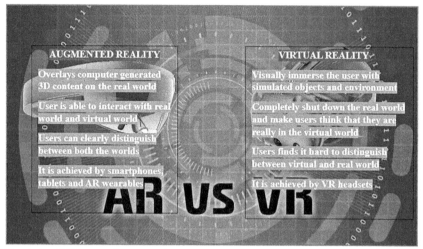

Fig. 4.2. Difference Between AR and VR. *Source*: Created by author.

stores like ASOS, Gucci, etc. to assist customers in finding the ideal size and style without needing to visit a store in person.

Virtual Try-Ons – When a customer is uncertain about how a product will appear on them, they frequently hesitate to purchase it. In a manner akin to virtual changing rooms, companies and merchants are utilising AR technology to enable customers to try caps, eyeglasses, and other accessories.

Space Visualisation – When a sofa isn't in the room, it might be challenging to imagine how it will look. Without needing to make a purchase right away, AR can assist clients in seeing how huge furniture pieces would fit into their residences or offices. E.g., with the Ikea AR app, customers can take a room scan and arrange computer-generated, to-scale images of the things they want in it.

4.1.3 Cashless Shopping

Consumers make use of cash transactions more often than they were before the pandemic, according to Kotkowski and Polasik (2021), which raises questions about financial inclusion. People are adjusting their purchasing habits because they are afraid to use cash. There are national variations in paying patterns due to several factors that are distinct to each country. With more and more people adopting cashless transactions like UPIs, mobile wallets, and cards that are contactless these days, Tripathi and Dave (2022) stated that electronic transactions have become more visible, responsible, scalable, and accountable – although cyber security is still necessary. Since all small merchants use online payments these days, accessibility to them is essential.

4.1.4 Logistics Robots

Logistics robots are autonomous systems designed to streamline goods flows, optimise safety, and increase productivity in warehouses. Companies are integrating robots into their processes to reduce error risk and increase productivity. McKinsey's research highlights the critical point for robots in omnichannel storage facilities. Robotics projects a 23% yearly increase for the logistics automation marketplace, which is expected to arrive at $51 billion by the year 2030 (Mecalux, 2022). Technological advancements in storage have prompted businesses to look into novel approaches to process optimisation:

Product Storage – The storing of items is a frequently encountered robotics use in logistics facilities. Modern technology is used to automate storage chores by controlling movements within the facility.

Internal Material Transportation – The transportation of items interferes with the work of operators and equipment handlers, who devote a large portion of their time to these duties. Internal goods movement automation is a useful robotic app for high-through operations.

Order Picking – One of the most expensive and intricate tasks in any warehouse is order processing. Furthermore, automation expedites and simplifies picking using the goods-to-person approach. By using this selection approach, workers can assemble purchases without requiring to travel because automated systems deliver the products to them.

4.1.5 Self-Checkout

In total, 60% of consumers dislike waiting in queues for checkout, and many may prefer self-checkout options. Self-checkouts allow customers to scan products and make payments without store staff assistance, enhancing customer satisfaction and saving money. Technological giants like Amazon and Walmart are interested in self-checkout equipment. Benefits include faster checkout times, shorter waits, increased storage capacity, and improved employee productivity. Retailers should gradually introduce self-checkout technology.

4.1.6 Electronic Shelf Labels (ESLs)

ESLs are small, battery-operated screens that replace traditional paper labelling at the shelf border. They connect wirelessly to a central server, creating a dynamic price automation system. ESLs can automate retail pricing tactics, ensuring accurate pricing at the right time and seamless omnichannel sales. Retailers can buy ESL parts from multiple manufacturers with confidence, knowing that each part can function with others if a global ESL standard is established. Implementing ESL improves customer satisfaction, environmental friendliness, resource management efficiency, and accuracy and speed.

4.2 New Retail Technologies

4.2.1 Drones and Robots Making Autonomous Delivery

Last-mile delivery is extremely challenging in cities with a high population due to rising traffic jams, vehicle parking restrictions, and environmental constraints (Akeb et al., 2018). As a result, within the past 10 years, novel last-mile delivery alternatives have appeared. Over the past 10 years, automation technology has improved significantly and created a wide range of novel business opportunities in the last-mile logistics sector. More precisely, it is anticipated that automated goods delivery would be a viable solution for up to 80% of business-to-customer (B2C) deliveries (Grolms, 2019). In certain circumstances, Unmanned Aerial Vehicles (UAVs) are unable to make deliveries for too many reasons, including their low carrying capacity, limited flying span, and inability to comply with regulations in cities. The self-driving delivery robot is one type of autonomous delivery that shows promise and has limited coverage. It would have appeared futuristic to see robots carrying packages to clients before COVID-19 (Chen et al., 2021). In the framework of city logistics, such robots' characteristics are most appropriate for last-mile deliveries. For instance, the Starship robot, which weighs a maximum of 45 kg, can deliver a payload containing not more than 2.6 kg to clients across a 4-mile range while moving at a pedestrian pace (Kottasova, 2015). Another example is that ANYmal may ascend over challenging surfaces including obstacles, staircases (up to 45°), and other ground barriers in addition to having a payload capacity of as much as 10 kg (Hutter et al., 2017). As a last illustration, consider the FedEx SameDay Bot, which can deliver packages from house to house within a radius of three miles and has a maximum pace of 16 kilometres per hour.

4.2.2 Sustainable Retail Technology

It is one of the retail technology trends that is becoming more and more popular across all industries, not just in retail. Customers have grown increasingly concerned with a brand's ethical standing, and green buying is becoming popular. A better-balanced future can be facilitated by innovative as well as sustainable technologies without compromising productivity or company expansion. To reduce waste and increase productivity, some strategies include moving to a cloud-based paradigm, digitising operations, and enhancing workflows with computer vision as well as Big Data (Canorea, 2021). The appointment of sustainability officers to some businesses is a positive development since it concentrates the possibility for proactive measures. There is a growing push in the general marketplace to invest in businesses that prioritise sustainability. Businesses should not attempt to accelerate their sustainability initiatives, as they will probably take years to mature. However, beginning with basic measures like purchasing fresher more power-efficient computing devices and other energy-efficient gadgets, as well as making sure that equipment is turned down whenever not in use, organisations can start to save energy. It's imperative to inform staff members about company sustainability initiatives and provide them with guidance on how they may contribute (Mearian, 2022). Fig. 4.3 explains sustainable technology.

4.2.3 Supply Chain Control Solutions Powered By Machine Learning (ML), AI, and IoT

Research on AI and ML has traditionally been done in combination with other fields and sectors since they are thought to be related. For instance, one systematic

The Future of Smart Retail 73

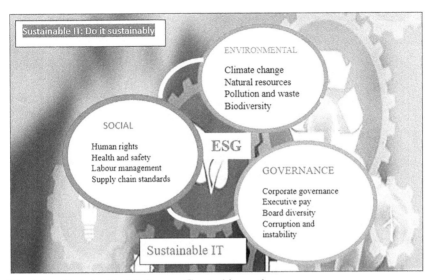

Fig. 4.3. Sustainable IT. *Source*: Created by author.

study of AI and ML techniques for energy demand side responsiveness was conducted (Antonopoulos et al., 2020). Similar to this, Kietzmann and Pitt (2020) provide some information on the uses of AI and ML that managers should be aware of. In addition, Haider et al. (2020) investigated the prospects, benefits, and direction of research in the field of IT for AI and ML in 5G network security. Canhoto and Clear (2020) have presented a paradigm for identifying the risk of value loss associated with business tools utilising AI and ML. Though it is technically a subset of AI, ML is revolutionising a wide range of industries. By using IT systems, trends within current databases as well as algorithms can be recognised, leading to the provision of suitable solutions and assisting in the process of making choices. To make clear how AI helps supply chain management research, numerous researchers have been aiming on this topic and produced scholarly articles (Feizabadi, 2020; Toorajipour et al., 2021; Younis et al., 2021). Talking about the IoT industry, present supply chain management is getting benefits from it. By cutting operating expenses, the IoT may automate and digitise supply chain activities to achieve optimal efficiency in operations. Supply chains have been transmuted by the widespread adoption of IoT devices. They are using the newest real-time surveillance technologies, such as GPS, and IoT gadgets in the Supply Chain (SC) process to monitor and track shipments. Near-field communication and RFID tags additionally are utilised by IoT devices for managing assets (Hussain et al., 2021). Fig. 4.4 shows features of the IoT-based supply chain.

Retail IoT solutions are being adopted by retailers to enhance the global consumer experience. Retailers and e-retailers have prospects in the following sectors thanks to the IoT revolution:

Marketing – Smartphones, which offer customised messages and exclusive offers, are essential during the shopping process. IoT devices use acquired data to identify particular gadgets and enable targeted marketing. These gadgets monitor

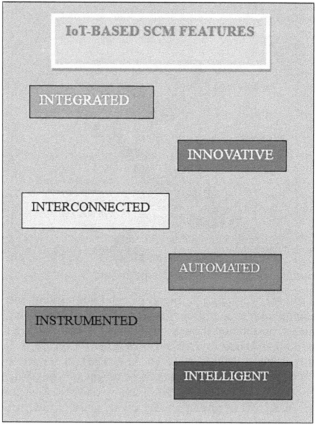

Fig. 4.4. Attributes of SCM Based on IoT. *Source*: Created by author.

everyday activities, purchasing patterns, and preferences, which enables targeted advertising. Users might visit stores again if applications and websites don't produce the expected outcomes.

Flexible Pricing and Advertising – Businesses may now more easily keep an eye on rivals, implement dynamic pricing, and modify promotions by using IoT and e-retail. Numerous marketing campaigns and fresh deals have resulted from this on well-known e-retail websites and applications.

Logistics – Efficient logistics using RFID and GPS track cargo steps, but unexpected delays can occur during lockdowns. Retailers use IoT solutions to inform customers and drivers, ensuring seamless supply chain management and logistics.

We probably make daily use of IoT devices. Some IoT gadgets that you might be familiar with are listed below:

Smart devices, like thermostats and security systems, utilise wireless connections to understand user instructions and function autonomously, assisting with daily tasks like setting adjustments and receiving door notifications.

Wearable technologies like smartwatches and Fitbits share data and track GPS locations.

Personal medical devices like pacemakers monitor vital signs and detect health issues remotely.

Autonomous vehicles rely on the internet for real-time information sharing. Sensors map surroundings, transmit camera footage, and respond to traffic signals.

4.2.4 Beacon Technology

The IT industry is talking a lot about beacon-based solutions for technology in this era of rapid technological advancement. Even though a lot of people are ignorant of this technology, it has been found to play a significant role in both enterprises and the lives of many individuals. The retail sector has seen a massive transformation because of this novel technology. The word 'Beacon' was first used by Apple in 2013. Experts in the field now refer to Beacon as simply 'iBeacon'. Beacons are tiny hardware components that emit radio frequencies to adjacent equipment. Mobile phones and other smart gadgets can pick up the radio signals that Beacon broadcasts (Yao et al., 2019). Beacon can be used to enhance connectivity and customer service because it is compatible with mobile gadgets. They are among the core ideas of the IoT (Zhuang et al., 2022). Beacons have the power to bring back the traditional brick-and-mortar retail paradigm since they can seamlessly connect your offline business with your internet presence. It enables merchants to better serve customers by providing them with improved customised experiences, personalised notifications, and loyalty advantages by knowing consumers through their data (Lin et al., 2022). At the same time, beacons provide insight into the connection between marketing campaigns and client conversions. Fig. 4.5 mentions the pros and cons of Beacon technology. Beacon can be used for the following purposes:

- Assist customers in navigating the store.
- Provide exclusive cuisine and jersey discounts to sports fans.
- Inform clients who are in-store about deals and discounts.
- Encourage clients to do in-store activities.
- As a loyalty initiative, use beacons.
- Observe consumer's in-store movement.

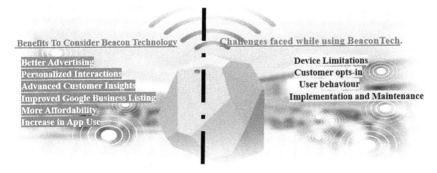

Fig. 4.5. Advantages and Challenges of Beacon Technology. *Source*: Created by author.

4.2.5 Smart Labels

Using sophisticated labelling systems to make items 'smarter' is essential to optimise the industrial procedures performed in an Industry 4.0 smart plant along with leveraging some of the innovations. There are two approaches to carry out this smart connection. If the products or parts have the necessary software or hardware embedded, the first involves communicating directly with them. A second strategy must be used, though, to add temporary exterior hardware or software using intelligent smart labelling or tags. This is because the entire hardware or software is typically not operational till the final phases of construction. This second method turns ordinary objects into smart, is more suitable for use in the product's production, and in certain situations can even be applied after the good has been delivered (Fernandez-Carames & Fraga-Lamas, 2018). Fig. 4.6 demonstrates the evolution of label technology. Also, the following features should be there to make the labelling system smart:

- Smart labels should provide information on product conditions using data from actuators, sensors, and related systems. They should identify occurrences once a product exits a processing stage and mirror this on both the smart label and a central traceability repository.
- Industry 4.0 smart labels should replace printed instructions by specifying tasks for an item at a specific point, and updating task information regularly as the product moves through the production process.
- The labels should also indicate final product attributes to users. Additionally, suppliers should be notified when a component runs out, and additional work is required.

4.2.6 Omnichannel Revolution

The goal of omnichannel retailing is to give customers a consistent experience from exploring to order fulfilment through both online and offline channels. The

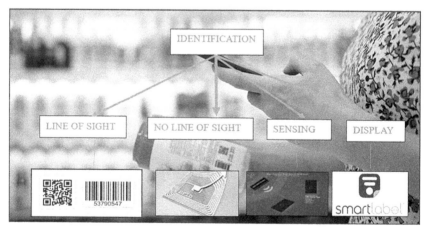

Fig. 4.6. Label Technology Evolution. *Source*: Created by author.

foundation of omnichannel retail is the idea that combining multiple points of contact creates value and makes an overall product that is superior to the combination of its parts. Fig. 4.7 shows the visualisation of omnichannel retailing. Furthermore, there is not a universal omnichannel marketing plan. Every business modifies its approach based on its industry and clientele. Omnichannel retail is becoming more and more important due to the growth of e-commerce, shifting consumer behaviour, and fierce rivalry in the retail industry. There has been a significant increase in the use of omnichannel 'retailing' in corporate earnings calls since 2020 (Hole et al., 2019).

The omnichannel revolution relies on technology to gather customer data and integrate loyalty and incentives into membership programmes. This shift benefits both physical and online shopping, offering seamless, personalised, and flexible experiences. However, omnichannel retail faces challenges such as organisational barriers, culture, and a need to question traditional methods. Retailers must ensure technology partners are affordable and compatible with their existing infrastructure, and that traditional methods are questioned to adapt to the changing landscape.

5. Findings

Technologies are developing quickly. Numerous of these innovations are significantly changing the retail industry. Retailing is being drastically changed by new technologies including drones, 5G networks, VR, AR, IoT, and micro-cloud computing. Specifically, after the COVID-19 pandemic, technology is enabling retail to adapt to novel and unanticipated situations. IoT technology has a positive impact on in-store and online shopping, which is advantageous for both

Fig. 4.7. Visualization of Omnichannel Retailing. *Source*: Created by author.

consumers and companies. For designers and developers who prioritise the user experience, innovation is essential. Web developers will need to use data to create intelligent, tailored apps as IoT becomes increasingly commonplace. For the best digital change consulting services for retailing IoT solutions, speak with industry professionals. This chapter provides a comprehensive picture and better comprehension of technology and retailing with our analysis of technology classification, technological trends in retailing. It is our aim that the study routes and future scenarios we detail will help generate new ideas and research.

According to the analysis, pre-purchase services and technological apps are mostly gathering information on customer buying. With almost $60 billion in transactions, self-checkout, and electronic payment are, nevertheless, growing in popularity. The study suggests introducing AI-based services and applications progressively to bring new technologies and enhance the effectiveness and calibre of various stages of the purchasing process. It is important to avoid pushing the application too early or too aggressively, though, as users may reject or even fight it. For interactive apps and image processing offerings, technology suppliers should leverage voice and image processing technologies in the future.

6. Conclusion

The retail industry is vibrant and constantly expanding. A few of these advancements have an opportunity to shape retail's future by allowing businesses to tailor their offerings to the needs of consumers. This will assist firms in enhancing the client experience across their process of purchasing and in offering tailored responses to the expanding needs of customers.

These days, numerous benefits of investing in retail e-commerce options include increased mobile marketing abilities, fresh sources of income, customised insights, and loyalty to customers over time. Retailers set themselves up for success by utilising retail technology to fortify relationships with both customers and Consumer Packaged Goods brands. Since technology connects customers, gadgets, and data for a more intelligent shopping experience, market observers assert that a digital retail revolution is underway. For merchants who are receptive to new ideas and prepared to view the volatile and complicated retail sector of today from a different angle, technology offers an exceptional competitive edge. Retailers must keep up with the latest technological advancements to remain competitive as the supply chain grows more intricate and consumers become more astute, tech-savvy, gadget-literate, and clever about using multiple channels. Retailers need to have strong digital relationships to connect and communicate with consumers as well as to mould and influence experiences. Retailers create connections to assist customers in making decisions that benefit them both now and in the future. They serve as the architects for the ties that exist with customers. Affordably priced, user-friendly technology that maximises advantages for both shops and consumers is urgently needed.

Talking about India, with technological advancements, shifting consumer tastes and focus on sustainability, the retail sector in India has a bright and promising future. Providing flawless omnichannel encounters, utilising data analytics for customisation, accepting electronic payments, and supporting environmentally friendly practices will be the main priorities for retailers as they continue to adjust to such new developments. Its retail sector is well positioned to prosper in the dynamic market environment by adopting innovation and transformation and is also centred on omnichannel tactics, which offer customers a seamless experience by giving them a comprehensive, single glance at each retail business from the comfort of their home or place of business. These strategies apply a variety of channels, including online stores, phone sales, physical shops, mobile devices and apps, and different kinds of consumer transactions to give buyers a wide range of shopping options. Table 4.2 mentions some future research questions for studies related to AI-based retailing.

Table 4.2.   Future Research Questions/Directions.

Challenges	Which technological platforms can easily accommodate new sorts of retailers? How can the causal influence of adoption of technology drivers on adoption be estimated?
AK/VR tech.	Future research should explore the metaverse's potential for cross-reality experiences and the use of blockchain technology, specifically NFTs, to enhance customer value creation. More specifically, human factor theory development in VR shop design (i.e., social component, eye-tracking, etc.) should be the primary emphasis of future research.
AI/ IoT	How can businesses coordinate interactions between workers and customers as well as between service robots and customers to produce a seamless experience?
Omnichannel strategy	What areas should future research focus on regarding customer behaviours such as showrooming and webrooming, including the underlying causes and potential strategies for businesses to address value co-destruction effectively?

Source: Author's compilation.

References

Akeb, H., Moncef, B., & Durand, B. (2018). Building a collaborative solution in dense urban city settings to enhance parcel delivery: An effective crowd model in Paris. *Transportation Research Part E: Logistics and Transportation Review*, *119*, 223–233. https://doi.org/10.1016/j.tre.2018.04.007

Anantharaman, S., Verma, B., Mittal, A., & Aggarwal, A. (2023, December). Exploring vendor's critical attributes to success in engineering, procurement and construction companies in India. In R. K. Kaushal, F. Ali, S. EL-Sappagh, & R. Mittal (Eds.), *AIP conference proceedings* (Vol. 2916, No. 1). AIP Publishing.

Antonopoulos, I., Robu, V., Couraud, B., Kirli, D., Norbu, S., Kiprakis, A., Flynn, D., Elizondo-Gonzalez, S., & Wattam, S. (2020). Artificial intelligence and machine learning approach to energy demand-side response: A systematic review.

80 Ritu Kumari and Vinay Pal Singh

Renewable and Sustainable Energy Reviews, *130*, 109899. https://doi.org/10.1016/j.rser.2020.109899

Canhoto, A. I., & Clear, F. (2020). Artificial intelligence and machine learning as business tools: A framework for diagnosing value destruction potential. *Business Horizons*, *63*(2), 183–193. https://doi.org/10.1016/j.bushor.2019.11.003

Canorea, E. (2021). *The tech trends that will shape the future of the retail sector*. Plain Concepts. https://www.plainconcepts.com/tech-trends-retail-sector/

Chawla, U., Verma, B., & Mittal, A. (2024). Resistance to O2O technology platform adoption among small retailers: The influence of visibility and discoverability. *Technology in Society*, *76*, 102482.

Chen, C., Demir, E., Huang, Y., & Qiu, R. (2021). The adoption of self-driving delivery robots in last mile logistics. *Transportation Research Part E: Logistics and Transportation Review*, *146*, 102214. https://doi.org/10.1016/j.tre.2020.102214

Chui, M., Manyika, J., Miremadi, M., Henke, N., Chung, R., Nel, P., & Malhotra, S. (2018). *Notes from the AI frontier: Applications and value of deep learning*. McKinsey & Company. https://www.mckinsey.com/featured-insights/artificial-intelligence/notes-from-the-ai-frontier-applications-and-value-of-deep-learning

Doolittle, & McMillan. (2020). *Changes in food retail foot traffic during COVID-19*. McMillanDoolittle – Transforming Retail. https://www.mcmillandoolittle.com/changes-in-food-retail-foot-traffic-during-covid-19/

Feizabadi, J. (2020). Machine learning demand forecasting and supply chain performance. *International Journal of Logistics Research and Applications*, *25*(2), 1–24. https://doi.org/10.1080/%2013675567.2020.1803246

Fernandez-Carames, T. M., & Fraga-Lamas, P. (2018). A review on human-centered IoT-connected smart labels for the Industry 4.0. *IEEE Access*, *6*, 25939–25957. https://doi.org/10.1109/access.2018.2833501

Grewal, D., Ahlbom, C.-P., Beitelspacher, L., Noble, S. M., & Nordfält, J. (2018). In-store mobile phone use and customer shopping behavior: Evidence from the field. *Journal of Marketing*, *82*(4), 102–126. https://doi.org/10.1509/jm.17.0277

Grewal, D., Gauri, D. K., Roggeveen, A. L., & Sethuraman, R. (2021). Strategizing retailing in the new technology era. *Journal of Retailing*, *97*(1), 6–12. https://doi.org/10.1016/j.jretai.2021.02.004

Grewal, D., Noble, S. M., Roggeveen, A. L., & Nordfalt, J. (2019). The future of in-store technology. *Journal of the Academy of Marketing Science*, *48*(1), 96–113. https://doi.org/10.1007/s11747-019-00697-z

Grewal, D., & Roggeveen, A. L. (2020). Understanding retail experiences and customer journey management. *Journal of Retailing*, *96*(1), 3–8. https://doi.org/10.1016/j.jretai.2020.02.002

Grewal, D., Roggeveen, A. L., & Nordfält, J. (2017). The future of retailing. *Journal of Retailing*, *93*(1), 1–6.

Grolms, M. (2019). *Autonomous shuttles and delivery robots*. Advanced Science News. https://www.advancedsciencenews.com/autonomous-shuttles-and-+delivery-robots/

Guha, A., Grewal, D., Kopalle, P. K., Haenlein, M., Schneider, M. J., Jung, H., Moustafa, R., Hegde, D. R., & Hawkins, G. (2021). How artificial intelligence will affect the future of retailing. *Journal of Retailing*, *97*(1), 28–41.

Haider, N., Baig, M. Z., & Imran, M. (2020). *Artificial intelligence and machine learning in 5G network security: Opportunities, advantages, and future research trends*. ArXiv:2007.04490 [Cs]. https://arxiv.org/abs/2007.04490

Hole, Y., Pawar, Ms. Snehal., & Khedkar, E. B. (2019). Omni channel retailing: An opportunity and challenges in the Indian market. *Journal of Physics: Conference Series*, *1362*, 012121. https://doi.org/10.1088/1742-6596/1362/1/012121

Hussain, M., Javed, W., Hakeem, O., Yousafzai, A., Younas, A., Awan, M. J., Nobanee, H., & Zain, A. M. (2021). Blockchain-based IoT devices in supply chain management:

A systematic literature review. *Sustainability*, *13*(24), 13646. https://doi.org/10.3390/su132413646

Hutter, M., Gehring, C., Lauber, A., Gunther, F., Bellicoso, C. D., Tsounis, V., Fankhauser, P., Diethelm, R., Bachmann, S., Bloesch, M., Kolvenbach, H., Bjelonic, M., Isler, L., & Meyer, K. (2017). ANYmal – toward legged robots for harsh environments. *Advanced Robotics*, *31*(17), 918–931. https://doi.org/10.1080/01691864.2017.1378591

Ivanova, N. V. (2020). *The future of retail: Innovations and basic trends.* Innovative Economic Symposium. 10.1007/978-3-030-60929-0_21

Jose, J. (2023). *5 Technologies driving the future of retail – ET retail.* ETRetail.com. https://retail.economictimes.indiatimes.com/blog/5-technologies-driving-the-future-of-retail/100988116

Kietzmann, J., & Pitt, L. F. (2020). *Artificial intelligence and machine learning: What managers need to know.* Business Horizons. https://doi.org/10.1016/j.bushor.2019.11.005

Koch, J., Frommeyer, B., & Schewe, G. (2022). Managing the transition to eco-friendly packaging – An investigation of consumers' motives in online retail. *Journal of Cleaner Production*, *351*, 131504. https://doi.org/10.1016/j.jclepro.2022.131504

Kotkowski, R. P., & Polasik, M. (2021). COVID-19 pandemic increases the divide between cash and cashless payment users in Europe. *Economics Letters*, *209*, 110139. https://doi.org/10.1016/j.econlet.2021.110139

Kottasova, I. (2015). *Forget drones, here come delivery robots.* CNNMoney. https://money.cnn.com/2015/11/03/technology/starship-delivery-robots/%3fiid%3dEL

Kumar, V., & Ayodeji, O. G. (2020). E-retail factors for customer activation and retention: An empirical study from Indian e-commerce customers. *Journal of Retailing and Consumer Services*, *59*, 102399. https://doi.org/10.1016/j.jretconser.2020.102399

Lee, L., Inman, J., Argo, J., Bottger, T., Dholakia, U. M., Gilbride, T., van Ittersum, K., Kahn, B. E., Kalra, A., Lehmann, D. R., McAlister, L., Shankar, V., & Tsai, C. I. (2017). From browsing to buying and beyond: The needs-adaptive shopper journey model. *SSRN Electronic Journal.* https://doi.org/10.2139/ssrn.3093999

Lin, M. Y.-C., Nguyen, T. T., Cheng, E. Y.-L., Le, A. N. H., & Cheng, J. M. S. (2022). Proximity marketing and Bluetooth beacon technology: A dynamic mechanism leading to relationship program receptiveness. *Journal of Business Research*, *141*, 151–162. https://doi.org/10.1016/j.jbusres.2021.12.030

Madhukar, L. S. (2018). Demonetization and cashless transactions: Impact on retail business markets. *JournalNX*, *4*(1), 175–177. https://www.neliti.com/publications/342443/demonetization-and-cashless-transactions-impact-on-retail-business-markets

Mearian, L. (2022). *Why sustainable tech is becoming a top initiative for execs.* Computerworld. https://www.computerworld.com/article/3676637/why-sustainable-tech-is-becoming-a-top-initiative-for-execs.html

Mecalux. (2022). *Logistics robots: The rise of automation in warehousing.* www.interlakemecalux.com. https://www.interlakemecalux.com/blog/logistics-robots

Nakano, S., & Kondo, F. N. (2018). Customer segmentation with purchase channels and media touchpoints using single source panel data. *Journal of Retailing and Consumer Services*, *41*, 142–152. https://doi.org/10.1016/j.jretconser.2017.11.012

Oberoi, S., Arora, S., Verma, B., & Roy, K. K. (2024). What do we know about artificial intelligence and blockchain technology integration in the healthcare industry? In B. Singla & A. Mittal (Eds.), *Driving decentralization and disruption with digital technologies* (pp. 124–138). IGI Global.

PricewaterhouseCoopers, & Kanta. (2020). *Retailing 2020: Winning in a polarized world.* https://rasci.in/downloads/2012/Retailing_2020_Winning_Polarized_World.pdf

Saluja, S. (2023). *The future of the retail industry in India: Embracing innovation and digital transformation.* www.linkedin.com. https://www.linkedin.com/pulse/future-retail-industry-india-embracing-innovation-digital-saluja

Setia, P., Deng, K., & Jena, R. (2017). Internally or externally-oriented it competencies: A configuration theory perspective on how to build demand management agility. *ICIS 2017 Proceedings*. 1–17. https://aisel.aisnet.org/icis2017/Strategy/Presentations/26/

Shankar, V., Douglass, T., Hennessey, J., Kalyanam, K., Setia, P., Golmohammadi, A., Tirunillai, S., Bull, J. S., & Waddoups, R. (2021). How technology is changing retail. *Journal of Retailing, 97*(1), 13–27. https://www.sciencedirect.com/science/article/pii/S0022435920300695

Singhraul, B. P., & Garwal, Y. S. (2018). Cashless economy – Challenges and opportunities in India. *Pacific Business Review International, 10*(9), 54–63. http://www.pbr.co.in/2018/2018_month/March/6.pdf

Souiden, N., Ladhari, R., & Chiadmi, N.-E. (2019). New trends in retailing and services. *Journal of Retailing and Consumer Services, 50*, 286–288. https://doi.org/10.1016/j.jretconser.2018.07.023

Toorajipour, R., Sohrabpour, V., Nazarpour, A., Oghazi, P., & Fischl, M. (2021). Artificial intelligence in supply chain management: A systematic literature review. *Journal of Business Research, 122*(1), 502–517. https://doi.org/10.1016/j.jbusres.2020.09.009

Tripathi, S., & Dave, N. (2022). Cashless transactions through e-commerce platforms in post-Covid-19. *International Journal of Management, Public Policy and Research, 1*(2), 12–23. https://doi.org/10.55829/010203

Turner, S. (2023). *What is retail technology?* www.swiftly.com. https://www.swiftly.com/blog/what-is-retail-technology

Von Briel, F. (2018). The future of omnichannel retail: A four-stage Delphi study. *Technological Forecasting and Social Change, 132*, 217–229. https://doi.org/10.1016/j.techfore.2018.02.004

Winn, E. (2023). *Common technology challenges facing retailers*. TPP Retail. https://www.tppretail.com/common-technology-challenges-facing-retailers/#:~:text=Not%20enough%20devices&text=They%20might%20be%20challenged%20to

Xu, L. D., Xu, E. L., & Li, L. (2018). Industry 4.0: State of the art and future trends. *International Journal of Production Research, 56*(8), 2941–2962.

Yao, Y., Huang, Y., & Wang, Y. (2019). Unpacking people's understandings of Bluetooth Beacon systems: A location-based IoT technology. In N. Mead & D. Port (Eds.), *52nd Hawaii international conference on system sciences* (pp. 1638–1647).

Yarkova, A. (2018). *Key trends and technologies for retail in 2019*. RETAILER.ru. https://retailer.ru/kljuchevye-trendy-i-tehnologii-dlja-ritejla-v-2019-godu/

Younis, H., Sundarakani, B., & Alsharairi, M. (2021). Applications of artificial intelligence and machine learning within supply chains: Systematic review and future research directions. *Journal of Modelling in Management, 17*(3), 916–940. https://doi.org/10.1108/jm2-12-2020-0322

Zhang, L., & Hänninen, M. (2022). *Digital retail – Key trends and developments* (B. L. MacCarthy & D. Ivanov, Eds.). Elsevier. https://www.sciencedirect.com/science/article/abs/pii/B9780323916141000149

Zhuang, Y., Zhang, C., Jianzhu Huai, Li, Y., Chen, L., & Chen, R. (2022). Bluetooth localization technology: Principles, applications, and future trends. *IEEE Internet of Things Journal, 9*(23), 23506–23524. https://doi.org/10.1109/jiot.2022.3203414

Chapter 5

Influence Dynamism of Augmented Reality in Manufacturing Industries

John Paul Raj V., Nara Srujana Rani, Sathish Pachiyappan and Saravanan Vellaiyan

School of Business and Management, Christ (Deemed to be University), Bangalore, India

Abstract

Augmented reality (AR) has emerged as one of the significant transformative technologies in today's business world. This technology overlays digital information and virtual objects onto the real world, and it is viewed in smartphones, tablets, and AR glasses. It enhances user experience, facilitates interactive learning, and provides real-time information or supports customers to make decisions. This chapter tries to find the impact of AR on customer's experience and willingness to buy furniture evidence from the manufacturing concern. Cross-sectional study was conducted with the help of a structured questionnaire. The data have been collected from 384 respondents who have exposure towards AR. Further, correlation analysis is employed to find the relationship and also regression analysis is used to check the influence level. The findings of the research reveal that most of the respondents found that AR very much useful in checking the furniture placement in home, and also it has helped respondents to make purchase decisions. Positive correlation was found between AR and customer's experience and willingness to buy furniture. The study further finds that there is a significant impact of AR on customer's experience and willingness to buy furniture. The findings of the study strengthen business organisations to effectively utilise AR to improve customer's experience and willingness to buy furniture.

Keywords: Augmented reality; customer experience; willingness to buy; furniture; easy to use; personalised to use

---

Augmenting Retail Reality: Blockchain, AR, VR, and the Internet of Things, Part A, 83–96
Copyright © 2025 by John Paul Raj V., Nara Srujana Rani, Sathish Pachiyappan and Saravanan Vellaiyan
Published under exclusive licence by Emerald Publishing Limited
doi:10.1108/978-1-83608-634-520241012

Introduction

AR is a technology that allows users to overlay digital information in the real world to improve their view of and interact with it. The term AR is used to describe systems that superimpose computer-generated information onto the natural environment (Doil et al., 2003). Mobile devices, such as smartphones and tablets, as well as specialist headgear, like Microsoft's HoloLens or Magic Leap's One, can be used to experience AR (De Pace et al., 2018). For AR to function, the real world must first be captured using the device's camera before any specific objects or locations can be identified and tracked using computer vision algorithms. Once it has been located, the AR application can superimpose digital content over the real world to give the user an engaging and immersive experience.

A variety of formats for digital content are possible, including three-dimensional (3D) models, animations, movies, text, and sound (De Pace et al., 2018). In recent years, AR technology has experienced substantial growth, and AR enhances the existing environment rather than replacing it (Doil et al., 2003). The following are a handful of the main elements advancing AR technology. AR technology is becoming more widely adopted across various industries, including retail, entertainment, healthcare, education, and manufacturing (Nee & Ong, 2013). As more companies look to capitalise on the advantages of this technology, this rising acceptance is fuelling the growth of the AR market. Hardware and software improvements: Creating more sophisticated hardware and software has increased AR technology's efficiency and performance (Romano et al., 2020). Due to this, AR technology is now more widely available and more straightforward to use, which has increased acceptance (Doil et al., 2003). Increased funding and investment: The AR market has received significant funding and investment in recent years, which has aided in accelerating the sector's innovation and growth. As a result, new AR applications and goods have been developed (Egger & Masood, n.d.), propelling the market's expansion. Consumers increasingly seek immersive and interactive experiences, and AR technology offers a means of delivering these experiences. The expansion of AR technology in sectors like entertainment, gaming, and retail is driven by this need (Bottani & Vignali, 2019). Overall, it is anticipated that AR technology will continue to develop in the years to come as it gets more sophisticated, approachable, and incorporated into a variety of businesses.

Overview of the Indian AR Market

India had 1.2 billion mobile subscribers as of 2021, of whom 750 million use smartphones. Most of the young people in Tier 2 and Tier 3 cities are technologically literate, allowing businesses and app developers to offer AR-based experiences. The consumer space's retail and gaming sectors are where AR is most frequently deployed. In India, AR technology is picking up steam as several businesses and startups investigate its possibilities in various sectors. In India, the following sectors are employing AR technology: Education: By giving students engaging and immersive content, AR technology is being used in India to improve learning.

Many educational institutions have incorporated AR technology into their teaching approaches to make learning more exciting and efficient. Retail: To give customers an immersive shopping experience, AR technology is being applied in India's retail sector. Healthcare: In India, AR technology is utilised to mimic and see medical processes and help operating room staff. It is also used to instruct medical students and help patients comprehend their ailments. Medical education, diagnostics, surgery, and fitness all use AR extensively. Tourism: To give guests an engaging and immersive experience, AR technology is applied in the Indian tourism sector. For instance, the Taj Mahal app uses AR to give users a virtual monument tour. Entertainment: To give people interactive experiences, AR technology is being applied in India's entertainment sector. The present surroundings create a playing area for AR games. Usually, portable gaming consoles, cellphones, and tablets are used to play AR games. Overall, as AR technology advances and becomes more widely available, new opportunities for creativity and innovation across numerous industries will arise.

AR in the Furniture Industry

The furniture market is fast changing because AR gives customers an engaging and dynamic buying experience (Lindén, 2019). Customers can use AR technology to arrange furniture virtually before purchasing. The inability to touch and engage with the object in person has been one of the main obstacles to buying furniture online (Young & Smith, 2016). Some ways furniture retailers use AR technology are visualisation, customisation, engagement, and cost saving. Elements that come under customer experience with AR in furniture are augmented product image, ease of use, personalised use, and better access to information (Chawla et al., 2024; Oberoi et al., 2024; Ramdani et al., 2022). The types of AR used in furniture companies are marker-based AR, marker-less AR, and projection-based AR. Marker-based AR: With this sort of AR, a printed image or marker is scanned by the camera of a smartphone or tablet, causing a 3D image of furniture to emerge on the device's screen (Ramdani et al., 2022). Customers may move the gadget about to view the furniture from various perspectives and understand how it might look in their room. Marker-less AR: With this sort of AR, a 3D image of furniture is placed inside a real-world scene by using a smartphone or tablet camera to identify objects like walls and floors (Carvalho et al., n.d.). Customers can do this without a printed marker to visualise how the furniture might look in their room. Projection-based AR: With this sort of AR, a 3D representation of furniture is projected onto a real-world setting, like an empty wall or floor (Hartanto et al., 2019).

Customers can then move the furniture around or modify its size to engage with it. Mixed reality enables customers to engage with virtual furnishings in an actual setting by fusing the digital and physical worlds (Kurniawan & Fadryan, 2019). Specialised hardware, such as Microsoft's HoloLens, is needed for this kind of AR, which superimposes digital visuals over the real world. To improve the shopping experience, boost sales, and let buyers visualise how furniture might look in their spaces, furniture makers may integrate one or more of these AR technologies. The kind of AR implemented may vary depending on the company's budget, the required technical know-how, and the desired level of engagement. IKEA uses a particular sort of AR: The mobile app from Swedish furniture company IKEA uses marker-less AR to let users realistically arrange furniture in their rooms (Ozturkcan, 2021). IKEA Place is a function that places a 3D image of furniture inside a real-world location using the camera of a smartphone or tablet to identify the features of the surrounding area, such as walls and flooring (Whang et al., 2021). Before purchasing, customers may view how the furniture will fit and appear in their homes. Accordingly, the customers may take the decision regarding the purchase of furniture items. Hence, AR plays a major role in taking decisions on purchase of furniture. With this background, the study aims to find the influential factors to use AR by the customer for buying furniture in the manufacturing industry.

One important barrier to incorporating AR into production environments is the initial cost of deployment, which includes hardware, software development, and employee training. Furthermore, the complexity of integrating AR technologies into existing production processes makes it difficult, since it requires collaboration between different departments and careful evaluation of compatibility issues with the existing infrastructure. Despite these limitations, the potential benefits of AR in terms of productivity, quality, and safety highlight the need of overcoming these barriers to wider implementation in manufacturing environments.

Empirical Studies

AR significantly and positively influences user experience by impinging on various product quality characteristics. AR-enriched user experience produces higher user satisfaction and user willingness to buy (Poushneh & Vasquez-Parraga, 2017). Consumers with positive attitudes are more willing to use a mobile AR (MAR) app again. Positive attitudes, in turn, favour the future success of MAR apps and reinforce consumer continuance intentions (Anantharaman et al., 2023; Qin et al., 2021a). AR can help buyers make fewer but more informed product choices before purchasing. Additionally, they found proof that AR can lower brand value, allowing developing brands a chance to interact with consumers. Findings indicate that at the point of purchase, AR can help with product duration and drive hedonic value through playfulness. Finally, at the post-purchase stage, findings show that AR can influence consumer choice confidence and can also amplify cognitive dissonance (Romano et al., 2020). AR experiences aid consumers in comprehending and forecasting a product's performance, which boosts purchase intention. Collective dissonance rises when buyers hear unfavourable feedback about a product they've chosen, which lowers purchasing intention and cognitive control. The findings offer marketing professionals and mobile service providers guidance on how to make use of AR technologies (Whang et al., 2021). Marketers can improve AR campaigns and different types of consumer engagement, including user–brand engagement, user–user engagement, and user–bystander engagement, by comprehending and addressing the dynamics between various active and passive AR ingredients (Scholz & Smith, 2016). Including AR objects in a mobile application involves careful design considerations, including determining users' needs, enabling natural interaction, and involving users in the programme through a realistic avatar (Dirin & Laine, 2018). The augmented technology used for customising furniture must be practical, intriguing, real, easy to use, and intuitive (Young & Smith, 2016). Based on the empirical studies, the following hypothesis is formulated.

The AR application is appreciated regardless of age, gender, and experience (Egaji et al., 2019). A study looked at how media aspects of AR affected customer behaviour. By drawing comparisons with earlier interactive technologies and their media characteristics – interactivity, hypertextuality, modality, connectivity, location-specificity, mobility, and virtuality – this chapter looks at how AR functions and its current commercial applications. Both smart device apps and big interactive screens are examples of AR tools that use media features. With this information, marketers may better understand how AR can be used as a tool in different purchasing channels for particular reasons. This study provided insight into some of the most recent developments in AR and the kinds of customer reactions this technology may generate (Javornik, 2016). Employing an AR retail application (app) could influence customers' intentions to buy (Watson et al., 2018). AR can improve a consumer's online purchasing experience by letting them view an extension of their physical selves that is real and realistic (Huang et al., 2019.

Brand involvement facilitated by AR increases user satisfaction with the app experience and intends to use the brand in the future (McLean & Wilson, 2019). AR enables customer creativity in a unique way that differs from earlier conceptions of creativity due to its connection to customer involvement. The usage of AR raises everyone's level of creative involvement, allowing them to gain more from AR-enabled purchasing decisions. However, the strength of this effect is critically dependent on the assessment orientation of the client. For highly assessment-oriented customers, AR makes it easier for them to compare products within the appropriate decision context. This leads to a better regulatory fit, which is demonstrated by increased customer engagement and the resulting imagination and anticipated satisfaction (Jessen et al., 2020). Generation Z women's perceptions of augmentation positively impact their body image, self-esteem, and actual purchasing behaviour. However, while Generation Z women's body image and self-esteem are positively impacted by their trust in social media celebrities, the addictive use of social media has no discernible effects (Ameen et al., 2022).

The main topic of discussion is the app's ability to demonstrate that IKEA understood the challenges associated with the furniture purchasing process and was willing to invest in providing its consumers with technology-based support (Ozturkcan, 2021). Consumer inspiration is a mediating construct between the advantages users gain from AR apps and shifts in brand perception. The student offers fresh insights into AR marketing theory and recommends that marketers assess MAR apps based on their ability to inspire (Rauschnabel et al., 2019). MAR applications are thought to alter consumer behaviour and are linked to rising user valuations of stores that offer them (Dacko, 2017). AR can boost virtual self-personalisation, produce hedonic and utilitarian value, and improve decision-making (Hébert-Lavoie et al., 2021). In retail and commercial applications

88   John Paul Raj V. et al.

such as branding, advanced visualisation, personalisation, improved customer experience, etc., integrating deep learning systems and AR techniques shows promising outcomes (Cruz et al., 2019). The significance of customer attitudes in service interactions and how customer attitude may affect customer perceived value (Alimamy & Al-Imamy, 2021). Inventory turnover, more significant average sales, cheaper expenses, fewer customer returns, higher levels of related item selling, and improved customer service outcomes are all anticipated benefits of a successful AR strategy for a brand or retailer. Few businesses employ AR, create a highly integrated AR plan, or integrate AR into their marketing initiatives despite these benefits that can increase revenue and customer loyalty (Berman & Pollack, 2021). Classification shows how varied AR marketing experiences might be useful to customers in ways that differ from current marketing strategies and highlights areas that should use more research (Chylinski et al., 2020).

Overall, the review concludes that AR has enormous potential to transform the way consumers buy furniture in the manufacturing industry. Consumers may see how different furniture pieces will appear and fit in their homes before making a purchase by overlaying virtual furniture models onto real-world environments using AR-enabled devices such as smartphones or smart glasses. This immersive experience improves the purchasing experience by allowing clients to virtually try out different furniture designs, styles, colours, and combinations in real time, bypassing the traditional restrictions of internet shopping and showroom visits. Furthermore, AR may provide personalised recommendations based on consumer tastes, room size, and existing décor, allowing for more informed and gratifying purchasing decisions. As AR technology advances and becomes more available, its integration into furniture purchasing experiences has the potential to reshape the industry landscape, providing manufacturers with new channels for engaging customers, increasing brand loyalty, and boosting the sales.

While the broad literature analysis sheds light on the positive effects of AR on user experience, customer behaviour, and marketing outcomes, there is a significant study gap that requires additional investigation. Existing research focuses mostly on the benefits and positive outcomes of AR applications in a variety of contexts, such as retail, branding, and consumer interactions. However, there is a lack of study which is related to influential factors for buying products using AR. In the technological world, many companies are trying to adopt new technology like AR in order to attract more customers towards their product. Also, companies wanted to know the willingness of the customer to buy the product using AR for further improvement. In order to fulfil the research gap, the study aims to find to what extent the customer is willing to buy the product using AR in the manufacturing concern. Also, this research would be a great insight to concern in order to understand the various factors for using AR to buy the product.

Objectives

This chapter aims to understand the demographic profile of the respondents and also find the relationship between the customer experience using AR and willingness to buy furniture in the manufacturing concern. Also, to what extent the AR influences the customer to buy furniture?

Hypotheses

H_1 – There is a significant relationship between AR and willingness to buy furniture.

H_2 – Positive influence of easy to use and willingness to buy furniture.

H_3 – Positive influence of personalised to use and willingness to buy furniture.

H_4 – Positive influence of better access to information and willingness to buy furniture.

H_5 – Positive influence of increases or augments product image and willingness to buy furniture.

Research Framework

The study formulated the research framework which is given in Fig. 5.1. AR is measured by four constructs such as easy to use, personalised to use, better access to information, and increases or augments product image are considered as explanatory variables. Willingness to buy is considered as an endogenous variable.

Methodology

The variables and constructs were identified through a review of the literature. The research questionnaire was created with questions categorised as easy to use, personalised to use, better access to information, and increases or augments product image to assess AR and willingness to purchase. Because the population is limitless, convenience sampling is used under non-probability sampling to select a sample from the population. A total of 384 samples have been obtained from respondents. A structured questionnaire was constructed with all of the different

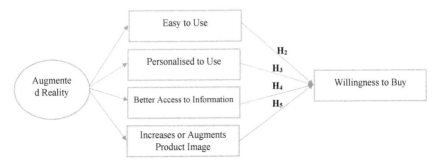

Fig. 5.1. Research Framework. *Source*: Author's work.

90 John Paul Raj V. et al.

types of questions connected to the study that would be required to analyse the findings. To assess the concept, each item was measured using a 5-point Likert scale. Respondents assessed the measure's assertions on a Likert scale of 1–5, with 1 representing 'strongly disagree' and 5 representing 'strongly agree'. To fulfil the objectives, descriptive statistics were employed to determine the characteristics of each variable. Correlation analysis was performed to determine whether a link existed, and regression analysis was used to assess the influence of exogenous variables on endogenous variables in the study.

Results and Discussion

Demographic Profile of the Respondents

Demographic factors reported by respondents include gender, age, purchasing frequency, and customer experience. The demographic attributes of 384 respondents are evaluated using percentage analysis. The proportion of research shows that out of 384 consumers, 213 (46%) are males and 171 (54%) are females. According to age indicators, the majority of respondents are between the ages of 26 and 35 (63%) and 16 and 25 (24%), followed by respondents between the ages of 36 and 45 (10%) and 46 and 55 (2%), respectively. The lowest proportion (0.5%) is among those over the age of 45.

Regarding online purchasing, 344 (90%) of 384 respondents prefer it, while the remaining 40 (10%) do not. Regarding the use of AR before purchasing, 175 (46) respondents stated that they are not currently using it but will try it in the future before purchasing, followed by 140 (36%) respondents who are already using it before purchasing, and the remaining 69 (18%) have not used AR before purchasing any product.

Reliability Test

Table 5.1 shows the Cronbach's (alpha) ratings, which indicate the reliability of the study constructs. The word 'number of items' refers to the questionnaire's total number of questions, which is 25, excluding demographic information. The data reveal that the values include easy to use ($\alpha = 0.936$), personalised ($\alpha = 0.912$),

Table 5.1.   Results of Reliability Analysis.

Constructs	No. of Items	Reliability (Cronbach's Alpha)
Easy to use	5	0.936
Personalised to use	5	0.912
Better access to information	5	0.916
Increases or augments product image	5	0.946
Willingness to buy	5	0.932

Source: Author's calculation.

Augmented Reality in Manufacturing Industries **91**

better access to information (α = 0.916), increase or augment product image (α = 0.946), and willingness to buy (α = 0.932). The fact that all of the alpha values are more than 0.90 indicates that the study's instrument is fairly reliable.

Correlation Analysis

In order to identify the relationship between the variables of the study, correlation analysis is done. Table 5.2 denotes the outcome of the correlation matrix.

Table 5.2 shows that the correlation analysis demonstrates substantial correlations between the research study's primary constructs. To begin, the 'easy to use' has positive relationships with all other constructs, implying that as perceived ease of use grows, so does the possibility of personalisation, better access to information, improved product image, and a higher inclination to buy. The extraordinarily large positive correlation ($r = 0.766$, $p < 0.01$) between easy to use and willingness to buy is especially notable, demonstrating that a user-friendly interface is substantially linked to greater consumer willingness to make a purchase. Furthermore, the moderate positive correlations (varying from 0.542 to 0.624) between easy to use and other constructs, such as personalised to use, better access to information, and increases or augments product image, point to a complex interaction between these variables.

Second, the constructs connected to personalisation and information accessibility have substantial positive connections. Personalised to use has a substantial positive association ($r = 0.777$, $p < 0.01$) with 'Willingness to Buy', highlighting the potential influence of personalised user experiences on consumer purchase intentions. Furthermore, the modest positive correlations (varying from 0.561 to 0.672) between personalised to use and other constructs, such as better access to information and increases or augments product image, highlight the interdependence of these elements in shaping consumer impressions. Hence, H_1 is accepted.

Table 5.2.   Correlation Analysis.

Constructs	Easy to Use	Personalised to Use	Better Access to Information	Increases or Augments Product Image	Willingness to Buy
Easy to use	1				
Personalised to use	0.542*	1			
Better access to information	0.624**	0.561**	1		
Increases or augments product image	0.562*	0.672*	0.601**	1	
Willingness to buy	0.766*	0.777*	0.725*	0.732*	1

Source: Author's calculation.

* and ** are statistically significant at 1% and 5%, respectively (two-tailed).

Regression Analysis

To check the influence of explanatory variables such as easy to use, personalised to use, better access to information, and increases or augments product image on willingness to buy furniture, multiple linear regression was used. Table 5.3 provides the summary of the regression outcome.

Table 5.3 shows the results of a multiple linear regression to predict willingness to buy furniture using AR. The model consists of four predictor variables: easy to use, personalised to use, better access to information, and increases or augments product image. The constant term is 0.943, and the standardised coefficients (β) for the predictor variables help understand their individual contributions to the dependent variable. It is observed that easy to use has positive and significant influence on willingness to buy ($\beta = 0.22$, $r < 0.01$) which indicates one-unit increase in perceived ease of use leads to a 0.220 unit rise in willingness to buy furniture using AR. Similarly, personalised to use ($\beta = 0.24$, $r < 0.05$) and better access to information ($\beta = 0.20$, $r < 0.05$) have positive and significant influence on willingness to buy at 5% significance level. However, on the other hand, increases or augments product image does not have significant influence on willingness to buy furniture using AR since the p value is greater than 5%. The overall model indicated by R^2 which indicates changes in the willingness to buy furniture is explained by changes in the explanatory variables such as easy to use, personalised to use, better access to information, and increases or augments product image. The probability value of F statistics $F(4,379) = 164.82$, p < 0.000) indicates that all the explanatory variables such as easy to use, personalised experience, better access to information and Increases or Augments Product Image are jointly significant to predict the willingness to buy. Finally, the customers are willing to buy furniture using AR by considering easy to use, personalised to use, and better access to information. Hence, H_2, H_3, and H_4 are accepted.

Table 5.3. Results of the Multiple Linear Regression Analysis for Predicting Willingness to Buy ($n = 384$).

Variables	β	Standard Error	t-statistics	p-Level
Constant	0.943	0.127	7.405	0.000*
Easy to use	0.220	0.078	2.839	0.005*
Personalised to use	0.246	0.095	2.582	0.010**
Better access to information	0.207	0.100	2.071	0.039**
Increases or augments product image	0.09	0.094	1.053	0.293

Source: Author's calculation.

$R^2 = 0.634$, adjusted $R^2 = 0.630$, $F(4,379) = 164.82$, $p < 0.000$; * and ** significant at 1% and 5%, respectively.

Implications

From the findings, AR has a big impact on customers' experiences and their propensity to purchase furniture in the manufacturing industry. AR provides a more immersive and personalised buying experience by enabling buyers to see furniture goods in their own living spaces before making a purchase. Virtual try-on of several components increases consumer satisfaction and chance of purchase by fostering a sense of confidence and connection with the product. As a result, furniture manufacturers embracing AR technologies stand to gain a competitive edge in the market, with implications for improved customer engagement, conversion rates, and overall business.

Limitations and Scope for Future Study

The study's sample size may restrict its generalisability. The study may focus on a restricted geographic area or demographic, limiting the capacity to generalise the findings to a larger population. The study considered only four factors to measure the AR in order to be willing to purchase the furniture by the customers. There are other factors that can be considered to measure the AR to purchase the furniture by the customers in future studies. Further, the study only focused on customers willing to purchase the furniture using AR in the furniture industry. In future, the researcher can do the research in other industries such as textiles, healthcare, cement, etc. in order to know the usage of AR by a customer for the purchase.

Conclusion

This research examines the impact of ease of use, personalisation, improved access to information, and increased or enhanced product image on buyers' propensity to purchase furniture via AR. According to the findings, perceived simplicity of use, personalisation features, and improved access to information all have a substantial impact on purchasers' desire to purchase furniture through AR. The findings have significant implications for marketing strategies and product development, highlighting the importance of user-friendly interfaces, customised experiences, and conveniently accessible information in increasing the use of AR for furniture purchasing. Future efforts might be directed towards improving these critical factors in order to improve the overall consumer experience and boost desire to employ AR technology in the furniture retail industry.

References

Alimamy, S., & Al-Imamy, S. Y. (2021). Customer perceived value through quality augmented reality experiences in retail: The mediating effect of customer attitudes. *Journal of Marketing Communications, 28*(4), 428–447. https://doi.org/10.1080/135 27266.2021.1897648

Ameen, N., Cheah, J., & Kumar, S. (2022). It's all part of the customer journey: The impact of augmented reality, chatbots, and social media on the body image and self-esteem of Generation Z female consumers. *Psychology & Marketing, 39*(11), 2110–2129. https://doi.org/10.1002/mar.21715

Anantharaman, S., Verma, B., Mittal, A., & Aggarwal, A. (2023, December). Exploring vendor's critical attributes to success in engineering, procurement and construction companies in India. In J. Singh, R. K. Kaushal, F. Ali, S. El-Sappagh, & R. Mittal (Eds.), *AIP conference proceedings* (Vol. 2916, No. 1). AIP Publishing.

Berman, B., & Pollack, D. (2021). Strategies for the successful implementation of augmented reality. *Business Horizons, 64*(5), 621–630. https://doi.org/10.1016/j.bushor.2021.02.027

Bottani, E., & Vignali, G. (2019). Augmented reality technology in the manufacturing industry: A review of the last decade. *IISE Transactions, 51*(3), 284–310. https://doi.org/10.1080/24725854.2018.1493244

Carvalho, E., Maçães, G., Brito, P., Varajão, I., & Sousa, N. (2011). *Use of Augmented Reality in the furniture industry*. First Experiment@ Int. Conference (exp.at'11), Lisboa, Portugal.

Chawla, U., Verma, B., & Mittal, A. (2024). Resistance to O2O technology platform adoption among small retailers: The influence of visibility and discoverability. *Technology in Society, 76*, 102482.

Chylinski, M., Heller, J., Hilken, T., De Ruyter, K., Mahr, D., & De Ruyter, K. (2020). Augmented reality marketing: a technology-enabled approach to situated customer experience. *Australasian Marketing Journal (AMJ), 28*(4), 374–384. https://doi.org/10.1016/j.ausmj.2020.04.004

Cruz, E., Orts-Escolano, S., Gomez-Donoso, F., Rizo, C., Rangel, J. C., Mora, H., & Cazorla, M. (2019). An augmented reality application for improving shopping experience in large retail stores. *Virtual Reality, 23*(3), 281–291. https://doi.org/10.1007/s10055-018-0338-3

Dacko, S. G. (2017). Enabling smart retail settings via mobile augmented reality shopping apps. *Technological Forecasting and Social Change, 124*, 243–256. https://doi.org/10.1016/j.techfore.2016.09.032

De Pace, F., Manuri, F., & Sanna, A. (2018). Augmented reality in Industry 4.0. *American Journal of Computer Science and Information Technology, 6*(1), 1–17. https://doi.org/10.21767/2349-3917.100017

Dirin, A., & Laine, T. H. (2018). User experience in mobile augmented reality: emotions, challenges, opportunities and best practices. *Computers, 7*(2), 33. https://doi.org/10.3390/computers7020033

Doil, F., Schreiber, W., Alt, T., & Patron, C. (2003). Augmented reality for manufacturing planning. In J. Deisinger & A. Kunz (Eds.), *Eurographics workshop on virtual environments* (pp. 71–76). ACM.

Egaji, O. A., Asghar, I., Warren, W., Griffiths, M., & Evans, S. (2019). An augmented reality application for personalised diamond shopping. In *2019 25th international conference on automation and computing (ICAC)* (pp. 1–7). IEEE. https://doi.org/10.23919/iconac.2019.8895045

Egger, J., & Masood, T. (n.d.). Augmented reality in support of intelligent manufacturing a systematic literature review. *Computers & Industrial Engineering, 140*(February 2020), 106195.

Hartanto, H. A., Makrie, I. K., Yesmaya, V., & Halfian, P. G. (2019). The development of furniture assembly instruction based on augmented-reality. *ComTech: Computer, Mathematics and Engineering Applications, 10*(2), 75–81. https://doi.org/10.21512/comtech.v10i2.5853

Hébert-Lavoie, M., Ozell, B., & Doyon-Poulin, P. (2021). The relationship between immersion and psychophysiological indicators. *PRESENCE: Virtual and Augmented Reality, 30*(winter), 233–262.

Huang, T. L., Mathews, S., & Chou, C. Y. (2019). Enhancing online rapport experience via augmented reality. *Journal of Services Marketing, 33*(7), 851–865. https://doi.org/10.1108/jsm-12-2018-0366

Javornik, A. (2016). Augmented reality: Research agenda for studying the impact of its media characteristics on consumer behaviour. *Journal of Retailing and Consumer Services, 30*, 252–261. https://doi.org/10.1016/j.jretconser.2016.02.004

Jessen, A., Hilken, T., Chylinski, M., Mahr, D., Heller, J., Keeling, D. I., & de Ruyter, K. (2020). The playground effect: How augmented reality drives creative customer engagement. *Journal of Business Research, 116*, 85–98. https://doi.org/10.1016/j.jbusres.2020.05.002

Kurniawan, B., & Fadryan, E. (2019, October 11). *Furniture online shopping using augmented reality.* https://doi.org/10.4108/eai.18-7-2019.2287836

Lindén, L. (2019). Utilizing augmented reality as a B2C marketing tool in the furniture retail industry. https://www.theseus.fi/bitstream/handle/10024/262926/Thesis%20final%20version%20Lauri%20Linde%CC%81n.pdf?sequence=2

McLean, G., & Wilson, A. (2019). Shopping in the digital world: Examining customer engagement through augmented reality mobile applications. *Computers in Human Behavior, 101*, 210–224. https://doi.org/10.1016/j.chb.2019.07.002

Nee, A. Y. C., & Ong, S.-K. (2013). Virtual and augmented reality applications in manufacturing. *IFAC Proceedings Volumes, 46*(9), 15–26.

Oberoi, S., Arora, S., Verma, B., & Roy, K. K. (2024). What do we know about artificial intelligence and blockchain technology integration in the healthcare industry? In *Driving decentralization and disruption with digital technologies* (pp. 124–138). IGI Global.

Ozturkcan, S. (2021). Service innovation: Using augmented reality in the IKEA Place app. *Journal of Information Technology Teaching Cases, 11*(1), 8–13. https://doi.org/10.1177/2043886920947110

Poushneh, A., & Vasquez-Parraga, A. Z. (2017). Discernible impact of augmented reality on retail customer's experience, satisfaction and willingness to buy. *Journal of Retailing and Consumer Services, 34*, 229–234. https://doi.org/10.1016/j.jretconser.2016.10.005

Qin, H., Osatuyi, B., & Xu, L. (2021a). How mobile augmented reality applications affect continuous use and purchase intentions: A cognition-affect-conation perspective. *Journal of Retailing and Consumer Services, 63*, 102680. https://doi.org/10.1016/j.jretconser.2021.102680

Qin, H., Peak, D. A., & Prybutok, V. R. (2021b). A virtual market in your pocket: How does mobile augmented reality (MAR) influence consumer decision making? *Journal of Retailing and Consumer Services, 58*, 102337. https://doi.org/10.1016/j.jretconser.2020.102337

Ramdani, M. A., Belgiawan, P. F., Aprilianty, F., & Purwanegara, M. S. (2022). Consumer perception and the evaluation to adopt augmented reality in furniture retail mobile application. *Binus Business Review, 13*(1), 41–56. https://doi.org/10.21512/bbr.v13i1.7801

Rauschnabel, P. A., Felix, R., & Hinsch, C. (2019). Augmented reality marketing: How mobile AR-apps can improve brands through inspiration. *Journal of Retailing and Consumer Services, 49*, 43–53. https://doi.org/10.1016/j.jretconser.2019.03.004

Romano, B., Sands, S., & Pallant, J. I. (2020). Augmented reality and the customer journey: An exploratory study. *Australasian Marketing Journal, 29*(4), 354–363. https://doi.org/10.1016/j.ausmj.2020.06.010

Scholz, J., & Smith, A. N. (2016). Augmented reality: Designing immersive experiences that maximize consumer engagement. *Business Horizons, 59*(2), 149–161. https://doi.org/10.1016/j.bushor.2015.10.003

Watson, A., Alexander, B., & Salavati, L. (2018). The impact of experiential augmented reality applications on fashion purchase intention. *International Journal of Retail &*

Distribution Management, *48*(5), 433–451. https://doi.org/10.1108/ijrdm-06-2017-0117

Whang, J. B., Song, J. H., Choi, B., & Lee, J. H. (2021). The effect of augmented reality on purchase intention of beauty products: The roles of consumers' control. *Journal of Business Research*, *133*, 275–284. https://doi.org/10.1016/j.jbusres.2021.04.057

Young, T. C., & Smith, S. (2016). An interactive augmented reality furniture customization system. In *Virtual, Augmented and Mixed Reality: 8th International Conference*, VAMR 2016, held as Part of HCI International 2016, Toronto, Canada, July 17–22, 2016. Proceedings 8 (pp. 662–668). Springer International Publishing.

Chapter 6

Innovation or Intrusion? Examining Employee Willingness to Collaborate With AI-Powered Service Robots in Retail

Meenal Arora[a], Ridhima Goel[b] and Jagdeep Singla[b]

[a]*Chitkara Business School, Chitkara University, Rajpura, India*
[b]*Institute of Management Studies and Research, Maharshi Dayanand University, Rohtak, Haryana, India*

Abstract

This chapter examines the significant transformations brought about by the incorporation of service robots in the ever-changing retail industry. In the retail industry, advanced technologies, including artificial intelligence (AI), co-bots, robotics, and automation, are transforming the experiences of customers and employees in response to the surge in human–robot collaboration (HRC) and worldwide investments in innovative projects. The primary goal of the research is to examine the impact of incorporating service robots on employees' willingness to work in a retail sector that fosters collaboration between humans and robots while improving the performance. The research highlights the key factors influencing employee perspectives and inclinations for collaborating with service robots in retail environments, as determined by an in-depth review of academic research and industrial insights. The results demonstrate the positive influence of service robots on improving HRC, optimising inventory management, and enhancing overall operational efficiency in the retail sector. The conclusion emphasises the need to adopt a holistic approach to successfully use the potential of service robots, with the aim of establishing a retail ecosystem that is both sustainable and harmonious. The presence of service robots in the retail industry has significant implications, offering a competitive advantage. The research results reveal stakeholders' perspectives on the

---

Augmenting Retail Reality: Blockchain, AR, VR, and the Internet of Things, Part A, 97–116
Copyright © 2025 by Meenal Arora, Ridhima Goel and Jagdeep Singla
Published under exclusive licence by Emerald Publishing Limited
doi:10.1108/978-1-83608-634-520241014

98 Meenal Arora et al.

crucial role of service robots in driving future development and maintaining long-term benefits. This chapter offers a comprehensive review of innovative technology in the retail marketplace, offering significant insights into the transformative potential of service robots.

Keywords: Service robots; artificial intelligence (AI); retail; human–robot collaboration (HRC); employee performance; robotics; willingness to collaborate (WTC)

Introduction

The arrival of the robots is imminent. According to industrial studies, the market for service robots is projected to increase from $41.5 billion in 2023 to more than $84.8 billion by 2028, with a compound annual growth rate (CAGR) of 15.4% (Market and Market, 2023). Robots have been deployed for a long time in places like assembly lines, warehouses, and order fulfilment centres. However, socially assistive service robots are being implemented extensively in frontline operations across various industries, such as health services, tourism, and retail (Ivanov & Webster, 2019). These robots may substitute or work alongside human staff. Service robots are specifically engineered to function in human contexts. Organisations now anticipate substantially higher revenues and commercial worth from their investments in the field of robotics (Yu et al., 2022). Furthermore, the use of service robots may aid in addressing the dilemma of shortages in labour (Bowen & Morosan, 2018).

Researchers saw the possibility of cooperation between robots and humans in the middle of the 20th century. Therefore, they investigated the notion by giving tasks that could be accomplished concurrently or sequentially, with each side working independently (Graham & Ume, 1997). While prioritising the safeguarding of human welfare, this approach resulted in prolonged periods of inactivity for a specific resource. Subsequently, researchers transitioned to voice-controlled collaboration, employing modes of communication that restrict the flow of data in one direction (Inkulu et al., 2021). The development of HRC technologies over time has reflected how these technologies have adapted to shifting needs. Initial methodologies emerged, including digital sensor-driven systems and voice or gesture manipulation. These were succeeded by augmented reality (AR) tools, which were facilitated by advanced visual sensors. These tools enabled interactive communication, which not only mitigated risks but also enhanced resource management and efficiency (Frey & Osborne, 2017; Graham & Ume, 1997). The integration of the Internet of Things has facilitated the development of cyber-physical systems and advanced communication devices. According to Inkulu et al. (2021), the aforementioned advancements have resulted in the emergence of a distinct category of collaborative robots that are regulated by human interaction, hence enhancing the efficacy of collaborative endeavours between humans and robots.

Retail executives face increasing demands to drive their firms ahead in the fiercely competitive landscape. AI is regarded as an innovative technology that may enhance the competitive advantage of retail organisations (Ivanov & Webster, 2019; Kaartemo & Helkkula, 2018; Matzner et al., 2018). Retail executives have shown a keen interest in integrating AI into their business operations (Meyer et al., 2020). The notion of deploying service robots in the aisles of retail stores, once seen as futuristic, has now materialised (Bogue, 2019; Grewal et al., 2020). Frontline service robots are self-governing and flexible interfaces that function inside a system, participating in interactions, communication, and providing services to an organisation's clients (Paluch et al., 2021; Wirtz et al., 2018).

According to Gray and Suri (2017), future projections suggest that over 30% of current full-time professions will evolve into advanced augmented services. This development creates prospects for the collaborative administration of assistance by humans and robotics. The advent of a 'human-in-the-loop' framework, uniting the intelligence of robots and mankind, has the potential to boost operational outcomes (Gray & Suri, 2017). Consequently, as automation may eradicate specific manual chores that have traditionally been carried out by the human workforce, it simultaneously establishes novel opportunities that require a transformation in professional realms. Work allocation is done to both human beings and robots in accordance with their individual competencies, implying that there are, in fact, no winners or losers in this changing dynamic (Khoa et al., 2022). The current transformation in professional spheres necessitates a reassessment of the competencies and responsibilities of human staff. In order to collaborate efficiently with robotics, they will be required to adjust and obtain fresh proficiencies.

A global outbreak of the pandemic has accelerated the pace of robotisation, as users are increasingly opting for contactless and touchless interactions to minimise health concerns (Le et al., 2022). In the retail sector, frontline employees (FLEs) are increasingly thriving from the presence of an extensive spectrum of service robots. These robots are assigned to do extensive frontline tasks that demand them to engage with consumers, contribute to discussions, and participate in social interactions (Tuomi et al., 2020). The concept of HRC is becoming more pertinent instead of completely substituting human personnel (Khoa et al., 2022; Paluch et al., 2021). Collaborative robots facilitate individuals interacting directly with robots, encouraging teamwork in which humans and robots collaborate as partners rather than independently (Le et al., 2022). The robot must be socially proficient and adaptable in order to collaborate successfully with humans (Tanevska et al., 2020).

As a cohesive component of the team, the robot assimilates the explicit or implicit intents of the whole group in order to accomplish shared objectives. However, to make it successful, the robot has to comprehend the team's objectives, beliefs, and ambitions while simultaneously expressing their own intentions (Bauer et al., 2008; Seeber et al., 2020). This collaborative strategy, in which individuals partner up with robots to establish a heterogeneous group focused on enhancing the supply of services, is known as co-botics. Within the realm of co-botics, robots do not supplant human beings; instead, they augment their capabilities by performing menial duties, thereby enabling humans to focus more intently on higher-level activities. Hence, this chapter focuses on the integration of AI and service robotics in the retail business and how employees perceive it.

In spite of the futuristic perception associated with service robotics, academics and professionals in various industries are diligently scrutinising the impact of robotics on working humans. Some concern has arisen about how employees react to teaming with increasingly intelligent and humanoid robotics, specifically in relation to interpersonal responsibilities. According to the insights of Bröhl et al. (2019), it has been suggested that the level of acceptance of technology serves a vital part when assessing the success of HRC or interaction. Furthermore, an increasing number of academicians have emphasised comprehending employees' perspectives regarding collaboration and working with robots across different industries (Ivanov & Webster, 2019; Qureshi & Syed, 2014; Yu et al., 2022). The findings of this research on human–robot interactions (HRIs) reveal a spectrum of emotions associated with the use of robots. Some academics believe that employees' interactions with service robots are self-motivating (Parvez et al., 2022; Przegalinska et al., 2019).

Existing research has delved into customers' perceptions regarding interaction with service robots (Christou et al., 2022). Few studies have discussed employees' perspectives on teaming with robots (Bhargava et al., 2020; Parvez et al., 2022) and HRC (Henschel et al., 2020; Libert et al., 2020). Despite these insights, many questions remain unanswered, necessitating a comprehensive review of the scholarly literature.

Remarkably, there has only been a limited amount of study conducted on the subject of HRC in the retail industry (Guha & Grewal, 2022; Noble et al., 2022). Employees may experience advantageous outcomes due to technological advancements in critical business realms, involving enhanced customer communication capabilities and the ability to archive and assess client information (Huang & Rust, 2020). On the contrary, employees might perceive technological advances as a rivalry and a potential menace (Jörling et al., 2019). As a result, our chapter aims to investigate the following question by synthesising existing literature in this domain:

RQ1: Which factors influence the willingness of the employees to work in collaboration with the service robots?

Literature Review

Introduction of AI

The advent of the digital era has led to the emergence of different strategies, with the modern conceptualisation of Industry 4.0 encompassing innovative digitalisation (Lasi et al., 2014; Molitor, 2020). Although Industry 4.0 is still in its early stages, experts are already predicting a possible fifth industrial revolution, known as Industry 5.0, which would usher in an evolving era of human and robotic collaboration and connection. Industry 5.0 aims to combine human innovation and artistry with robotic efficiency, performance, and stability (Kiran et al., 2020). This phenomenon results in a growing reliance on robots in daily activities, which in turn creates opportunities for further exploration and investigation (Chatterji et al., 2023; Henschel et al., 2020; Libert et al., 2020).

The three categories of AI based on capabilities are delineated as follows: artificial superintelligence (ASI), artificial general intelligence (AGI), and artificial narrow intelligence (ANI). Super AI represents a theoretical capacity for intelligent agents to surpass the cognitive capabilities of even the most exceptional human minds, yet current technological limitations preclude the realisation of such systems (Abonamah et al., 2021; IBM, 2023). General AI is conceptualised as the ability to possess human-like cognitive faculties, allowing it to tackle a broad spectrum of intellectual challenges and attracting significant attention in contemporary AI research endeavours. However, practical implementations of AGI remain elusive. Narrow AI, commonly referred to as 'weak' AI, predominates in contemporary applications. ANI systems excel in executing specific tasks, whether it be driving vehicles or speech and image recognition. These systems operate within well-defined task boundaries, continually refining their abilities through real-time interactions with their environment. Nevertheless, Narrow AI lacks the versatility of General AI and is constrained to the singular task for which they are designed (Abonamah et al., 2021). As General AI advances, it holds the potential to lead to the development of service robotics, wherein autonomous systems can adapt to various tasks and environments, revolutionising industries and everyday life.

Service Robots

In 2022, the sales of service robots designed for professional applications reached a cumulative figure of 158,000 units, reflecting a notable surge of 48%. The impetus behind companies opting for automation is prominently underscored by a scarcity of staff, which is a compelling catalyst for adopting robotic solutions (International Federation of Robotics, 2023).

In the literature of service robots, it is defined as 'system-based autonomous and adaptable interfaces that interact, communicate, and deliver service to an organization's customers' (Wirtz et al., 2018). Robots can be classified based on various characteristics such as anthropomorphism, task orientation, or representation (Wirtz et al., 2018). In this discussion, we specifically focus on service robots that have a physical human-like appearance, such as Pepper and Sophia, and exclude virtual assistants like Alexa. The reason for this focus is that a human-like embodiment allows these robots to engage in dynamic interactions with humans (Tung & Law, 2017). Frontline service robots demonstrate a unique ability to make independent decisions by analysing data collected from its sensors, cameras, and microphones (Wirtz et al., 2018). A concrete demonstration of this capability is its capacity to autonomously monitor shelves, detecting and correcting any incorrect placement of merchandise (Bogue, 2019).

Service Robots and AI

Digital service technologies are undergoing a rapid shift due to software and hardware innovation. In the domain of software, a myriad of significant innovations have surfaced, leading to the age of AI, data analytics, and the compelling domain of generative AI, which is shown by an amazing programme like Chat-GPT. This digital era has also been fuelled by natural language processing (NLP), biometrics, and machine learning (ML), while cloud computing and geotagging represent unexplored domains that tempt us to explore further. The expanding metaverse, AR, and virtual reality (VR) all encourage us to overcome the limitations of the real world and investigate domains that possess infinite opportunities (Anantharaman et al., 2023; Chawla et al., 2024; Wirtz et al., 2023). In addition, hardware innovation is booming, providing real-world examples of our aspirations for technology. The digital environment is populated with automated transportation and service robotics, providing futuristic insights where technology seamlessly enhances individual activities (Dwivedi et al., 2023; Mariani & Borghi, 2023).

The technological emergence served as a major transformation between human interaction and multiple industries (Dwivedi et al., 2023; Lu et al., 2020; Wirtz et al., 2023). AI-enabled service robots supplement and replace human employees in various contexts, ranging from fully automated employees to service providers and delivery agents (Pitardi et al., 2021; Wirtz et al., 2023). Service robots are becoming essential parts of the work setting for frontline staff. In a study, Abdelhakim et al. (2023) predicted that robot technology would positively affect the working environment, revenue phase, and overall effectiveness in the near future. These robots may improve the service experience by providing clients with more reliable services and enhancing their enjoyment during interactions (Xu et al., 2020).

Service Robots in Retail

The use of frontline service robots in retail settings has been shown to increase operational efficiency by continually sustaining productivity without experiencing exhaustion. These robots demonstrate remarkable competence in activities such as monitoring stocks, outperforming human counterparts with regard to both speed and accuracy (Joseph, 2023). According to the International Federation of Robotics (2020), there has been a substantial rise of 32% in the global sales of commercial service robots between 2018 and 2019, driven by the numerous advantages they deliver. Furthermore, the International Federation of Robotics (2023) anticipates that robots will play an increasingly significant position in numerous professional duties in the near future.

The integration of service robots in human services may encounter public opposition owing to apprehensions over the apparent absence of human interaction and ethical ramifications, such as the possible rise in unemployment (Lu et al., 2022). Service robots, acting as replacements for human employees, have the potential to disrupt the conventional notion of service, presenting psychological obstacles that leaders must confront. Although intelligent robots are becoming more capable and finding new uses, it is widely recognised that they cannot completely replace human workers (Kaleefathullah et al., 2020). Although robots have the ability to polarise employment and either replace or augment human labour, consumers currently rely more on human help than technical support (Xu et al., 2023). As a result, organisations are placing more importance on the cooperation between humans and robots.

Humans and Service Robots Collaboration

Collaboration, outlined by Ring and Van De Ven (1994), is the process of teamwork that is influenced by the actions and interpretations of the individuals engaged. The notion highlights the societal viewpoint that impacts individuals' willingness to cooperate (Paluch et al., 2021). Social aspects include individual traits, interpersonal connections, and the perceived level of trust shared by individuals (Chan & Tung, 2019; Yilmaz & Hunt, 2001).

The continuous progress in robotic capabilities is augmenting their efficacy in human interaction. The integration of natural language processing signifies a substantial advancement in enhancing the connection between robots and humans. Anticipated future improvements include the integration of biometrics, including face and voice recognition technologies. These characteristics are anticipated to empower robots to recognise people and provide exceedingly customised services to clients (Wirtz et al., 2018). The expanding capabilities of robots are increasing the variety of service situations in which they may function. They are shifting from being mechanical workers behind the scenes to becoming socially skilled workers in the forefront (Marinova et al., 2016). Within the HRI field, there is a growing trend of referring to robots as co-workers, team members, and/or colleagues (Gombolay et al., 2015; Molitor & Renkema, 2022). Collaborative robots have been thoroughly examined in industrial environments (Molitor & Renkema, 2022), but the interest in this subject has only lately increased among researchers studying service-related fields (Lu et al., 2020). Vatan and Dogan (2021) assert that service robots possess the ability to engage with employees and consumers via many means, therefore presenting robots as entities capable of social interaction. According to Huang and Rust (2020), the researchers discovered that when humans and machines work together more closely, it may improve the quality of service and increase the market share. In a study, Goel et al. (2024) emphasised the need to comprehend the interdependence between technology and employees, especially during the current digital era, in order to prioritise higher performance at work. Organisations have distinct obstacles in guaranteeing human–robot cooperation and convincing workers to cooperate with robots (Bröhl et al., 2019).

The efficacy of service robots in the retail industry is yet insufficiently investigated, as shown by the scarcity of existing research (Belanche et al., 2019). Although robots are widely used in several fields, there is a noticeable paucity of empirical research that particularly investigates the quality of customer–robot interactions in retail environments (Belanche et al., 2019). Prior studies have mostly focused on service robots in the healthcare sector, the hotel industry (Sakshi et al., 2019), and financial organisations (Kaur et al., 2021). In order to address this lack of research, the present study seeks to investigate the factors that impact the collaboration between employees and service robots in a retail setting.

Service robots demonstrate adaptability in managing both administrative activities, such as those in a warehouse, and customer-facing jobs, including contacts with customers (Tuomi et al., 2020). The existing research, together with the popular press, has provided several instances that demonstrate the wide-ranging effects of robots on different parts of jobs, both in good and bad ways (Bertacchini et al., 2017; Kim et al., 2021). Robots may assist retail FLEs by taking over time-consuming, labour-intensive, and repetitive duties, allowing them to dedicate more time to important operations (Huang & Rust, 2020; Wirtz et al., 2018).

Frontline Employees and Service Robots in Retail

The adoption of service robots in the retail sector is a rising field that has captured the interest of researchers and professionals (De Gauquier et al., 2020). According to Wirtz et al. (2018), service robots are interfaces that are self-sufficient and flexible, and they collaborate with clients to provide services to an organisation. These functions may be classified into front-office duties (such as direct consumer engagement, such as giving product details) and back-office duties (working behind the curtains, such as aiding assembly line personnel).

While current research mostly focuses on analysing the influence of service robots on employees, it is essential to comprehend the attitudes of frontline personnel about their collaboration with these robots. Employee happiness in this service profit chain is directly correlated with the satisfaction of customers (Lu et al., 2020). Therefore, it is crucial to understand the expectations and mindsets of employees on the front line towards robots in the workplace in order to successfully adopt them in the retail setting.

According to recent research evaluations conducted by Lu et al. (2020), service robots have the potential to deliver advantages such as less repetitive tasks and the promotion of cooperation between humans and robots. However, they may also have negative effects, including a decrease in personal freedom and an increase in employment instability. Existing research has mostly been conceptual in nature (e.g., Frey & Osborne, 2017; Wirtz et al., 2018), accompanied by little empirical investigation (e.g., Yu et al., 2022), notably in the under-researched area of retailing (Lu et al., 2020).

Through exploratory research involving interviews with frontline employees across multiple retail segments (e.g., grocery, electronics, fashion), Meyer et al. (2020) uncovered pertinent information regarding the reception and opposition of service robots. The identification of employee apprehensions over a decline in their social standing was acknowledged. However, the implementation of adequate training on collaborating with robots resulted in successful empowerment. Further investigation should focus on instances whereby individuals possess prior exposure to working alongside robots, thus enhancing our comprehension of the employee–robot interaction (Lu et al., 2020). Hence, retailers have to formulate appropriate methods to expedite the integration of robots among their employees on the front lines.

According to Bhargava et al. (2020), robots are now being expected to function at the intersection of the digital, real-time, and social domains. The following brings up several benefits as well as possible obstacles. The complex interaction between these factors places robots at the pinnacle of the retail industry and in different industries. Therefore, the main objective of this study is to investigate the factors impacting the willingness of employees to collaborate with robots in the retail sector by adopting a qualitative approach, as depicted in Fig. 6.1.

Factors Impacting the Willingness of Employees to Collaborate With Robots

Emotional Demands (ED) in the Workplace

The workplace is characterised by the ongoing need to address challenging requests or concerns from clients, co-workers, or managers, which may lead to emotional distress (Tesi et al., 2018). The anthropomorphism of service robots, evolving with human-like behaviour, significantly impacts employees' perception and adaptation in the digital workplace (Epley, 2018; Tojib et al., 2023). ED play a crucial role in HRC, reflecting the essence of service settings, where employees engage in psychological labour while interacting with clients (Choi et al., 2019). The dynamics of HRC include triadic interactions involving consumers, staff, and robotics, leading to heightened emotional engagement (Odekerken-Schröder et al., 2021).

However, the implementation and anthropomorphism of AI-powered service robotics have been linked to negative impacts on consumer and employee well-being, prompting a reassessment of the role of both employees and customers in the overall workplace environment (Cheng et al., 2022; Makridis & Mishra, 2022; Tojib et al., 2023). Although service robots cannot fully substitute human employees, they do alter employees' roles, positioning them as enablers, innovators, and coordinators within the organisational structure. Likewise, customers are assuming new roles as active contributors to the adoption and utilisation of technological advancements (Tojib et al., 2023; Vatan & Dogan, 2021; Willems et al., 2022).

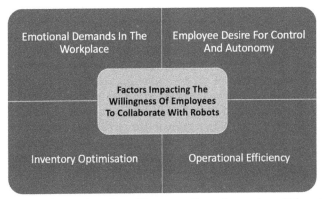

Fig. 6.1. Factors impacting the willingness of employees to collaborate with robots (Author(s) Representation)

Retailers have been focusing on personalising merchandise and brands to resonate with clients by giving them anthropomorphic traits and personalities (Cheng et al., 2022). Despite this, humanoid robots elicit both positive and negative responses during interactions and the development of trust and reliability (Kim et al., 2021; Liao & Huang, 2024).

Moreover, ED assume greater significance in job attributes in the context of HRC. The adoption of service robots has the potential to result in an upward trend in visitor grievances (Choi et al., 2019). Staff members might discover themselves overseeing perched demands associated with robotics introduction, directions, and troubleshooting, causing heightened emotional stimulation (Lu et al., 2020).

Employee Desire for Control and Autonomy (Paluch et al., 2021)

The successful incorporation of intriguing technological advances within an organisation is considerably affected by the personality traits and characteristics of the anticipated user (Lin & Mattila, 2021; Paluch et al., 2021). Employee attributes comprise people's personal features and perspectives in their work-related duties and interactions (Carson et al., 2004). These inherent traits are associated with the capacity to work well in a team, adapt to changes, and handle pressure (Paluch et al., 2021).

In the service delivery context, staff members' personality traits, such as responsiveness and emotional expression, have been determined as essential for customer satisfaction and service recovery (Keh et al., 2013; Komunda & Osarenkhoe, 2012). These attributes constitute the cognitive and psychological foundation during employee willingness to perform tasks, engagement, work fulfilment, and, eventually, collaborative performance (Lee & Way, 2010). According to Gwinner et al. (2005), employees' traits influence adaptive behaviour and the potential to customise services in a frontline work setting. It is essential to consider these characteristics when developing a human and service robot collaboration model, as they might either support or hinder employees' dedication and involvement in collaborative arrangements. Frontline staff members' capacity to meet client requirements is significantly impacted by their need for control (Bitner et al., 2000). Employees' views of control positively correlate with job satisfaction, dedication, participation, and performance (Lu et al., 2016).

According to Lee and Ravichandran (2019), results are favourably impacted by the subjective perception of control rather than the degree of authority. Individuals with a strong inclination towards control are inclined to exert independent judgement and encounter difficulty in adjusting to a perceived loss of authority (Rijsdijk & Hultink, 2003). Within the realm of professional stress, higher degrees of control are positively associated with employees' overall wellness (Lu et al., 2016). Employees' willingness to work with frontline service robots is heavily influenced by their desire to control.

A parallel observation can be noted pertaining to the prominence of the desire for autonomy, particularly among personnel occupying frontline roles that demand an empathetic assessment of service environments and comprehension of unique customer requirements (Surprenant & Solomon, 1987). Autonomy, referred to as the amount of freedom individuals have to effectively carry out their activities independently, is vital for worker productivity, stimulating fundamental human desires for individual growth, learning, and advancement (Ryan & Frederick, 1997; Schaufeli & Bakker, 2004). The employees' desire for autonomy is especially relevant given the convoluted and demanding nature of job duties (Slåtten & Mehmetoglu, 2011). Establishing mutually beneficial partnerships for employees who collaborate with service robots involves understanding and accomplishing this fundamental desire for autonomy.

Inventory Optimisation

AI is crucial in enhancing inventory management and improving stocking tactics across diverse sectors. Companies such as H&M and Walmart use AI to effectively monitor their stock levels. Tally, a company, has created a retail trade robot that uses AI to independently oversee shelves by detecting vacant areas and incorrectly positioned objects (Mahmoud et al., 2020). Within the field of predictive analytics, AI aids professionals in creating models that enable robots to independently handle tasks related to stocking, inventory, and ordering. This ensures that individuals can receive requested items in a timely manner (Javaid et al., 2020).

AI-driven service robots significantly enhance efficiency in managerial tasks and replenishment of inventories. These robots independently monitor inventory levels, perform audits, and replenish shelves, leading to enhanced operational efficiency and cost reduction (IBM, 2023; LinkedIn, 2023). In addition to traditional inventory duties, Exotec Solution, a French robotics company, has developed robots with the ability to scale racks, retrieve orders, and transport them to designated sites (Mahmoud et al., 2020). Wearable robots, such as different exoskeletons, reduce the likelihood of accidents caused by lifting big objects in warehouse activities (Tang & Veelenturf, 2019).

Major retailers like Walmart and prominent delivery companies such as UPS and FedEx are heavily engaged in autonomous delivery initiatives, including drones and vans (Bogue, 2019). The client initiates an order, which is then handled by an automation system that is connected to a warehouse (Centobelli et al., 2021). The system proceeds to process and deliver the order within a short span of time (Market and Market, 2023). These advancements demonstrate the smooth incorporation of AI and robotics in transforming inventory management, stocking, and last-mile delivery systems in the retail industry.

Operational Efficiency

The retail industry expects productivity, service quality, and operational efficiency improvements by incorporating service robots into their operations (Le et al., 2022; Pillai et al., 2021; Xu et al., 2023). The extensive use of these robots by diverse businesses relies on their efficiency, which is described as their capacity to properly and swiftly complete tasks (Coronado et al., 2022). Efficient robotic services optimise operations and provide timely customer support, contributing to time savings (Choi et al., 2019). Robots play a major role in enhancing efficiency for non-customer-facing tasks in retail, including maintenance, inventory audits, and pricing modifications. They have an enormous impact on distribution facilities and warehouses, automating processes such as selection, packaging, and organising, hence improving order fulfilment while minimising errors.

In addition, robots navigate retail aisles to effectively replenish shelves, allowing human workers to allocate their time towards more intricate activities (LinkedIn, 2023). This has the potential to lower the need for workers in certain activities. Certain robots are actively engaged in customer-facing responsibilities, such as interacting with customers and delivering marketing or product-related information while also assisting sales personnel (Forgan, 2020; Guha & Grewal, 2022). Efficient robotic performance boosts customer satisfaction along with perceived value by reducing errors (Javaid et al., 2020). The reliability and stability of efficient robotic services help customers have a good opinion of the business by lowering doubt and guaranteeing a consistent level of service quality (Lin & Mattila, 2021). Furthermore, the use of effective robotic services indirectly enhances productivity by performing activities at a faster rate, thus enabling human employees to dedicate their attention to more valuable interactions. This eventually leads to an improvement in the overall quality of service experiences (Belanche et al., 2019).

Conclusion

Ultimately, the use of service robots in automation has extended beyond traditional work settings, infiltrating plenty of human environments. The swift advancement of technology, especially in service-oriented industries such as retail, is causing significant and fundamental changes. Service robots first boost the operational efficiency of retail procedures (Tuomi et al., 2020).

In this study, we aimed to explore the willingness of employees in the retail industry to collaborate with service robots. Through a comprehensive analysis of existing literature, we synthesised various factors influencing this willingness. Our study uniquely contributes to the field by providing insights specifically tailored to the retail context, shedding light on the nuances and challenges faced by employees in this industry. This research addresses a void in the current body of literature and serves as a unique endeavour that breakthroughs the field of robotics by encouraging further studies in the future. It addresses the current need for additional investigation in the collaborative robot working environment, particularly in the retailing industry. In the digital era of Industry 4.0, achieving success for an organisation depends on effective technology adoption and acceptance in the workplace. To achieve synergy between humans and robots in Industry 5.0, it is crucial to have a profound comprehension of the crucial factors involved (Pillai et al., 2021). The retail industry has seen a revolution due to digitisation and automation, resulting in the adoption of robots and substantial transformations in organisational environments, service costings, and performance (Tuomi et al., 2020).

Service robots, which are specifically developed for tasks related to livestock or humanoid beings, provide the possibility of strategic implementation in many service sectors, such as airports, hotels, and restaurants. Scientists have developed theories and tactics for management to enhance cooperation with robots in every sector (Vrontis et al., 2021). These developments draw attention to robots' characteristics, attributes, and potential in the modern business community, increasing workers' knowledge of and attitudes towards robots (McLeay et al., 2020). In specific contexts, AI has already occupied leadership or equivalent positions to human personnel (Jarrahi, 2018). Nowadays, industries are readily agreeing to integrate the work and creativity of human employees along with the effectiveness and performance of humanoid service robots (Kiran et al., 2020).

In the retail industry, the use of bots for greeting and concierge services, in addition to AI-powered chatbots for human contact, promotes personnel security, enabling them to address more intricate human engagements. Our research findings are essential for retail managers who need to evaluate the effectiveness and optimal positioning of service robots and estimate the time it takes to recoup the investment (De Gauquier et al., 2020).

Implications of This Study

The implications of employing these technologies extend far beyond mere adoption; they encompass sustaining competitiveness, generating memorable experiences, and establishing enduring human relations within the retail industry. Our findings underscore the pivotal role of seamless cooperation between human employees and intelligent technologies, with AI and robotics serving as invaluable partners in propelling retail into a new era of excellence.

This chapter provides invaluable insights into how workers perceive and interact with service robots in collaborative work settings. Building upon previous research (Hinds et al., 2004), our study illuminates the collaborative dynamics of HRI in the workplace, emphasising the interplay between employee characteristics and robot capabilities. Our qualitative research has identified key factors driving workers' engagement with service robots, including their perceptions of rewards and potential risks, thereby offering actionable insights for fostering constructive cooperation between intelligent technology and human beings in professional environments (Paluch et al., 2021).

Organisations deploying service robots must navigate a myriad of managerial considerations to ensure successful integration. Our research highlights the considerable efficiency gains offered by service robot technologies, including substantial cost reductions, decreased error rates, and lower workforce requirements (Bughin et al., 2018). As we transition towards a more technologically advanced environment, our approach equips managers with the tools to address employee apprehensions surrounding the integration of humans and service robots into their daily work routines.

Crucially, decision-makers must carefully select HRC features that align with work requirements and individual characteristics. Facilitating this decision-making process is essential for integrating automation, AI, and employees into diverse work processes, ultimately enhancing collaboration effectiveness. By viewing robots and humans as complementary assets, organisations can strengthen both frontline and back-end operations, simplify tasks for staff members, and foster a positive work environment conducive to retaining skilled individuals in the future.

Limitations and Future Recommendations of This Study

The current study offers a thorough synthesis of existing literature concerning the factors impacting employees' willingness to collaborate with service robots in the retail industry. However, it is essential to acknowledge certain limitations stemming from methodological choices, which may impact the study's generalisability.

A significant limitation of our study is its dependence on an extensive review of existing literature, which restricts our ability to perform empirical analysis and evaluate the relative impact of various factors. By integrating quantitative and qualitative methods in future research endeavours, we can deepen the understanding of the pivotal relationship between humans and service robots in retail workplaces. This will facilitate the development of strategies to promote effective collaboration and improve organisational outcomes. Further, this approach may help in systematically examining the perceived benefits, risks, job characteristics, and individual differences that may influence employees' willingness and behaviours to collaborate with service robotics within retail settings. Additionally, longitudinal studies could offer valuable insights into the evolving dynamics of HRI over time. Moreover, the inherent subjectivity in the study selection process may introduce bias, potentially compromising the objectivity of the findings.

However, despite these limitations, the current study plays a crucial role in consolidating knowledge and highlighting research gaps in the domain of service robots and employee collaboration within the retail industry.

References

Abdelhakim, A. S., Abou-Shouk, M., Ab Rahman, N. A. F. W., & Farooq, A. (2023). The fast-food employees' usage intention of robots: A cross-cultural study. *Tourism Management Perspectives, 45*, 101049. https://doi.org/10.1016/j.tmp.2022.101049

Abonamah, A. A., Tariq, M. U., & Shilbayeh, S. (2021). On the commoditization of artificial intelligence. *Frontiers in Psychology, 12*. https://doi.org/10.3389/fpsyg.2021.696346

Anantharaman, S., Verma, B., Mittal, A., & Aggarwal, A. (2023, December). Exploring vendor's critical attributes to success in engineering, procurement and construction companies in India. *In AIP Conference Proceedings* https://doi.org/10.1063/5.0179963.

Bauer, A., Wollherr, D., & Buss, M. (2008). Human–robot collaboration: A survey. *International Journal of Humanoid Robotics, 5*(01), 47–66. https://doi.org/10.1142/s0219843608001303

Belanche, D., Casaló, L. V., Flavián, C., & Schepers, J. (2019). Service robot implementation: A theoretical framework and research agenda. *The Service Industries Journal, 40*(3–4), 203–225. https://doi.org/10.1080/02642069.2019.1672666

Bertacchini, F., Bilotta, E., & Pantano, P. (2017). Shopping with a robotic companion. *Computers in Human Behavior, 77*, 382–395. https://doi.org/10.1016/j.chb.2017.02.064

Bhargava, A., Bester, M., & Bolton, L. (2020). Employees' perceptions of the implementation of robotics, artificial intelligence, and automation (RAIA) on job satisfaction, job security, and employability. *Journal of Technology in Behavioral Science, 6*(1), 106–113. https://doi.org/10.1007/s41347-020-00153-8

Bitner, M. J., Brown, S. W., & Meuter, M. L. (2000). Technology infusion in service encounters. *Journal of the Academy of Marketing Science, 28*(1), 138–149. https://doi.org/10.1177/0092070300281013

Bogue, R. (2019). Strong prospects for robots in retail. *Industrial Robot: The International Journal of Robotics Research and Application, 46*(3), 326–331. https://doi.org/10.1108/ir-01-2019-0023

Bowen, J., & Morosan, C. (2018). Beware hospitality industry: The robots are coming. *Worldwide Hospitality and Tourism Themes, 10*(6), 726–733. https://doi.org/10.1108/whatt-07-2018-0045

Bröhl, C., Nelles, J., Brandl, C., Mertens, A., & Nitsch, V. (2019). Human–robot collaboration acceptance model: Development and comparison for Germany, Japan, China and the USA. *International Journal of Social Robotics, 11*(5), 709–726. https://doi.org/10.1007/s12369-019-00593-0

Bughin, J., Hazan, E., Lund, S., Dahlström, P., Wiesinger, A., & Subramaniam, A. (2018). *Skill shift: Automation and the future of the workforce.* McKinsey Global Institute Report No. 1/2018.

Carson, E., Ranzijn, R., Winefield, A., & Marsden, H. (2004). Intellectual capital: Mapping employee and work group attributes. *Journal of Intellectual Capital, 5*(3), 443–463. https://doi.org/10.1108/14691930410550390

Centobelli, P., Cerchione, R., Esposito, E., Passaro, R., & Shashi. (2021). Determinants of the transition towards circular economy in SMEs: A sustainable supply chain management perspective. *International Journal of Production Economics, 242*, 108297. https://doi.org/10.1016/j.ijpe.2021.108297

Chan, A. P. H., & Tung, V. W. S. (2019). Examining the effects of robotic service on brand experience: The moderating role of hotel segment. *Journal of Travel & Tourism Marketing, 36*(4), 458–468. https://doi.org/10.1080/10548408.2019.1568953

Chatterji, N., Manohar, S., & Verma, B. (2023). Assessing the influence of graduate characteristics on employer satisfaction: A multi-dimensional analysis. *The Open Psychology Journal, 16*(1).

Chawla, U., Verma, B., & Mittal, A. (2024). Resistance to O2O technology platform adoption among small retailers: The influence of visibility and discoverability. *Technology in Society, 76*, 102482.

Cheng, X., Zhang, X., Cohen, J., & Mou, J. (2022). Human vs. AI: Understanding the impact of anthropomorphism on consumer response to chatbots from the perspective of trust and relationship norms. *Information Processing & Management, 59*(3), 102940. https://doi.org/10.1016/j.ipm.2022.102940

Choi, Y., Choi, M., Oh, M. M., & Kim, S. S. (2019). Service robots in hotels: Understanding the service quality perceptions of human-robot interaction. *Journal of Hospitality Marketing & Management, 29*(6), 613–635. https://doi.org/10.1080/19368623.2020.1703871

Christou, I. T., Kefalakis, N., Soldatos, J. K., & Despotopoulou, A. M. (2022). End-to-end industrial IoT platform for Quality 4.0 applications. *Computers in Industry, 137*, 103591. https://doi.org/10.1016/j.compind.2021.103591

Coronado, E., Kiyokawa, T., Ricardez, G. A. G., Ramirez-Alpizar, I. G., Venture, G., & Yamanobe, N. (2022). Evaluating quality in human-robot interaction: A systematic search and classification of performance and human-centered factors, measures and metrics towards an industry 5.0. *Journal of Manufacturing Systems, 63*, 392–410. https://doi.org/10.1016/j.jmsy.2022.04.007

De Gauquier, L., Brengman, M., & Willems, K. (2020). The rise of service robots in retailing: Literature review on success factors and pitfalls. *Retail Futures, 15*–35. https://doi.org/10.1108/978-1-83867-663-620201007

Dwivedi, Y. K., Sharma, A., Rana, N. P., Giannakis, M., Goel, P., & Dutot, V. (2023). Evolution of artificial intelligence research in technological forecasting and social change: Research topics, trends, and future directions. *Technological Forecasting and Social Change*, *192*, 122579. https://doi.org/10.1016/j.techfore.2023.122579

Epley, N. (2018). A mind like mine: The exceptionally ordinary underpinnings of anthropomorphism. *Journal of the Association for Consumer Research*, *3*(4), 591–598. https://doi.org/10.1086/699516

Forgan, B. (2020). What robots can do for retail. *Harvard Business Review*, October 1.

Frey, C. B., & Osborne, M. A. (2017). The future of employment: How susceptible are jobs to computerisation? *Technological Forecasting and Social Change*, *114*, 254–280 https://doi.org/10.1016/j.techfore.2016.08.019

Goel, R., Singla, J., Mittal, A., & Arora, M. (2024). A decade analysis of employees' well-being and performance while working from home: A bibliometric approach. *Information Discovery and Delivery*. Vol. ahead-of-print, No. ahead-of-print. https://doi.org/10.1108/idd-03-2023-0030

Gombolay, M. C., Gutierrez, R. A., Clarke, S. G., Sturla, G. F., & Shah, J. A. (2015). Decision-making authority, team efficiency and human worker satisfaction in mixed human–robot teams. *Autonomous Robots*, *39*(3), 293–312. https://doi.org/10.1007/s10514-015-9457-9

Graham, G. M., & Ume, I. (1997). Automated system for laser ultrasonic sensing of weld penetration. *Mechatronics*, *7*(8), 711–721. https://doi.org/10.1016/s0957-4158(97)00031-7

Gray, M. L., & Suri, S. (2017). The humans working behind the AI curtain. *Harvard Business Review*. https://hbr.org/2017/01/the-humans-working-behind-the-ai-curtain

Grewal, D., Noble, S. D., Roggeveen, A. L., & Nordfält, J. (2020). The future of in-store technology. *Journal of the Academy of Marketing Science*, *48*(1), 96–113.

Guha, A., & Grewal, D. (2022). How robots will affect the future of retailing. *AMS Review*, *12*(3–4), 245–252. https://doi.org/10.1007/s13162-022-00241-3

Gwinner, K. P., Bitner, M. J., Brown, S. W., & Kumar, A. (2005b). Service customization through employee adaptiveness. *Journal of Service Research*, *8*(2), 131–148. https://doi.org/10.1177/1094670505279699

Henschel, A., Hortensius, R., & Cross, E. S. (2020). Social cognition in the age of human–robot interaction. *Trends in Neurosciences*, *43*(6), 373–384. https://doi.org/10.1016/j.tins.2020.03.013

Hinds, P. J., Roberts, T. L., & Jones, H. (2004). Whose job is it anyway? A study of human-robot interaction in a collaborative task. *Human-Computer Interaction*, *19*(1–2), 151–181. https://doi.org/10.1080/07370024.2004.9667343

Huang, M. H., & Rust, R. T. (2020). Engaged to a robot? The role of AI in service. *Journal of Service Research*, *24*(1), 30–41. https://doi.org/10.1177/1094670520902266

IBM. (2023). Understanding the different types of artificial intelligence. https://www.ibm.com/blog/understanding-the-different-types-of-artificial-intelligence/

Inkulu, A. K., Bahubalendruni, M. R., Dara, A., & K., S. (2021). Challenges and opportunities in human robot collaboration context of Industry 4.0 - a state of the art review. *Industrial Robot: The International Journal of Robotics Research and Application*, *49*(2), 226–239. https://doi.org/10.1108/ir-04-2021-0077

International Federation of Robotics. (2020) Service robots record: Sales worldwide up 32%. https://ifr.org/ifr-press-releases/news/service-robots-record-sales-worldwide-up-32

International Federation of Robotics. (2023). Staff shortage boosts service robots Sales up 48%. https://ifr.org/ifr-press-releases/news/staff-shortage-boosts-service-robots-sales-up-48

Ivanov, S., & Webster, C. (2019). Economic fundamentals of the use of robots, artificial intelligence, and service automation in travel, tourism, and hospitality. *Robots, Artificial Intelligence, and Service Automation in Travel, Tourism and Hospitality*, 39–55. https://doi.org/10.1108/978-1-78756-687-320191002

Jarrahi, M. H. (2018). Artificial intelligence and the future of work: Human-AI symbiosis in organizational decision making. *Business Horizons, 61*(4), 577–586. https://doi.org/10.1016/j.bushor.2018.03.007

Javaid, M., Haleem, A., Vaishya, R., Bahl, S., Suman, R., & Vaish, A. (2020). Industry 4.0 technologies and their applications in fighting COVID-19 pandemic. *Diabetes & Metabolic Syndrome: Clinical Research & Reviews, 14*(4), 419–422. https://doi.org/10.1016/j.dsx.2020.04.032

Jörling, M., Böhm, R., & Paluch, S. (2019). Service robots: Drivers of perceived responsibility for service outcomes. *Journal of Service Research, 22*(4), 404–420. https://doi.org/10.1177/1094670519842334

Joseph, J. (2023). What are service robots and how they benefit mankind? https://robots.net/tech-reviews/what-are-service-robots/

Kaartemo, V., & Helkkula, A. (2018). A systematic review of artificial intelligence and robots in value co-creation: Current status and future research avenues. *Journal of Creating Value, 4*(2), 211–228. https://doi.org/10.1177/2394964318805625

Kaleefathullah, A. A., Merat, N., Lee, Y. M., Eisma, Y. B., Madigan, R., Garcia, J., & Winter, J. D. (2020). External human–machine interfaces can be misleading: An examination of trust development and misuse in a CAVE-based pedestrian simulation environment. *Human Factors: The Journal of the Human Factors and Ergonomics Society, 64*(6), 1070–1085. https://doi.org/10.1177/0018720820970751

Kaur, B., Kiran, S., Grima, S., & Rupeika-Apoga, R. (2021). Digital banking in Northern India: The risks on customer satisfaction. *Risks, 9*(11), 209. https://doi.org/10.3390/risks9110209

Keh, H. T., Ren, R., Hill, S. R., & Li, X. (2013). The beautiful, the cheerful, and the helpful: The effects of service employee attributes on customer satisfaction. *Psychology & Marketing, 30*(3), 211–226. https://doi.org/10.1002/mar.20599

Khoa, D. T., Gip, H. Q., Guchait, P., & Wang, C. Y. (2022). Competition or collaboration for human–robot relationship: A critical reflection on future cobotics in hospitality. *International Journal of Contemporary Hospitality Management, 35*(6), 2202–2215. https://doi.org/10.1108/ijchm-04-2022-0434

Kim, S. S., Kim, J., Badu-Baiden, F., Giroux, M., & Choi, Y. (2021). Preference for robot service or human service in hotels? Impacts of the COVID-19 pandemic. *International Journal of Hospitality Management, 93*, 102795. https://doi.org/10.1016/j.ijhm.2020.102795

Kiran, D., Sharma, I., & Garg, I. (2020). Industry 5.0 and smart cities: A futuristic approach. *European Journal of Molecular & Clinical Medicine, 7*(8), 2750–2756.

Komunda, M., & Osarenkhoe, A. (2012). Remedy or cure for service failure? *Business Process Management Journal, 18*(1), 82–103. https://doi.org/10.1108/14637151211215028

Lasi, H., Fettke, P., Kemper, H. G., Feld, T., & Hoffmann, M. (2014). Industry 4.0. *Business & Information Systems Engineering, 6*(4), 239–242. https://doi.org/10.1007/s12599-014-0334-4

Le, K. B. Q., Sajtos, L., & Fernandez, K. V. (2022). Employee-(ro)bot collaboration in service: An interdependence perspective. *Journal of Service Management, 34*(2), 176–207. https://doi.org/10.1108/josm-06-2021-0232

Lee, C., & Way, K. (2010). Individual employment characteristics of hotel employees that play a role in employee satisfaction and work retention. *International Journal of Hospitality Management, 29*(3), 344–353. https://doi.org/10.1016/j.ijhm.2009.08.008

Lee, S. A., & Ravichandran, S. (2019). Impact of employees' job control perceptions on their work-related responses in the hospitality industry. *International Journal of Contemporary Hospitality Management, 31*(7), 2720–2738. https://doi.org/10.1108/ijchm-09-2018-0784

Liao, J., & Huang, J. (2024). Think like a robot: How interactions with humanoid service robots affect consumers' decision strategies. *Journal of Retailing and Consumer Services, 76*, 103575. https://doi.org/10.1016/j.jretconser.2023.103575

Libert, K., Cadieux, N., & Mosconi, E. (2020). Human-machine interaction and human resource management perspective for collaborative robotics implementation and adoption. In *53rd Hawaii international conference on system sciences*, Maui, HI.

Lin, I. Y., & Mattila, A. S. (2021). The value of service robots from the hotel guest's perspective: A mixed-method approach. *International Journal of Hospitality Management, 94*, 102876. https://doi.org/10.1016/j.ijhm.2021.102876

LinkedIn. (2023). *How AI and robots revolutionise retail.* https://www.linkedin.com/pulse/how-ai-robots-revolutionise-retail

Lu, H., Diaz, D. J., Czarnecki, N. J., Zhu, C., Kim, W., Shroff, R., . . . Alper, H. S. (2022). Machine learning-aided engineering of hydrolases for PET depolymerization. *Nature, 604*(7907), 662–667. https://doi.org/10.1038/s41586-022-04599-z

Lu, L., Lu, A. C. C., Gursoy, D., & Neale, N. R. (2016). Work engagement, job satisfaction, and turnover intentions. *International Journal of Contemporary Hospitality Management, 28*(4), 737–761. https://doi.org/10.1108/ijchm-07-2014-0360

Lu, V., Wirtz, J., Kunz, W. H., Paluch, S., Gruber, T., Martins, A., & Patterson, P. (2020). Service robots, customers, and service employees: What can we learn from the academic literature and where are the gaps? *SSRN Electronic Journal, 30*(3), 361–391. https://doi.org/10.2139/ssrn.3806199

Mahmoud, A. B., Tehseen, S., & Fuxman, L. (2020). The dark side of artificial intelligence in retail innovation. *Retail Futures*, 165–180. https://doi.org/10.1108/978-1-83867-663-620201019

Makridis, C. A., & Mishra, S. (2022). Artificial intelligence as a service, economic growth, and well-being. *Journal of Service Research, 25*(4), 505–520. https://doi.org/10.1177/10946705221120218

Mariani, M. M., & Borghi, M. (2023). Artificial intelligence in service industries: Customers' assessment of service production and resilient service operations. *International Journal of Production Research, 62*(15), 1–17. https://doi.org/10.1080/00207543.2022.2160027

Marinova, D., de Ruyter, K., Huang, M. H., Meuter, M. L., & Challagalla, G. (2016). Getting smart. *Journal of Service Research, 20*(1), 29–42. https://doi.org/10.1177/1094670516679273

Market and Market. (2023). *Service robotics market.* https://www.marketsandmarkets.com/Market-Reports/service-robotics-market-681.html

Matzner, M., Büttgen, M., Demirkan, H., Spohrer, J., Alter, S., Fritzsche, A., & Neely, A. (2018). Digital transformation in service management. *Journal of Service Management Research, 2*(2), 3–21. https://doi.org/10.15358/2511-8676-2018-2-3

McLeay, F., Osburg, V. S., Yoganathan, V., & Patterson, A. (2020). Replaced by a robot: Service implications in the age of the machine. *Journal of Service Research, 24*(1), 104–121. https://doi.org/10.1177/1094670520933354

Meyer, P., Jonas, J. M., & Roth, A. (2020). Frontline employees' acceptance of and resistance to service robots in stationary retail – An exploratory interview study. *Journal of Service Management Research, 4*(1), 21–34. https://doi.org/10.15358/2511-8676-2020-1-21

Molitor, M. (2020). *Effective human-robot collaboration in the Industry 4.0 context: Implications for human resource management* (pp. 1–54). Master's thesis, University of Twente.

Molitor, M., & Renkema, M. (2022). Human-robot collaboration in a smart industry context: Does HRM matter? In T. Bondarouk & M. R. Olivas-Lujan (Eds.), *Smart industry – Better management (advanced series in management)* (Vol. 28, pp. 105–123). Emerald.

Noble, S. M., Mende, M., Grewal, D., & Parasuraman, A. (2022). The fifth industrial revolution: How harmonious human–machine collaboration is triggering a retail and service [r]evolution. *Journal of Retailing, 98*(2), 199–208. https://doi.org/10.1016/j.jretai.2022.04.003

Odekerken-Schröder, G., Mennens, K., Steins, M., & Mahr, D. (2021). The service triad: An empirical study of service robots, customers and frontline employees. *Journal of Service Management, 33*(2), 246–292. https://doi.org/10.1108/josm-10-2020-0372

Paluch, S., Tuzovic, S., Holz, H. F., Kies, A., & Jörling, M. (2021). 'My colleague is a robot' – exploring frontline employees' willingness to work with collaborative service robots. *Journal of Service Management, 33*(2), 363–388. https://doi.org/10.1108/josm-11-2020-0406

Parvez, M. O., Arasli, H., Ozturen, A., Lodhi, R. N., & Ongsakul, V. (2022). Antecedents of human-robot collaboration: Theoretical extension of the technology acceptance model. *Journal of Hospitality and Tourism Technology, 13*(2), 240–263. https://doi.org/10.1108/jhtt-09-2021-0267

Pillai, S. G., Haldorai, K., Seo, W. S., & Kim, W. G. (2021). COVID-19 and hospitality 5.0: Redefining hospitality operations. *International Journal of Hospitality Management, 94*, 102869. https://doi.org/10.1016/j.ijhm.2021.102869

Pitardi, V., Wirtz, J., Paluch, S., & Kunz, W. H. (2021). Service robots, agency and embarrassing service encounters. *Journal of Service Management, 33*(2), 389–414. https://doi.org/10.1108/josm-12-2020-0435

Przegalinska, A., Ciechanowski, L., Stroz, A., Gloor, P., & Mazurek, G. (2019). In bot we trust: A new methodology of chatbot performance measures. *Business Horizons, 62*(6), 785–797. https://doi.org/10.1016/j.bushor.2019.08.005

Qureshi, M. O., & Syed, R. S. (2014). The impact of robotics on employment and motivation of employees in the service sector, with special reference to health care. *Safety and Health at Work, 5*(4), 198–202. https://doi.org/10.1016/j.shaw.2014.07.003

Rijsdijk, S. A., & Hultink, E. J. (2003). Honey, have you seen our hamster?' consumer evaluations of autonomous domestic products. *Journal of Product Innovation Management, 20*(3), 204–216. https://doi.org/10.1111/1540-5885.2003003

Ring, P. S., & Van De Ven, A. H. (1994). Developmental processes of cooperative interorganizational relationships. *Academy of Management Review, 19*(1), 90–118. https://doi.org/10.5465/amr.1994.9410122009

Ryan, R. M., & Frederick, C. (1997). On energy, personality, and health: Subjective vitality as a dynamic reflection of well-being. *Journal of Personality, 65*(3), 529–565. https://doi.org/10.1111/j.1467-6494.1997.tb00326.x

Sakshi, S., Cerchione, R., & Bansal, H. (2019). Measuring the impact of sustainability policy and practices in tourism and hospitality industry. *Business Strategy and the Environment, 29*(3), 1109–1126. https://doi.org/10.1002/bse.2420

Schaufeli, W. B., & Bakker, A. B. (2004). Job demands, job resources, and their relationship with burnout and engagement: A multi-sample study. *Journal of Organizational Behavior, 25*(3), 293–315. https://doi.org/10.1002/job.248

Seeber, I., Waizenegger, L., Seidel, S., Morana, S., Benbasat, I., & Lowry, P. B. (2020). Collaborating with technology-based autonomous agents. *Internet Research, 30*(1), 1–18. https://doi.org/10.1108/intr-12-2019-0503

Slåtten, T., & Mehmetoglu, M. (2011). Antecedents and effects of engaged frontline employees. *Managing Service Quality: An International Journal, 21*(1), 88–107. https://doi.org/10.1108/09604521111100261

Surprenant, C. F., & Solomon, M. R. (1987). Predictability and personalization in the service encounter. *Journal of Marketing, 51*(2), 86–96. https://doi.org/10.1177/002224298705100207

Tanevska, A., Rea, F., Sandini, G., Cañamero, L., & Sciutti, A. (2020). A socially adaptable framework for human-robot interaction. *Frontiers in Robotics and AI, 7*, 121. https://doi.org/10.3389/frobt.2020.00121

Tang, C. S., & Veelenturf, L. P. (2019). The strategic role of logistics in the industry 4.0 era. *Transportation Research Part E: Logistics and Transportation Review, 129*, 1–11. https://doi.org/10.1016/j.tre.2019.06.004

Tesi, A., Aiello, A., & Giannetti, E. (2018). The work-related well-being of social workers: Framing job demands, psychological well-being, and work engagement. *Journal of Social Work, 19*(1), 121–141. https://doi.org/10.1177/1468017318757397

Tojib, D., Sujan, R., Ma, J., & Tsarenko, Y. (2023). How does service robot anthropomorphism affect human co-workers? *Journal of Service Management, 34*(4), 750–769. https://doi.org/10.1108/josm-03-2022-0090

Tung, V. W. S., & Law, R. (2017). The potential for tourism and hospitality experience research in human-robot interactions. *International Journal of Contemporary Hospitality Management, 29*(10), 2498–2513. https://doi.org/10.1108/ijchm-09-2016-0520

Tuomi, A., Tussyadiah, I. P., & Stienmetz, J. (2020). Applications and implications of service robots in hospitality. *Cornell Hospitality Quarterly, 62*(2), 232–247. https://doi.org/10.1177/1938965520923961

Vatan, A., & Dogan, S. (2021). What do hotel employees think about service robots? A qualitative study in Turkey. *Tourism Management Perspectives, 37*, 100775. https://doi.org/10.1016/j.tmp.2020.100775

Vrontis, D., Christofi, M., Pereira, V., Tarba, S., Makrides, A., & Trichina, E. (2021). Artificial intelligence, robotics, advanced technologies and human resource management: A systematic review. *The International Journal of Human Resource Management, 33*(6), 1237–1266. https://doi.org/10.1080/09585192.2020.1871398

Willems, K., Verhulst, N., De Gauquier, L., & Brengman, M. (2022). Frontline employee expectations on working with physical robots in retailing. *Journal of Service Management, 34*(3), 467–492. https://doi.org/10.1108/josm-09-2020-0340

Wirtz, J., Hofmeister, J., Chew, P. Y. P., & Ding, X. D. (2023). Digital service technologies, service robots, AI, and the strategic pathways to cost-effective service excellence. *The Service Industries Journal, 43*(15–16), 1173–1196. https://doi.org/10.1080/02642069.2023.2226596

Wirtz, J., Patterson, P. G., Kunz, W. H., Gruber, T., Lu, V. N., Paluch, S., & Martins, A. (2018). Brave new world: Service robots in the frontline. *Journal of Service Management, 29*(5), 907–931. https://doi.org/10.1108/josm-04-2018-0119

Xu, J., Hsiao, A., Reid, S., & Ma, E. (2023). Working with service robots? A systematic literature review of hospitality employees' perspectives. *International Journal of Hospitality Management, 113*, 103523. https://doi.org/10.1016/j.ijhm.2023.103523

Xu, S., Stienmetz, J., & Ashton, M. (2020). How will service robots redefine leadership in hotel management? A Delphi approach. *International Journal of Contemporary Hospitality Management, 32*(6), 2217–2237. https://doi.org/10.1108/ijchm-05-2019-0505

Yilmaz, C., & Hunt, S. D. (2001). Salesperson cooperation: The influence of relational, task, organizational, and personal factors. *Journal of the Academy of Marketing Science, 29*(4), 335–357.

Yu, X., Xu, S., & Ashton, M. (2022). Antecedents and outcomes of artificial intelligence adoption and application in the workplace: The socio-technical system theory perspective. *Information Technology & People, 36*(1), 454–474. https://doi.org/10.1108/itp-04-2021-0254

Chapter 7

Measuring the Adoption of IoT in OTT Platforms

Isha Kalra[a,b] and Meenu Gupta[a]

[a]*Maharishi Markandeshwar (Deemed to be University), Mullana – Ambala, Haryana, India*
[b]*School of Commerce & Business Management, Geeta University, Panipat, Haryana, India*

Abstract

The digital content distribution environment is undergoing a dramatic transformation due to the convergence of internet of things (IoT) and over-the-top (OTT) platforms, which provide users with personalised and immersive experiences. OTT streaming platforms have not only grabbed the attention of customers for entertainment and quality content for binge-watch but also successfully changed the industry market trends. An empirical analysis of the deployment of IoT technology in OTT platforms is presented in this chapter. This chapter tries to explore the perception of viewers towards adoption of IoT in OTT streaming platforms. The unified theory of acceptance and use of technology-2 (UTAUT2) model is the main framework for this chapter, and one-way analysis of variance (ANOVA) and stepwise regression is applied to analyse the responses. Findings suggested the consumer characteristics have significant effect on the attitude of the consumers. On the other hand, security and privacy issues with data become major obstacles. In order to balance innovation and user protection, the study concluded with recommendations for OTT service providers and legislators on how to support the responsible and successful implementation of IoT technology in the media and entertainment sector. The findings highlighted that viewers are adopting IoT while streaming OTT platforms. This chapter will help the interested parties and

---

Augmenting Retail Reality: Blockchain, AR, VR, and the Internet of Things, Part A, 117–141
Copyright © 2025 by Isha Kalra and Meenu Gupta
Published under exclusive licence by Emerald Publishing Limited
doi:10.1108/978-1-83608-634-520241017

organisations by providing them insights regarding consumer behaviour across OTT services which they can utilise to formulate strategies.

Keywords: Adoption; attitude; behaviour; internet of things (IoT); over-the-top; trust; intention

Introduction

The emergence of OTT platforms has substantially changed the digital entertainment market by distributing material directly over the internet and upending established broadcasting methods. The IoT has become a disruptive force in the digital age, providing creative ways to improve the usability and functioning of OTT platforms (Chakraborty et al., 2023; Singh et al., 2024). This chapter delves into the complex role that digitalisation plays in OTT media, looking at how it affects user engagement, content distribution, data analytics, and the general progression of the entertainment sector (Haridas & Deepak, 2020; Sundaravel & Elangovan, 2020). Entertainment experiences are now personalised, interactive, and seamlessly integrated due to the IoT's integration with OTT platforms (Hallur et al., 2021). Technology is crucial in determining how the digital television sector develops in the future, from data analytics and targeted advertising to content distribution and user interaction (Given et al., 2012; Hallur et al., 2023). To preserve user happiness and trust in this changing digital environment, stakeholders must successfully negotiate the difficulties relating to data security and privacy.

IoT makes smart content distribution possible by allowing device-to-device connection. Consumers can start watching material on one device and move easily to another. In addition to increasing user convenience, cross-device integration encourages prolonged viewing sessions, which strengthens OTT platform loyalty (Chen et al., 2023; Shu et al., 2018). The revolution in content delivery and customisation brought about by IoT is one of the main contributions to OTT platforms (Park & Kwon, 2019). The growing number of IoT-capable gadgets, such as wearables, smart TVs, and streaming devices, make it possible to easily gather and evaluate user interactions and preferences (Dovile, 2017; Gubbi et al., 2013). By using a data-driven strategy, OTT providers can offer viewers personalised content recommendations that make for a more engaging and customised experience (Lin et al., 2017; Singh & Tomar, 2018; Trad, 2024). IoT sensors are essential for keeping an eye on the quality of service (QoS) in OTT platforms. Real-time data from linked devices allow parameters to be dynamically adjusted based on network conditions, helping to maximise streaming quality. This guarantees viewers a reliable and excellent watching experience during Covid-19 (Yaqoub et al., 2023).

Through interactive experiences, OTT platforms can now offer improved user engagement due to IoT connectivity (Mohan et al., 2021). Using synchronisation, second-screen applications for smartphones or tablets offer extra information, trivia, or interactive components to enhance the user-content relationship (Botta et al., 2016; Trad, 2024). Strong data security and privacy must be ensured as the amount of data acquired by IoT devices rises. OTT platforms need to put in place thorough safeguards to protect user data, taking into account issues with privacy and security (Kim et al., 2021). Targeted advertising is one way that IoT-driven data analytics help OTT companies make money. Advertisers might potentially increase OTT providers' advertisement income by delivering more tailored and relevant adverts by utilising the data collected from linked devices (Chen et al., 2023; Gubbi et al., 2013). In an effort to comprehend how users of internet streaming services have adapted the technology, Mobile technologies are adopted. Previous research has also been done on smartphone adoption, mobile marketing, and mobile usage adoption in relation to technology adoption (Camilleri & Camilleri, 2019; Taylor & Todd, 1995; Weinswig, 2016). The research explains why people use fitness apps on smartphones and analyses consumer acceptance of mobile marketing (Dhiman et al., 2020; Eneizan et al., 2019; Nikolopoulou et al., 2020). Additionally, the adoption of online streaming platforms is the main focus of this study.

Streaming services are influencing users' viewing habits while also providing them with the content they desire. The content of an online video distributor or streaming service influences whether or not a consumer will purchase it (Bandyopadhyay & Bandyopadhyay, 2010; Kohli, 2020). Even while streaming services are steadily replacing traditional television, their reach is still limited by piracy, a lack of traditional content, and affordability in rural areas. On the other hand, their expansion in urban markets is significantly influenced by internet accessibility (You et al., 2021).

Adoption of Technology

With the introduction of internet streaming services, the approach to entertainment consumption has completely changed, moving away from traditional media consumption and towards digital platforms (GWI, 2019). OTT services provide a wide variety of on-demand entertainment options and have become widely available due to the increase in the consumption of digital material. The way that cutting-edge features and innovations are seamlessly integrated into these platforms is an example of how technology is being adopted in this environment. Modern technologies that offer users tailored viewing recommendations include artificial intelligence (AI), IoT, and machine learning (Munoz-Leiva et al., 2017; Nagy, 2018). These technologies are essential to content recommendation systems. Adaptive streaming technology additionally guarantees a seamless and buffer-free viewing experience on a variety of devices. The widespread usage of OTT streaming services is facilitated by the integration of user-friendly interfaces, cross-device synchronisation, and high-definition streaming capabilities (Davis, 1989; Parnami & Jain, 2021).

Performance Expectancy

Streaming services are impacting the watching habits of users and providing them with content demanded. Customers are willing to adopt new OTT media platforms, according to a study, and are impacted by content, subscription, age, language, time spent on platform, and existing usage (Lee et al., 2021). Content is the main decider regarding the purchase of a streaming service or online video distributor (Kohli, 2020; Verma & Tandon, 2022). Within the framework of OTT streaming services, the UTAUT paradigm is a vital tool for comprehending user behaviour and adoption. 'Performance expectancy' is one of its fundamental concepts that is particularly important in determining whether or not people choose to use OTT streaming platforms (Venkatesh et al., 2003). Performance expectancy is the measure of how much the user believes utilising the technology will improve their performance and how capable the system is (Venkatesh et al., 2012). Performance expectations in the context of OTT streaming are closely related to the user interface, streaming speed, perceived effectiveness and quality of content delivery, and overall service reliability (Scherer et al., 2019). According to user choices and behaviour, IoT devices frequently offer personalised experiences (Mohan et al., 2021). When users feel that an OTT streaming platform produces high-performance results, such as fluid video, they are more likely to adopt and stick with it (Nagy, 2018; Park, 2010).

The longevity of OTT streaming services and their user experience are greatly influenced by IoT performance expectations. It speaks to what consumers believe and anticipate from the streaming platform in terms of its overall performance, quality, and functionality. Performance expectations can make a big difference in a competitive OTT streaming market with respect to IoT (Yoon & Kim, 2022). Instantaneous and dependable streaming experiences are highly valued by users, and platforms that emphasise and deliver on this promise gain a competitive advantage (Niehaves & Plattfaut, 2014). Greater user involvement is fostered by high performance expectations. When users are confident in the dependability and performance of the streaming service, they are more inclined to explore content and engage in interactive features on the platform for longer. Users expect the IoT to customise services and recommendations to meet their unique needs (Wallace & Sheetz, 2014).

One of the main strategies for getting people to embrace and stick with the OTT platform is a positive performance expectation. When consumers regularly enjoy high-quality streaming, they are more likely to remain subscribers and use the service over the long run (Venkatesh et al., 2003, 2012). Meeting or surpassing consumers' expectations increases their overall happiness with the OTT streaming service when they have high expectations for uninterrupted streaming, fast content loading, and little interruptions. IoT plays a crucial role for enhancing the user's expectations. When performance expectations are regularly satisfied, users are more inclined to adopt technical advancements offered by OTT streaming platforms (Camilleri, 2021; Davis, 1989, Venkatesh & Bala, 2008). This entails implementing more sophisticated elements that improve the watching experience overall, such as immersive audio and greater resolutions. IoT increases efficiency by requiring less time and effort to complete numerous tasks.

Effort Expectancy (EE)

The UTAUT model now includes effort expectation, a key indicator of how well people will accept new technology. EE is defined as a 'degree of ease of use in handling any technical breakthrough with less efforts' (Davis, 1989; Moore & Benbasat, 1991; Thompson et al., 1991; Venkatesh et al., 2003). Customers do not feel that use of OTT service is complicated. Further, it has also been found that EE has a positive impact on the personal decisions because OTT services are clear and understandable (Im et al., 2010; Venkatesh et al., 2003). It highlighted how simple and convenient it is to use the streaming platform after implementation of IoT. OTT solutions that save time and are convenient are valued by customers. An overall more efficient and user-friendly experience is enhanced by EE, which lowers the number of steps required to start streaming video. User engagement is directly impacted by EE. Users are more likely to interact with the platform and spend more time there when it has a simplified and easy-to-use interface enabled by IoT, which decreases the work required to find and consume content (Camilleri, 2020). Users can surmount a steep learning curve by utilising OTT platforms that prioritise low EE. When a service is simple to use and comprehend, users are more likely to continue with it, which lowers annoyance and encourages them to explore features without feeling overwhelmed (Camilleri, 2021; Venkatesh & Bala, 2008).

One important aspect influencing users' adoption of OTT streaming services is effort anticipation. Platforms with an intuitive user interface enabled by IoT make it easy for users to browse, find content, and use features that are more likely to draw in new members. Users' ability to find content is influenced by their effort expectations (Niehaves & Plattfaut, 2014; Vijayasarathy, 2004). Users need not exert as much effort searching for material that suits their interests when using platforms with efficient search features, user-friendly categorisation, and tailored suggestions (Venkatesh et al., 2012). IoT offers an easy-to-use platform that makes material more accessible. EE contributes to a smooth and enjoyable watching experience by guaranteeing that users can easily locate and access the content they want.

IoT also permits the compatibility with a range of devices to OTT streaming platforms. Users need less effort to flip between screens when a platform is compatible with smart TVs, smartphones, tablets, and other devices (Venkatesh et al., 2003). Platforms that simplify the process of subscribing, unsubscribing, and managing account settings are incorporated with the help of IoT and AI as they enhance the user experience (Venkatesh, 2022). There is a clear relationship between EE and customer satisfaction. An OTT streaming service that reduces the amount of work involved in different interactions from account management to content discovery is more likely to satisfy its users (Dolan et al., 2019; Khan, 2017).

Facilitating Conditions

The success and user experience of OTT streaming services are greatly influenced by the facilitating conditions that are created. The term 'facilitating conditions' describes the outside elements that help or impede consumers from using and profiting from the streaming platform. Facilitating conditions refers to the users' cognition regarding the availability of resources in the environment, such as those at home or at work, to complete a task effectively (Venkatesh et al., 2003). Facilitating conditions favourably affect Behavioural Intention (BI) and use behaviour of customers of OTT platforms as well as IoT adopters. Encouraging user interactions with the streaming service depends on the availability of technical assistance. Frequently Asked Questions (FAQs), troubleshooting instructions, and easily understandable support channels all help to quickly resolve user concerns

122 Isha Kalra and Meenu Gupta

and improve overall user happiness (Ray et al., 2019). IoT, internet speed, and stability also have a major impact on how well OTT viewers receive the content. Users must be able to obtain a dependable, fast internet connection in order to guarantee buffer-free, interruption-free streaming (Dhir et al., 2017).

Having a variety of excellent content available is one of the facilitating conditions. A carefully chosen content library guarantee enabled by IoT offers a wide range of options for users, accommodating a variety of tastes and enhancing the streaming experience (Mohan et al., 2021; Troise & Camilleri, 2021). One of the supporting requirements is that the OTT streaming service works with a variety of devices (Smock et al., 2011). User ease and accessibility are improved by platforms that fluidly support a variety of devices, including gaming consoles, smartphones, tablets, and smart TVs (Leung, 2015; Malik et al., 2016).

Encouraging conditions require a safe and privacy-compliant workplace (Venkatesh et al., 2012). In order to build trust and confidence in the OTT streaming service, users need to feel confident that their viewing preferences and personal information are secure which can be secured by IoT. Legal and licencing issues have an impact on content availability (Given et al., 2012; GWI, 2019). Facilitating conditions include ensuring that the content library complies with regulatory norms, obtaining the required licences, and the OTT platform abiding by copyright laws. Reaching a wider audience and growing the user base are facilitated by regional content restrictions and availability in multiple locations. By guaranteeing that consumers have access to the newest features, performance gains, and an ever-evolving and fulfilling streaming experience, frequent updates and enhancements to the OTT platform help to facilitate conditions (Joo & Sang, 2013). A brief overview of some prominent studies related to adoption of OTT is given in Table 7.1.

Trust

In the world of OTT streaming services, trust is essential as it has a significant impact on users' choices, contentment, and sustained involvement. The dependability of the material offered by OTT streaming services is directly related to trust. Trust is described as 'the willingness of a party to be vulnerable to the actions of another party based on the expectation that the other will perform a particular action important to the trustor, irrespective of the ability to monitor or control that other party' (Gefen et al., 2003). Consumers want reliable, high-calibre content, and a reliable platform makes sure that content is authentic, compliant with licencing terms, and not distributed without permission. Users give over their viewing habits and personal information to OTT streaming services (Vijayasarathy, 2004). It is impossible to overestimate the importance of trust in this area. Strong data security protocols, adoption of IoT, and a dedication to user privacy foster confidence and reassure users that their private data are treated with care. The dependability of the streaming service is the foundation for trust. Consumers anticipate uninterrupted streaming, low interruptions, and constant uptime. When a platform lives up to these expectations, its user base becomes more dependable and devoted (Camilleri, 2021; Venkatesh & Bala, 2008).

Table 7.1. Major Contributors in Literature.

Author (s)	Objective	Statistical Methods	Findings
Camilleri and Falzon (2021)	To investigate the way individuals used and were satisfied with streaming services during Covid-19.	Confirmatory factor analysis and Structural equation models (SEM)	The perceived utility and user-friendliness of streaming platforms were found to be important predictors of the individuals' intentions to use the indicated technologies.
Steiner and Xu (2020)	Investigating the main factors of viewers' binge-watching behaviours	Qualitative and inductive method	The results show that cultural inclusion, relaxation, catching up, a sense of accomplishment, and an enhanced viewing experience are the main reasons for viewers' binge-watch.
Tefertiller and Sheehan (2019)	To determine the driving forces for modern television watching	Principal component analysis	Stress reduction, calming entertainment, habitual viewing, information seeking, and social connection were found to be the five motivational elements for watching television.
Chen (2019)	To investigate the competition between Taiwan's traditional television and OTT TV platforms	Principal component analysis	OTT TV and traditional TV share a high level of similarity on amusement and ease of use.
Lee et al. (2018)	To study the elements that viewers take into account while selecting between internet streaming and cable television.	Principal component analysis and confirmatory factor analysis	The key elements such as cost, ease of use, and social trends are considered by the viewers while selecting between the adoption of cable and online media.
Tefertiller (2018)	To investigate the variables that most accurately forecast customers' decision to switch from cable television to video streaming	Principal component analysis	Stress management, habitual viewing, information seeking, and social connection were found to be the motivational elements for watching television.

Source: Author's compilation.

124   *Isha Kalra and Meenu Gupta*

IoT helps to enhance the trust by a prompt and efficient customer service system. Users should be aware that they can readily contact support if they run into problems. Reputable platforms give top priority to customer service, quickly and effectively resolving user issues (Wallace & Sheetz, 2014). Informing users about terms of service, subscription fees, and platform updates fosters trust and facilitates their ability to make wise choices (Venkatesh et al., 2012, 2022). The accuracy of content suggestions depends on trust. Users are more likely to trust the platform's ability to grasp their interests and preferences when they receive personalised recommendations based on their watching history and preferences (Munoz-Leiva et al., 2017; Nagy, 2018). When switching between devices, users anticipate a seamless experience provided by IoT. Consistency in content, user interface, and platform preferences are hallmarks of a reliable OTT streaming service.

Other users' experiences have the power to sway trust. Building confidence in the platform's dependability, content quality, and general user happiness is facilitated by positive community comments and user reviews (Herrero & San Martin, 2017; Rauniar et al., 2014). When users perceive that the OTT platform is dedicated to constant improvement, their trust is reinforced. Consistent upgrades, additions, and improvements demonstrate a commitment to offering a state-of-the-art and dynamic streaming experience.

Attitude

Attitude refers to how users feel, think, and assess OTT platforms, content, and the streaming experience. A user's loyalty to an OTT platform is strongly influenced by their thoughts regarding it. Consistent long-term usage and positive views are influenced by a positive and pleasurable streaming experience (Ajzen, 1991). Users' decisions to renew their subscriptions are influenced by their attitudes. A positive outlook that is cultivated by an engaging content line-up, usability, and general contentment increases the probability that consumers will stick with their subscriptions (Scherer et al., 2019; Yang & Lee, 2018).

Users' propensity to refer other people to an OTT platform is greatly influenced by their attitude. Positive, contented consumers are more likely to spread the word about their experiences, which can result in recommendations from satisfied users that draw in new ones (Nagaraj et al., 2021; Tefertiller, 2020). Positive opinions on the genres, recommendations, and content library encourage users to explore and take in a wider range of offerings, which in turn increases viewership. Overall customer satisfaction is strongly correlated with attitude (Rogers, 2003). Positive sentiments show satisfaction with the streaming experience, but negative sentiments could suggest discontent. Positive attitudes and increased levels of satisfaction can be fostered by platforms that proactively seek to comprehend and conform to user preferences. Good opinions about adoption of IoT, distinctive features and user experience all help a platform gain a competitive advantage since consumers are more inclined to select and stick with a platform with ease of use (Harwood, 1999; Kaur et al., 2020).

A notable gap is found out in the realm of OTT platforms. Previous research has focused on the adoption of technology among consumers, but it is not integrated with OTT streaming and IoT. Moreover, the crucial impact of consumer attitude towards adoption of IoT in case of OTT platforms is still unknown, offering a fascinating direction for further investigation. By bridging these gaps, we may gain a comprehensive picture of customer behaviour and the factors that contribute to or hinder the success of OTT services.

Thus, the present study aims to address following research questions:

RQ1: What are the factors affecting the attitude of consumers towards OTT streaming platforms?

RQ2: Do consumer characteristics moderate the behaviour towards adoption of IoT in OTT platforms?

Users' receptivity to embracing new OTT platform features and technology is influenced by their attitude. Positive attitudes can be shaped by platforms that effectively address user concerns and highlight the benefits of innovations, which will facilitate the adoption of new features. Users' attitudes influence how open they are to receiving personalised suggestions and content discovery tools. Content discovery algorithms perform better when users have a positive perspective of the platform's capacity to recognise and accommodate their personal preferences (Smock et al., 2011). Users' perceptions of the brand linked to OTT platforms are greatly influenced by their attitudes. While a bad attitude could result in brand mistrust, a positive attitude helps to build a positive brand image (Greenwood & Long, 2011). For OTT streaming to be successful, a positive brand perception must be established and maintained.

This chapter is divided into four sections. The first section consists of an introduction, and the second section includes a theoretical framework. In the second section, research methodology and questionnaire development are also discussed. The third section describes the data analysis, and the fourth section includes the findings and limitations of the study.

Theoretical Framework

The factors that determine the UTAUT model are price value, hedonic motivation, social influence, performance expectancy, EE, and facilitating conditions. The UTAUT1 and UTAUT2 hypotheses were initially put forth in 2012 (Venkatesh, 2022). Researchers have several reasons to use UTAUT2 as a theoretical framework when analysing how advances in technology are adopted in customer circumstances, including the fact that it has received over 6,000 citations in IS and other domains (Tamilmani et al., 2018, 2021). The context of the user and how they adapted to the technology are examined in UTAUT2 studies (Venkatesh et al., 2012). Researchers have examined how different users have adopted OTT content using the UTAUT2 theory. Furthermore, UTAUT2 has been widely used in studies to assist researchers in better understanding the trend of technology adoption across a variety of disciplines (Herrero & San Martin, 2017; Venkatesh & Davis, 2000). In this chapter, only five variables are taken as shown in Fig. 7.1, namely performance expectancy, EE, facilitating conditions, trust and attitude towards OTT for measuring the perception of viewers towards OTT platforms in adoption of IoT. In Table 7.2, a brief description of all the selected variables of the present study is given.

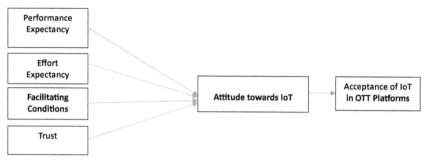

Fig. 7.1. Theoretical Framework. *Source*: Author's compilation.

Table 7.2. Definition of Variables.

Variables	Definition
Performance expectancy	The extent to which a technology benefits the user when performing a particular activity (Venkatesh et al., 2012).
EE	Degree of ease of use in handling any technical breakthrough with less efforts (Venkatesh et al., 2012).
Facilitating conditions	Facilitating conditions refer to the users' cognition regarding the availability of resources in the environment, such as those at home or at work, to complete a task effectively (Venkatesh et al., 2012).
Trust	The willingness of a party to be vulnerable to the actions of another party based on the expectation that the other will perform a particular action important to the trustor, irrespective of the ability to monitor or control the other party (Gefen et al., 2003).
Attitude towards using	The extent to which a viewer perceives the use of an AI-based system in OTT positively or negatively (Ajzen, 1991).

Source: Author's compilation.

Hypotheses Development

H1: Perception of viewers differ significantly based on their age regarding the adoption of IoT in OTT streaming platforms.

H2: Perception of viewers differ significantly based on their operating knowledge of smart device regarding the adoption of IoT in OTT streaming platforms.

H3: Perception of viewers differ significantly based on their experience regarding the adoption of IoT in OTT streaming platforms.

H4: Antecedents of OTT platforms have a positive impact on the intention to adopt IoT in OTT streaming platforms.

Research Methodology

The present study was conducted in the National Capital Region (NCR), Delhi (India). The sample type is basically convenient and purposive. Exploratory and descriptive research design is used to analyse the data. Primary data are collected from the OTT viewers. A standardised questionnaire based on technology acceptance model is developed to examine the attitude of viewers towards OTT platforms. Each item is rated at 5-point Likert scale ranging from 'Strongly disagree' to 'Strongly agree'. Out of a total of 192 responses, 171 were selected for the study. Both online and offline questionnaires are used to record the responses of the viewers. The study is performed in NCR, Delhi. The respondents have marked their level of agreement on the survey instrument regarding adoption of OTT platforms. The constructs were presented in the appendix and tried and tested in other studies also (Joo & Sang, 2013; Munoz-Leiva et al., 2017; Yang & Lee, 2018).

Analysis

IBM Statistical Package for Social Science (SPSS) was used to analyse the data. To proceed with the analysis, internal consistency and reliability of the scale were measured with the help of Cronbach's alpha. The value of Cronbach's alpha was 0.732, which was found to be significant. Table 7.3 depicted the basic information of the respondents. The responses were collected from consumers of NCR and the maximum number of respondents lies in the age group of 18–25 years.

Table 7.3. Profiling of Respondents.

Particulars	Demographics	Frequency	Percentage
Age	18–25	55	32.2
	26–40	48	28.1
	41–50	41	24.0
	Above 50	27	15.8
Education	Primary	22	12.9
	Higher and secondary	38	22.2
	Graduation	57	33.3
	Postgraduation	54	31.6
Knowledge of smart device	Low	35	20.5
	Moderate	80	46.8
	High	56	32.7
Experience in OTT streaming	Less than 2 years	45	26.3
	2–4 years	57	33.3
	4–6 years	44	25.7
	More than 6 years	25	14.6

Source: Author's calculation.

128　Isha Kalra and Meenu Gupta

A moderate level of frequency of having knowledge of smart device was reported by the respondents. The responses of the participants were kept confidential, and identity of the respondents remain anonymous.

Composite reliability, average variance extracted, and Cronbach's alpha are used to check the internal consistency of the scale (Hair et al., 1998). In Table 7.4, the value of *average variance extracted*, Composite Reliability (CR), and Cronbach's alpha (CA) is mentioned. The value of average variance extracted was found to be significant for all factors.

Further, the value of Cronbach's alpha is 0.8, which is greater than 0.7 and signifies that the model was found to be reliable (Nunnally, 1978). The composite reliability of the construct was found to be significant and hence fulfils the condition of reliability (Fornell & Larcker, 1981). Table 7.4 indicated that the mean score of all the factors was greater than the midpoint of the scale as items were measured on 5-point Likert scale (Nunnally, 1978). This signifies that a positive attitude is shown by viewers towards adoption of IoT in OTT platforms.

The main objective of the study is to analyse the perception of viewers regarding adoption of IoT in OTT streaming platforms depending upon their age, experience, and knowledge of smart devices.

The difference in mean for two or more populations is examined using ANOVA (Anderson et al., 2011; Malhotra & Dash, 2011). So, to analyse the difference in the perception of viewers regarding adoption of IoT in OTT platforms, one-way ANOVA is used. In the same way, for exploring the perception of viewers on the basis of age, one-way ANOVA has been applied at a 5% level of significance. Table 7.5 depicts that mean values of all variables are greater than the midpoint scale, and adoption of IoT has a positive impact on the perception of viewers. This table depicted that there is a significant difference found in the perception of viewers on the basis of age regarding adoption of IoT. It indicated that perception of viewers differs significantly regarding OTT platforms according to different age groups.

Further, Table 7.6 represents the perception of viewers based on their knowledge of smart devices. To test the hypothesis *H2*, one-way ANOVA was implemented, and this table shows that the mean score of all variables is greater than the midpoint scale. This table shows that viewers have a positive perception towards adoption of IoT in OTT streaming platforms on the basis of their knowledge

Table 7.4.　Construct Reliability and Validity.

Factors	Items	Mean	SD	Variance	AVE	CR	CA
Performance expectancy	4	3.756	0.882	0.780	0.696	0.812	**0.825**
EE	4	4.052	0.716	0.514	0.671	0.843	**0.819**
Facilitating conditions	4	3.833	0.760	0.579	0.635	0.796	**0.823**
Trust	6	3.427	0.996	0.993	0.681	0.819	**0.796**
Attitude towards using	3	4.094	0.534	0.285	0.761	0.761	**0.818**
Intention	4	4.024	0.498	0.249	0.721	0.772	**0.818**

Source: Author's calculation.
Note: SD, standard deviation.

Table 7.5. Perception of Viewers Based on Age.

Factors	18–25 Years		26–40 Years		41–50 Years		More Than 50 Years		F	Significance (p-Value)
	Mean	SD	Mean	SD	Mean	SD	Mean	SD		
Performance expectancy	3.693	0.839	3.769	0.913	3.702	1.017	3.976	0.737	0.561	0.032
EE	3.830	0.783	4.186	0.727	4.185	0.474	4.167	0.730	2.783	0.043
Facilitating conditions	3.797	0.750	3.769	0.855	3.919	0.778	3.917	0.588	0.344	0.031
Trust	3.594	0.837	3.406	1.026	3.274	1.173	3.270	1.037	0.920	0.053
Attitude towards using	4.107	0.391	4.128	0.416	4.108	0.696	3.984	0.756	0.361	0.021

Source: Author's calculation.
Note: SD, standard deviation.
Significant at 5% level.

130   Isha Kalra and Meenu Gupta

of smart devices. In OTT streaming platforms, smart devices play a crucial role. In Table 7.6, a significant difference is found in the perception of viewers on the basis of knowledge of smart devices regarding adoption of IoT. This suggested that on the basis of knowledge of smart devices, perception of viewers differs significantly for the implementation of IoT in OTT streaming platforms.

In the adoption of IoT, exploring perception regarding the experience of the viewers is also very essential which depicts the significant level of adoption. Table 7.7 depicts the perception of viewers based on their experience in OTT streaming. This table shows that the mean value is greater than the midpoint, which signifies that IoT has a positive impact on the viewers' perception. Further, the highest mean value is found in case of attitude towards using the IoT. This table indicated that a significant difference is found in the perception of viewers towards adoption of IoT on the basis of experience of using OTT platforms.

In order to analyse the adoption of IoT on the OTT platforms, linear regression is applied. Following hypotheses are proposed to test the intention of viewers towards OTT platforms.

H4a: Performance expectancy has a positive impact on the intention to adopt IoT in OTT streaming platforms.

H4b: EE has a positive impact on the intention to adopt IoT in OTT streaming platforms.

H4c: Facilitating conditions has a positive impact on the intention to adopt IoT in OTT streaming platforms.

H4d: Trust has a positive impact on the intention to adopt IoT in OTT streaming platforms.

H4e: Attitude has a positive impact on the intention to adopt IoT in OTT streaming platforms.

Table 7.6.   Perception of Viewers Based on the Knowledge of Smart Device.

Factors	Low		Moderate		High		F	Significance (*p*-Value)
	Mean	SD	Mean	SD	Mean	SD		
Performance expectancy	3.884	0.725	3.662	1.004	3.828	0.761	0.843	0.041
EE	3.991	0.744	4.049	0.673	4.094	0.778	0.178	0.037
Facilitating conditions	3.795	0.887	3.792	0.781	3.922	0.644	0.443	0.043
Trust	3.643	0.827	3.390	1.016	3.352	1.061	0.833	0.047
Attitude towards using	4.131	0.429	4.132	0.524	4.015	0.607	0.733	0.025

Source: Author's calculation.
Note: SD, standard deviation.
Significant at 5% level.

Table 7.7. Perception of Viewers Based on Experience.

Factors	Less Than 2 Years		2–4 Years		4–6 Years		More Than 6 Years		F	Significance (p-Value)
	Mean	SD	Mean	SD	Mean	SD	Mean	SD		
Performance expectancy	3.750	0.993	3.793	0.777	3.664	0.956	3.852	0.812	0.788	0.024
EE	3.912	0.830	3.984	0.725	4.270	0.387	4.057	0.879	1.672	0.031
Facilitating conditions	3.676	0.903	3.814	0.700	3.993	0.677	3.864	0.755	0.913	0.045
Trust	3.369	1.015	3.401	1.047	3.469	0.961	3.508	0.974	0.073	0.011
Attitude towards using	4.072	0.573	4.121	0.336	4.070	0.690	4.121	0.540	0.365	0.039

Source: Author's calculation.
Note: SD, standard deviation.
Significant at 5% level.

132 Isha Kalra and Meenu Gupta

Table 7.8. Regression Analysis.

Dependent Variables Independent Variable	β	SE	p	Squared Multiple Correlation	Hypothesis
Performance expectancy Intention towards adopting IoT	0.037	0.048	0.000	0.766	*H4a**
EE Intention towards adopting IoT	0.077	0.059	0.056	0.530	*H4b**
Facilitating conditions Intention towards adopting IoT	0.153	0.055	0.034	0.556	*H4c**
Trust Intention towards adopting IoT	0.179	0.043	0.021	0.630	*H4d**
Attitude Intention towards adopting IoT	0.093	0.079	0.042	0.893	*H4e**

Source: Author's calculation.
Note: Intention towards using IoT = $\alpha + \beta_1$performance expectancy + β_2EE + $\beta_3$facilitating conditions + $\beta_4$trust + $\beta_5$attitude; β stands for standardised regression weight; SE stands for standard error.
Significant at 5% level.

In Table 7.8, the results indicated the values of standardised regression weights and standard error for performance expectancy, EE, trust, facilitating conditions, and attitude. It is found that p-value is less than 0.05. It is concluded that the intention of viewers towards usage of IoT is significantly affected by performance expectancy, EE, trust, facilitating conditions, and attitude. Standardised regression weights are calculated, which signify the positive influence of IoT on OTT platforms.

Furthermore, the variance explained by performance expectancy, EE, trust, facilitating conditions, and attitude is 76%, 53%, 55%, 63%, 89%, respectively, which signified the positive contribution towards adoption of IoT. It can be concluded that all five factors taken under this study affect the intention of the viewers and further affects the adoption of IoT.

Discussion and Conclusion

The epidemic has functioned as a stimulant for the OTT business in India. This is one of the sectors that has grown in popularity as a result of the current scenario. The digital revolution has reached its pinnacle and is still developing. With more families choosing for smart TVs, OTT entertainment is no longer limited to smartphones. Variable price models, inexpensive data packs, and premium high-definition quality content are further elements that have expanded OTT platform digital adoption (Madnani et al., 2020). Viewers will be able to see the popular OTT industry's rapid expansion due to implementation of IoT. Findings suggested that trust is the only factor in which significant difference is highlighted (Ratnasingam & Pavlou, 2003). Adoption of IoT in providing better streaming services will be very helpful in attracting the customers towards OTT platforms.

The survey highlighted the perception and attitude towards OTT platforms. Study depicted that adoption of IoT in OTT platforms can foster an ecosystem that improves user pleasure, adoption, and retention by addressing external variables including device compatibility, internet speed, technical assistance, accessibility of content, and legal considerations. Fulfilling these requirements effectively boosts the OTT streaming service's market competitiveness and overall success. Consumers anticipate little buffering and speedy loading of videos. Platforms that give priority to these elements improve the whole experience of delivering content. After the implementation of IoT, users are less likely to cancel their subscriptions or transfer platforms if they continuously receive high-quality streaming with no disruptions or technical concerns. When a streaming service regularly meets or beyond user expectations, viewers are more likely to stick with it, which fosters brand trust and demonstrates the company's dedication to providing an excellent viewing experience (Lingareddy & Damle, 2022; Trad, 2024). In addition to increasing customer happiness, meeting or above user expectations for streaming quality, dependability, and overall performance also fosters brand loyalty, favourable word of mouth, and a competitive edge.

In the highly competitive world of OTT streaming, platforms that place a high priority on user-friendly interfaces, effective navigation, and seamless interactions tend to generate positive user experiences, higher adoption, and continued user loyalty. Essentially, the adoption of IoT has offered effective OTT streaming services. It's the confidence consumers feel in the platform's honesty, dependability, and dedication to providing a safe and secure streaming experience. In the competitive market, platforms that value and foster trust are better positioned to draw in, hold onto, and satisfy a devoted user base.

This market is massive because of low-cost data services, subscription packs, and inexpensive handsets. Binge-watching is now feasible, which is enabled by IoT devices. There is no longer any need to wait for the next episode, as there is with cable television. These OTT platforms have entirely enslaved the Indian population. Further, adoption of IoT will be helpful in enriching the experience of viewers.

Practical Implications

The practical implications of adopting OTT streaming platforms, as analysed through the lens of the UTAUT, underscore the significance of performance expectancy and EE. For users, the appeal of these platforms lies in the diverse content libraries and personalised recommendations, emphasising the need for

134 Isha Kalra and Meenu Gupta

service providers to continuously enhance the perceived usefulness of their offerings. Simultaneously, streamlining user interfaces, improving navigation, and optimising overall user experiences are critical to bolstering the perceived ease of use by adopting IoT. Positive attitudes towards using OTT platforms are created by consistent supply of high-quality content and responsive platforms, ultimately influencing users' behavioural intents to adopt and actively engage with the technology.

The research extends the application of the UTAUT2 model beyond its traditional domains and contributes to the body of knowledge by validating in the context of IoT. The research bridges several interdisciplinary areas, including technology adoption, IoT, and digital media platforms. It contributes to the theoretical integration of concepts from these diverse fields, offering a comprehensive framework. This analysis provides an understanding of how and why viewers or consumers of OTT platforms might embrace IoT features, enriching the theoretical discourse on technology adoption. Furthermore, recognising external variables like social influence and facilitating conditions allows service providers to tailor their strategies, ensuring a supportive environment for users. In essence, the UTAUT model guides both users and service providers towards fostering a positive and seamless adoption of IoT experience in the realm of OTT streaming.

Future Research Directions

In the field of IoT and OTT streaming platforms, future research is expected to address a complex array of issues and possibilities. First and foremost, research must be done to determine how IoT devices might be used to improve OTT streaming user experiences. This investigation covers the incorporation of smart devices – like wearables, smart TVs, and voice-activated assistants – to customise interactive features, adaptive streaming, and content recommendations according to user preferences. Furthermore, it is critical to investigate how users view and interact with IoT-enabled features in OTT streaming services. This line of inquiry entails exploring user preferences for interactive features, personalised content recommendations, and the influence of contextual elements on their watching experiences. Furthermore, it's worthwhile to investigate how marketing and communication tactics affect customer views and promote trust in OTT platforms with IoT capabilities. In the rapidly changing world of OTT streaming platforms, ongoing research will be crucial to adapting strategies for changing customer expectations, as consumer behaviour is dynamic and driven by both technology improvements and societal changes. To sum up, by looking at these aspects, future studies will be able to provide a thorough knowledge of how consumers behave when it comes to IoT in OTT streaming, which will help industry players develop strategies that are both user-centred and efficient.

Author's Contribution

In this manuscript, each author contributes in a significant way. At every step, the results and their implications for this article were discussed by all the authors.

Availability of Information and Resources

The main article includes all pertinent information and data.

Declaration of Competing Interest

The authors affirm that they have no known financial or interpersonal conflicts that would have perceived to have an impact on the research presented in this study.

References

Anderson, D. R., Sweeney, D. J., & Williams, T. A. (2011). *Statistics for business and economics* (9th ed). Cengage Learning.

Ajzen, I. (1991). The theory of planned behavior. *Organizational Behavior and Human Decision Processes, 50*(2), 179–211.

Bandyopadhyay, K., & Bandyopadhyay, S. (2010). User acceptance of information technology across cultures. *International Journal of Intercultural Information Management, 2*(3), 218–231.

Botta, A., De Donato, W., Persico, V., & Pescapé, A. (2016). Integration of cloud computing and internet of things: A survey. *Future Generation Computer Systems, 56,* 684–700.

Camilleri, M. A. (2020). The online users' perceptions toward electronic government services. *Journal of Information, Communication and Ethics in Society, 18*(2), 221–235.

Camilleri, M. A. (2021). Strategic dialogic communication through digital media during COVID-19 crisis. Camilleri, M. A. (Ed.), *Strategic corporate communication in the digital age* (pp. 1–18). Emerald Publishing Limited, Leeds. https://doi.org/10.1108/978-1-80071-264-520211001

Camilleri, M. A., & Camilleri, A. C. (2019). The students' readiness to engage with mobile learning apps. *Interactive Technology and Smart Education, 17*(1), 28–38.

Camilleri, M. A., & Falzon, L. (2021). Understanding motivations to use online streaming services: Integrating the technology acceptance model (TAM) and the uses and gratifications theory (UGT). *Spanish Journal of Marketing-ESIC, 25*(2), 217–238.

Chakraborty, D., Siddiqui, M., Siddiqui, A., Paul, J., Dash, G., & Dal Mas, F. (2023). Watching is valuable: Consumer views–content consumption on OTT platforms. *Journal of Retailing and Consumer Services, 70,* 103148.

Chen, C. H., Chen, I. F., Tsaur, R. C., & Chui, L. Y. (2023). User behaviors analysis on OTT platform with an integration of technology acceptance model. *Quality & Quantity, 57*(6), 5673–5691.

Chen, Y. N. K. (2019). Competitions between OTT TV platforms and traditional television in Taiwan: A Niche analysis. *Telecommunications Policy, 43*(9), 101793.

Davis, F. D. (1989). Perceived usefulness, perceived ease of use, and user acceptance of information technology. *MIS Quarterly*, 319–340.

Dhiman, N., Arora, N., Dogra, N., & Gupta, A. (2020). Consumer adoption of smartphone fitness apps: An extended UTAUT2 perspective. *Journal of Indian Business Research, 12*(3), 363–388.

Dhir, A., Khalil, A., Lonka, K., & Tsai, C. C. (2017). Do educational affordances and gratifications drive intensive Facebook use among adolescents?. *Computers in Human Behavior, 68,* 40–50.

Dolan, R., Conduit, J., Frethey-Bentham, C., Fahy, J., & Goodman, S. (2019). Social media engagement behavior: A framework for engaging customers through social media content. *European Journal of Marketing*, *53*(10), 2213–2243.

Dovile, T. (2017). *Internet of Things (IoT) driven media recommendations for television viewers*. The concept of IoT TV. Retrieved from https://www.diva-portal.org/smash/get/diva2:1112935 /FULLTEXT01.pdf

Eneizan, B., Mohammed, A. G., Alnoor, A., Alabboodi, A. S., & Enaizan, O. (2019). Customer acceptance of mobile marketing in Jordan: An extended UTAUT2 model with trust and risk factors. *International Journal of Engineering Business Management*, *11*, 1847979019889484.

Fornell, C., & Larcker, D. F. (1981). Evaluating structural equation models with unobservable variables and measurement error. *Journal of Marketing Research*, *18*(1), 39–50.

Gefen, D., Karahanna, E., & Straub, D. W. (2003). Trust and TAM in online shopping: An integrated model. *MIS Quarterly*, *27*(1), 51–90.

Given, J., Curtis, R., & McCutcheon, M. (2012). Online video in Australia. *International Journal of Digital Television*, *3*(2), 141–162.

Greenwood, D. N., & Long, C. R. (2011). Attachment, belongingness needs, and relationship status predict imagined intimacy with media figures. *Communication Research*, *38*(2), 278–297.

Gubbi, J., Buyya, R., Marusic, S., & Palaniswami, M. (2013). Internet of things (IoT): A vision, architectural elements, and future directions. *Future Generation Computer Systems*, *29*(7), 1645–1660.

GWI. (2019). *Digital versus traditional media consumption. Global web index trend report 2019*. Global Web Index. www.globalwebindex.com/reports/traditional-vs-digital-media-consumption

Hair, J. F., Jr., Anderson, R. E., Tatham, R. L., & Black, W. C. (1998). *Multivariate data analysis* (5th Intl. ed.). Prentice Hall.

Hallur, G. G., Aslekar, A., & Prabhu, S. G. (2023). Digital solution for entertainment: An overview of over the top (OTT) and digital media. In S. Das, & S. Gochhait (Eds.), *Digital entertainment as next evolution in service sector* (pp. 35–53). Palgrave Macmillan. https://doi.org/10.1007/978-981-19-8121-0_3.

Hallur, G. G., Prabhu, S., & Aslekar, A. (2021). Entertainment in Era of AI, Big Data & IoT. In S. Das, & S. Gochhait (Eds.), *Digital entertainment* (pp 87–109). Palgrave Macmillan. https://doi.org/10.1007/978-981-15-9724-4_5.

Haridas, H., & Deepak, S. (2020). Customer perception towards networked streaming service providers with reference to amazon prime and Netflix. *International Journal of Recent Technology and Engineering (IJRTE)*, *9*(1), 513–517.

Harwood, J. (1999). Age identification, social identity gratifications, and television viewing. *Journal of Broadcasting & Electronic Media*, *43*(1), 123–136.

Im, I., Hong, S., & Kang, M. S. (2011). An international comparison of technology adoption: Testing the UTAUT model. *Information & Management*, *48*(1), 1–8.

Herrero, Á., & San Martín, H. (2017). Explaining the adoption of social networks sites for sharing user-generated content: A revision of the UTAUT2. *Computers in Human Behavior*, *71*, 209–217.

Joo, J., & Sang, Y. (2013). Exploring Koreans' smartphone usage: An integrated model of the technology acceptance model and uses and gratifications theory. *Computers in Human Behavior*, *29*(6), 2512–2518.

Kaur, P., Dhir, A., Chen, S., Malibari, A., & Almotairi, M. (2020). Why do people purchase virtual goods? A uses and gratification (U&G) theory perspective. *Telematics and Informatics*, *53*, 101376.

Khan, M. L. (2017). Social media engagement: What motivates user participation and consumption on YouTube?. *Computers in Human Behavior*, *66*, 236–247.

Kim, S., Baek, H., & Kim, D. H. (2021). OTT and live streaming services: Past, present, and future. *Telecommunications Policy*, *45*(9), 102244.

Kohli, C. (2020). The replacement of conventional television by streaming services. *International Journal of Research in Engineering, Science and Management, 3*(10), 59–67.

Lee, C. C., Nagpal, P., Ruane, S. G., & Lim, H. S. (2018). Factors affecting online streaming subscriptions. *Communications of the IIMA, 16*(1), 2.

Lee, S., Lee, S., Joo, H., & Nam, Y. (2021). Examining factors influencing early paid over-the-top video streaming market growth: A cross-country empirical study. *Sustainability, 13*(10), 5702.

Leung, L. (2015). Using tablet in solitude for stress reduction: An examination of desire for aloneness, leisure boredom, tablet activities, and location of use. *Computers in Human Behavior, 48*, 382–391.

Lin, J., Yu, W., Zhang, N., Yang, X., Zhang, H., & Zhao, W. (2017). A survey on internet of things: Architecture, enabling technologies, security and privacy, and applications. *IEEE Internet of Things Journal, 4*(5), 1125–1142.

Lingareddy, V., & Damle, M. (2022). Video streaming OTT platforms: A com- parative study of their streaming infrastructure with strategies implemented. In *2022 International interdisciplinary humanitarian conference for sustainability (IIHC)*, Bengaluru, India (pp. 29–35). doi: 10.1109/IIHC55949.2022.10060746.

Madnani, D., Fernandes, S., & Madnani, N. (2020). Analysing the impact of COVID-19 on over-the-top media platforms in India. *International Journal of Pervasive Computing and Communications, 16*(5), 457–475.

Malhotra, N. K., & Dash, S. (2011). *Marketing research: An applied orientation* (6th ed.). Pearson Education.

Malik, A., Dhir, A., & Nieminen, M. (2016). Uses and gratifications of digital photo sharing on Facebook. *Telematics and Informatics, 33*(1), 129–138.

Mohan, J. S., Challa, N. P., Swathi, P., & Kowshiki, N. (2021). Transforming OTT digital platform business using blockchain technology. *Blockchain Applications for Secure IoT Frameworks: Technologies Shaping the Future, 1*, 173.

Moore, G. C., & Benbasat, I. (1991). Development of an instrument to measure the perceptions of adopting an information technology innovation. *Information Systems Research, 2*(3), 192–222.

Munoz-Leiva, F., Climent-Climent, S., & Liébana-Cabanillas, F. (2017). Determinants of intention to use the mobile banking apps: An extension of the classic TAM model. *Spanish Journal of Marketing-ESIC, 21*(1), 25–38.

Nagaraj, S., Singh, S., & Yasa, V. R. (2021). Factors affecting consumers' willingness to subscribe to over-the-top (OTT) video streaming services in India. *Technology in Society, 65*, 101534.

Nagy, J. T. (2018). Evaluation of online video usage and learning satisfaction: An extension of the technology acceptance model. *International Review of Research in Open and Distance Learning, 19*(1), 160–184.

Niehaves, B., & Plattfaut, R. (2014). Internet adoption by the elderly: Employing IS technology acceptance theories for understanding the age-related digital divide. *European Journal of Information Systems, 23*, 708–726.

Nikolopoulou, K., Gialamas, V., & Lavidas, K. (2020). Acceptance of mobile phone by university students for their studies: An investigation applying UTAUT2 model. *Education and Information Technologies, 25*, 4139–4155.

Nunnally, J. C. (1978). *Psychometric theory* (2nd ed.) McGraw.

Park, N. (2010). Adoption and use of computer-based voice over Internet protocol phone service: Toward an integrated model. *Journal of Communication, 60*(1), 40–72.

Park, S., & Kwon, Y. (2019). Research on the relationship between the growth of OTT service market and the change in the structure of the Pay-TV market. *30th European Conference of the International Telecommunications Society (ITS): "Towards a Connected and Automated Society"*, Helsinki, Finland, 16th–19th June, 2019. Retrieved from https://hdl.handle.net/10419/205203.

Parnami, S., & Jain, T. (2021). A study on increase in the usage of OTT streaming services. *International Journal of Research in Engineering, Science and Management, 4*(8), 142–145.

Ratnasingam, P., & Pavlou, P. A. (2003). Technology trust in internet-based interorganizational electronic commerce. *Journal of Electronic Commerce in Organizations (JECO), 1*(1), 17–41.

Rauniar, R., Rawski, G., Yang, J., & Johnson, B. (2014). Technology acceptance model (TAM) and social media usage: An empirical study on Facebook. *Journal of Enterprise Information Management, 27*(1), 6–30.

Ray, A., Dhir, A., Bala, P. K., & Kaur, P. (2019). Why do people use food delivery apps (FDA)? A uses and gratification theory perspective. *Journal of Retailing and Consumer Services, 51,* 221–230.

Rogers, E. M. (2003). *Diffusion of innovations* (5th ed.). Simon and Schuster.

Scherer, R., Siddiq, F., & Tondeur, J. (2019). The technology acceptance model (TAM): A meta-analytic structural equation modeling approach to explaining teachers' adoption of digital technology in education. *Computers & Education, 128,* 13–35.

Shu, L., Zhang, D., Wu, D., Wang, S., & Zhang, Y. (2018). Edge computing in the internet of things: A survey. *IEEE Access, 6,* 6900–6919.

Singh, K. K., Makhania, J., & Mahapatra, M. (2024). Impact of ratings of content on OTT platforms and prediction of its success rate. *Multimedia Tools and Applications, 83*(2), 4791–4808.

Singh, K. K., & Tomar, D. S. (2018, August). Architecture, enabling technologies, security and privacy, and applications of internet of things: A survey. In *2018 2nd International Conference on I-SMAC (IoT in Social, Mobile, Analytics and Cloud) (I-SMAC)I-SMAC (IoT in Social, Mobile, Analytics and Cloud) (I-SMAC), 2018 2nd International Conference on,* Palladam, India (pp. 642–646). doi: 10.1109/I-SMAC.2018.8653708.

Smock, A. D., Ellison, N. B., Lampe, C., & Wohn, D. Y. (2011). Facebook as a toolkit: A uses and gratification approach to unbundling feature use. *Computers in human behavior, 27*(6), 2322–2329.

Steiner, E., & Xu, K. (2020). Binge-watching motivates change: Uses and gratifications of streaming video viewers challenge traditional TV research. *Convergence, 26*(1), 82–101.

Sundaravel, E., & Elangovan, N. (2020). Emergence and future of over-the-top (OTT) video services in India: An analytical research. *International Journal of Business, Management and Social Research, 8*(2), 489–499.

Tamilmani, K., Rana, N. P., Dwivedi, Y., Sahu, G. P., & Roderick, S. (2018). Exploring the role of price value' for understanding consumer adoption of technology: A review and meta-analysis of UTAUT2 based empirical studies. *PACIS 2018 Proceedings, 64.* https://aisel.aisnet.org/pacis2018/64.

Tamilmani, K., Rana, N. P., Wamba, S. F., & Dwivedi, R. (2021). The extended unified theory of acceptance and use of technology (UTAUT2): A systematic literature review and theory evaluation. *International Journal of Information Management, 57,* 102269.

Taylor, S., & Todd, P. A. (1995). Understanding information technology usage: A test of competing models. *Information Systems Research, 6*(2), 144–176.

Tefertiller, A. (2018). Media substitution in cable cord-cutting: The adoption of web-streaming television. *Journal of Broadcasting & Electronic Media, 62*(3), 390–407.

Tefertiller, A. (2020). Cable cord-cutting and streaming adoption: Advertising avoidance and technology acceptance in television innovation. *Telematics and Informatics, 51,* 101416.

Tefertiller, A., & Sheehan, K. (2019). TV in the streaming age: Motivations, behaviors, and satisfaction of post-network television. *Journal of Broadcasting & Electronic Media, 63*(4), 595–616.

Thompson, R. L., Higgins, C. A., & Howell, J. M. (1991). Personal computing: Toward a conceptual model of utilization. *MIS quarterly*, 125–143.

Trad, A. T. (2024). Business transformation projects: The impact of the over-the-top. In N. Kalorth (Ed.), *Exploring the impact of OTT media on global societies* (pp. 241–271). IGI Global. Retrieved from https://www.igi-global.com/chapter/business-transformation-projects/340646

Troise, C., & Camilleri, M. A. (2021). The use of digital media for marketing, CSR communication and stakeholder engagement. In M. A. Camilleri (Ed.), *Strategic corporate communication in the digital age* (pp. 161–174). Emerald Publishing Limited. https://doi.org/10.1108/978-1-80071-264-520211010

Venkatesh, V. (2022). Adoption and use of AI tools: A research agenda grounded in UTAUT. *Annals of Operations Research, 308*(1), 641–652.

Venkatesh, V., & Bala, H. (2008). Technology acceptance model 3 and a research agenda on interventions. *Decision Sciences, 39*(2), 273–315.

Venkatesh, V., & Davis, F. D. (2000). A theoretical extension of the technology acceptance model: Four longitudinal field studies. *Management Science, 46*(2), 186–204.

Venkatesh, V., Morris, M. G., Davis, G. B., & Davis, F. D. (2003). User acceptance of information technology: Toward a unified view. *MIS Quarterly, 27*(3), 425–478.

Venkatesh, V., Thong, J. Y., & Xu, X. (2012). Consumer acceptance and use of information technology: Extending the unified theory of acceptance and use of technology. *MIS Quarterly, 36*(1), 157–178.

Verma, B., & Tandon, U. (2022). Modelling barriers to wearable technologies in Indian context: Validating the moderating role of technology literacy. *Global Knowledge, Memory and Communication, 73*(6/7), 984–1004.

Vijayasarathy, L. R. (2004). Predicting consumer intentions to use on-line shopping: The case for an augmented technology acceptance model. *Information & Management, 41*(6), 747–762.

Wallace, L. G., & Sheetz, S. D. (2014). The adoption of software measures: A technology acceptance model (TAM) perspective. *Information & Management, 51*(2), 249–259.

Weinswig, D. (2016). Gen Z: Get ready for the most self-conscious, demanding consumer segment. *Fung Global Retail & Technology*, 1–19. Retrieved from https://deborah-weinswig.com/wp-content/uploads/2016/08/Gen-Z-Report-2016-by-Fung-Global-Retail-Tech-August-29-2016.pdf

Yang, H., & Lee, H. (2018). Exploring user acceptance of streaming media devices: An extended perspective of flow theory. *Information Systems and e-Business Management, 16*(1), 1–27.

Yaqoub, M., Jingwu, Z., & Ambekar, S. S. (2023). Pandemic impacts on cinema industry and over-the-top platforms in China. *Media International Australia, 191*(1), 105–128. https://doi.org/10.1177/1329878X221145975.

Yoon, S. Y., & Kim, J. B. (2022). A study on user satisfaction and intention to con-tinue use of OTT platform digital content provision service. *2022 IEEE/ACIS 7th international conference on Big Data, Cloud Computing, and Data Science (BCD)* (pp. 290–296). Danang, Vietnam. doi: 10.1109/BCD54882.2022.9900797.

You, C. S., Tu, S. T., Yan, Y. N., Wang, S. Y., & Chou, C. H. (2021, September). Discussion on the recent development of OTT platforms in Taiwan. In *2021 IEEE international conference on consumer electronics-Taiwan (ICCE-TW)* (pp. 1–2). Penghu, Taiwan. doi: 10.1109/ICCE-TW52618.2021.9603124.

Appendix: The Measuring Items

Concept	Question	Theory	Measurement
	In the context of IoT, viewers perceive that …		
Performance expectancy			
PE1	OTT is better than normal television subscriptions	Venkatesh et al. (2012)	5-point Likert scale
PE2	OTT allows to improve content watching experience	Venkatesh et al. (2012)	5-point Likert scale
PE3	OTT is a useful innovation	Venkatesh et al. (2012)	5-point Likert scale
PE4	Using OTT services allow me to save time	Venkatesh et al. (2012)	5-point Likert scale
EE			
EE1	Learning how to use OTT services is easy for me	Venkatesh et al. (2012)	5-point Likert scale
EE2	My interaction with OTT services is clear and understandable	Venkatesh et al. (2012)	5-point Likert scale
EE3	Find OTT services easy to use	Venkatesh et al. (2012)	5-point Likert scale
EE4	Using OTT services does not seem to be complicated for me	Venkatesh et al. (2012)	5-point Likert scale
Facilitating conditions			
FC1	I have the resources necessary to use OTT services	Venkatesh et al. (2012)	5-point Likert scale
FC2	I have the knowledge necessary to use OTT services	Venkatesh et al. (2012)	5-point Likert scale
FC3	OTT services is compatible with other technologies I use	Venkatesh et al. (2012)	5-point Likert scale

(Continued)

Concept	Question	Theory	Measurement
FC4	I can get help from others when I have difficulties using OTT service	Venkatesh et al. (2012)	5-point Likert scale
Trust			
T1	Reliable information is offered by OTT system	Gefen et al. (2003)	5-point Likert scale
T2	OTT advocates transparency in the system	Gefen et al. (2003)	5-point Likert scale
T3	OTT has essential abilities to carry out its work	Gefen et al. (2003)	5-point Likert scale
T4	OTT system takes into account the needs of its users	Gefen et al. (2003)	5-point Likert scale
T5	OTT system is open to the serve demands of its users	Gefen et al. (2003)	5-point Likert scale
T6	OTT system would not do anything unfair to the user	Gefen et al. (2003)	5-point Likert scale
Attitude towards using			
AT1	OTT is a good tool for innovations in video streaming	Ajzen (1991)	5-point Likert scale
AT2	OTT will be appropriate for video streaming	Ajzen (1991)	5-point Likert scale
AT3	Use of OTT on a regular basis will be valuable for me	Ajzen (1991)	5-point Likert scale

Chapter 8

Modern Consumerism and Retailing: The Metaverse Bound

Brian Kee Mun Wong[a], Foong Li Law[b] and Chin Ike Tan[b]

[a]*Swinburne University of Technology Sarawak Campus, Malaysia*
[b]*Asia Pacific University of Technology and Innovation, Malaysia*

Abstract

The emergence of consumerism has led to regulatory measures being integrated into business practices, but the influence of consumers in developing countries remains limited, resulting in businesses being less responsive. The digital retail landscape is undergoing a transformative revolution, driven by Industrial Revolution (IR) 4.0 technological advancements such as artificial intelligence (AI), wearables, virtual reality (VR), augmented reality (AR), and blockchain technology. This development focuses on convenience, personalisation, and emotional connections. Companies are adapting to modern consumer behaviour through various strategies, including online shopping, mobile commerce, data analytics, technology integration, user reviews, and contactless payments. The COVID-19 pandemic has accelerated this seismic shift in the retail industry, and online retail is expected to continue to grow post-pandemic, driven by these technologies. AI enhances the customer experience, wearables provide interactive engagement, VR offers immersive shopping, AR merges online and physical shopping, and blockchain ensures secure transactions in the emerging metaverse. As retail converges with the metaverse, the potential for borderless and personalised shopping experiences is enormous. Advances in VR technology could lead to interconnected virtual spaces that seamlessly connect physical and digital retail, providing immersive and personalised shopping experiences. However, challenges such as cost, learning curves, digital security, legal ambiguity, data privacy, financial risk, and ethical

---

Augmenting Retail Reality: Blockchain, AR, VR, and the Internet of Things, Part A, 143–166
Copyright © 2025 by Brian Kee Mun Wong, Foong Li Law and Chin Ike Tan
Published under exclusive licence by Emerald Publishing Limited
doi:10.1108/978-1-83608-634-520241020

144 Brian Kee Mun Wong et al.

considerations need to be addressed through vigilant and informed consumer engagement in this evolving digital landscape.

Keywords: Consumerism; digital retailing; metaverse; immersive technologies; consumer engagement

Introduction

Consumerism, as an evolving concept, goes beyond its modern association with consumer rights. Detaching it from this prevailing focus, consumerism is viewed as the collective conduct of consumers, generating shared features and ends. While it may face criticism for its narrow semantic scope, the listing of consumption-related acts is acknowledged as a partial historical account. Terms such as 'consumption', 'consuming', and 'consumerism', are employed as convenient shorthand expressions to encompass diverse actions (Pennell, 1999). This perspective emphasises the diversity of actions, especially in the early modern period. Modern consumerism, attributed to economic, social, and technological innovations like mass production, advertising, and credit selling, remains elusive as a pattern of meaningful conduct (Campbell, 2018).

The emergence of modern consumerism in 17th and 18th-century Western Europe challenged previous assumptions that consumerism flowed from industrialisation (Trentmann, 2004). It resulted from pre-industrial consumerism, influenced by growing wealth, cultural innovation translation, and compensation for social uncertainties. Modern consumerism encompasses a cultural and economic paradigm emphasising the continuous acquisition of goods and services. This phenomenon is characterised by several key elements such as high consumption rates, mass production and globalisation, marketing and advertising, planned obsolescence, credit culture, consumer rights and protections, and digital consumerism. Perhaps, the multifaceted phenomenon underscores the intricate interplay between cultural ideals, economic structures, and consumption patterns in contemporary society.

Rooted in the belief that increased acquisition enhances one's quality of life or social standing, modern consumerism is marked by high consumption rates (Chiarelli, 2014). It is closely linked to mass production and globalisation, facilitated by technological advances that enable the widespread availability and affordability of products. Products are typically designed with limited lifespans or quick obsolescence, encouraging frequent purchases (Bisschop et al., 2022). Hence, companies heavily invest in marketing and advertising to persuade consumers to make purchases, creating perceived needs for new items, even when existing ones are functional (Dwivedi et al., 2021). The availability of credit, including credit cards and loans, fuels modern consumerism by enabling purchases beyond immediate financial means, contributing to a culture of debt (Segal, 2023). The advent of e-commerce has led to digital consumerism, transforming shopping habits, and the retail landscape (Amin & Nor, 2013).

Over the years, modern consumerism has spurred varied ethical and moral commentary, adapting to new concerns like the green economy (Söderholm, 2020). Despite ethical critiques, consumerism has maintained intensity and expanded geographically, forming a pervasive aspect of contemporary urban life. Ethical commentary is considered intrinsic to consumerism, reflected in efforts to moderate excess, combat fraud, and question the moral validity of the phenomenon (Stearns, 2009). Hence, there is a need for increasing awareness and legislation aimed to protect consumer rights, ensure product safety, and prevent false advertising within the context of modern consumerism (Amin & Nor, 2013).

Transitioning to the digital realm, digital retailing integrates traditional physical retailing with online retail stores, moving towards omnichannel retailing (Jain & Werth, 2019). Often, it encompasses various technologies, undergoing a major transformation that emphasises the digitalisation of the retail industry through digital technologies (Hansen & Sia, 2015). The changing landscape places customer experience as a leading goal for retailers, representing a non-financial and complex objective in the digital retail environment (Cakir et al., 2019; Verhoef et al., 2009).

Evolution of Consumerism and Digital Retailing

The ascent of consumerism has empowered consumers to voice their concerns regarding dubious business practices, prompting an upswing in regulatory measures, especially in Western countries (Craig-Lees & Hill, 2002). Developed economies have responded by institutionalising consumerism within socio-political systems, leading to comprehensive regulations that businesses routinely integrate into their decision-making processes (Steiner & Steiner, 1997). In stark contrast, developing countries face lower pressure from the consumer movement, resulting in relatively low corporate responsiveness to consumerism. The prevalence of seller's market conditions in these least developed countries (LDCs) fosters a scenario where consumers, prioritising basic physiological needs, accept whatever is offered due to their limited voice in the marketplace (Kaynak, 1985; Reddy & Campbell, 1994).

The absence of a supportive macroeconomic environment further limits consumerism activities in LDCs to micro issues like product safety, packaging, and misleading advertising, while developed countries focus on macro issues such as pollution, poverty, and healthcare (Kaynak, 1985). Comparative research between Bangladeshi and Australian managers reveals that consumerism in developing countries, like Bangladesh, plays a constructive role, creating awareness, maintaining ethical conduct, and eliminating questionable practices. This aligns with Kaynak's (1985) consumerism life cycle (CLC) stages, providing empirical support for the evolution of consumerism in different countries (e.g. Barker, 1987; Barksdale & Perreault, 1980; Rajan Varadarajan & Thirunarayana, 1990; Rajan Varadarajan et al., 1992).

Simultaneously, as consumerism evolves, digital retailing undergoes a profound transformation to meet the demands of modern consumers, emphasising convenience, personalisation, and seamless online experiences (Koppens, 2021). This shift, driven by globalisation, rapid technological developments, and environmental concerns, has given rise to the platform economy. Major tech companies like Uber, Facebook, and Google influence online services, setting cultural expectations for speed and efficiency (Dekker & Okano-Heijmans, 2020). To adapt, businesses now integrate AR into digital marketing communications, allowing customers to visualise products virtually. This marks a departure from the traditional VR, with AR enhancing physical reality by incorporating virtual displays into the real world (Koppens, 2021).

As online customer engagement intensifies, businesses grapple with optimising service experiences, understanding customer journeys, and addressing the emotional aspects of e-commerce retailing. In the pursuit of cultivating customer satisfaction and fostering emotional bonds, businesses employ AR technologies like virtual fitting rooms (VFRs) as integral components of their marketing communication strategies, as highlighted by Koppens (2021). Through the interactive features and vibrant product representations facilitated by VFRs, companies craft distinctive and emotionally impactful customer experiences, responding adeptly to the dynamic shifts in the realm of digital retail. In fact, the transformation of digital retailing manifests across diverse dimensions:

1. **Revolutionising Online Shopping Experience**: The introduction of online platforms has fundamentally altered how consumers engage, offering unparalleled convenience and accessibility (Reinartz et al., 2019). This shift is further accentuated by the surge in mobile commerce, where platforms are meticulously tailored for smartphones.
2. **Ascendance of Mobile Commerce (m-commerce)**: The proliferation of mobile usage has been the catalyst for the upswing in mobile commerce (Pelet & Taieb, 2022). Websites are now intricately optimised for mobile devices, enriching the overall shopping experience.
3. **Harnessing Data Analytics and Machine Learning**: Retailers harness consumer data to curate personalised recommendations and deploy targeted advertisements, thereby intensifying consumer engagement (Dwivedi et al., 2021). The integration of social media allows consumers to seamlessly explore and purchase products (Appel et al., 2020).
4. **Pioneering Technological Advancements**: Innovations such as virtual try ons and AR directly confront consumer apprehensions, delivering a more immersive and interactive shopping experience (Yoo, 2023; Zhang et al., 2019). The embrace of subscription models, the proliferation of diverse e-commerce marketplaces, and the adoption of competitive pricing strategies have become pervasive trends (Bischof et al., 2020; Cano et al., 2023).
5. **Impact of User Reviews and Ratings**: Consumer trust and purchasing decisions are significantly influenced by user reviews and ratings, shaping the credibility and appeal of products and services (Chen et al., 2022).
6. **Rise of Contactless Payments**: The inclusion of mobile wallets and digital platforms has become integral, furnishing consumers with a secure and efficient checkout experience (Bezovski, 2016).

In a broader context, the evolution of digital retailing mirrors a responsive adaptation to the tenets of modern consumerism. The emphasis on convenience,

Modern Consumerism and Retailing *147*

personalisation, and seamless technology integration signifies a paradigm shift, and businesses that actively embrace these transformative changes position themselves to craft distinctive and emotionally resonant customer experiences within the dynamically evolving digital retail landscape. How exactly did the evolution of digital retailing occur and what are the digital technology enablers that are present within this space?

The Growth and Trend of Digital Retailing

Advances in technology have reshaped many industries from manufacturing to the entertainment industry. The retailing industry is no different. The landscape of modern consumerism practices and digital retailing is now experiencing an exponential seismic shift that is driven by advances, adoption, and disruption caused directly or indirectly by technology. Although many scholars have previously written about the role of technology in changing the landscape of retailing, it was the COVID-19 pandemic that accelerated the growth and adoption of technology by causing a worldwide disruption in the daily lifestyle of consumers. This change of lifestyle has caused many brick-and-mortar retailers to pivot and move rapidly towards technology-based solutions and practices as physical stores experiencing closures became more prevalent (Retail News Asia, 2020; Shankar et al., 2021).

The post-pandemic era is seeing more and more of the adoption and integration of technologies resulting in the growth of online retail penetration. This change in consumer and industry economics will experience a shift in digital retailing, gaining a significant share of the global retail profits. Based on the data from Statistica (Coppola, 2023), online sales in 2022 accounted for nearly 19% of global retail sales. This figure is estimated to reach 25% by 2027 as studies has shown that 87.6% of Generation Z prefer online shopping (Renouard, 2023), and this number is expected to rise over the next few decades as these centennials and indeed the preceding generations are becoming more dependent on technology, using it as an effective medium for communication, information, leisure, business, socialisation, consumerism, learning, and as ways to better engage and motivate them (Giray, 2022; Tan & Wong, 2016). To understand the impact technology plays as enablers vital to the rise of digital retailing, it is essential that we delve into each technology enabler.

AI

Central to this technology revolution is our ever-increasing dependence on AI. From autonomous vehicles to smart devices – AI is now becoming a significant presence in society and is fast becoming an essential part of our everyday lives, be it at work or at home. As this technology continues to evolve and become more powerful, capable, and accessible, society will also become more reliant and dependent on AI in the coming years. Indeed, the main role of AI is to reduce or, if possible, eliminate the need for human involvement in mundane tasks – to make decisions for humans or to provide us with enough information for humans to take the next step.

This is highly evident in the ecosystem of digital retail, where AI has and will revolutionise many essential aspects of this industry. From targeted online advertisements and recommendations based on consumer surfing patterns to enhanced modern chatbots trained on large language models, AI is the main driver in consumer/customer efficiency through customised shopping experiences (Anica-Popa et al., 2021). Through machine learning and deep learning algorithms, AI is able to take advantage of structured and unstructured data, enabling retailers to anticipate trends – thus inventorying effectively, predicting spending patterns, and optimising pricing strategies. These algorithms based on personalisation are also able to analyse consumer data and window-shopping habits to discern preferences and behaviours making for a more targeted customer experience.

An example of the use of AI and robotics in retail is the American home improvement chain, Lowe's Companies. Autonomous robots greet customers in their retail store and assist shoppers to find items in store. The robots use AI and computer vision technology to detect customers as they enter stores and proceed to communicate with them in multiple languages and to guide these customers to selected items using smart laser sensors (Taylor, 2016). At the same time, a second set of screens displays location-based special offers. As an added value, these autonomous robots called LoweBots simultaneously scan shelves using computer vision and AI technology to perform inventory tracking, assisting store assistants in restocking items on the shelves.

In fact, Lowe's is not the only major retail chain that uses AI and computer vision technology, Neiman Marcus, Sephora, and Walmarts are also using these technologies to improve customer search experience and at the same time improve store efficiency. However, moving forward, the integration of AI in immersive technologies such as extended reality (XR), AR, and VR will bring modern digital retail and consumerism closer to the holy grail of the envisioned metaverse concept.

Immersive Technologies

According to Tucci (2023), the metaverse is a digital reality where a vast population of the world will reside, work, socialise, shop, and play with each other, all within the confines of their own homes – very much like the movie, Ready Player One. It is a digital world where our on-screen avatars interact with other people and move from one digital experience or domain to another, be it a digital game, social space, work, or shopping experience. Our identities will be tied closely to these digital facsimiles of ourselves (Tucci, 2023).

The metaverse is an alternate universe albeit in a digital realm that has no boundaries and obeys no laws of physics. It is a perpetual and persistent multi-user environment merging the digital reality through the experiences and eyes of the physical reality (Mystakidis, 2022). The metaverse term was first used by Neal Stephenson in his 1992 novel, *Snow Crash*. In this chapter, we conceptualised it as a form of escapism to a reality where the digital realm replaces the physical realm. In fact, the term 'metaverse' consists of two keywords – 'meta' which implies transcending or going beyond the limits of something, and 'verse' which is short for universe.

Modern Consumerism and Retailing **149**

In short, it is a massive digital environment that runs parallel to our physical realm. The metaverse can exist in three forms – the first as an entirely separate reality. There is no connection between both realities – in fact, this is the most commonly practised state in the metaverse. The concept of metaverse where one can live, socialise, transact, and interact in a digital world is not something new. The first online massive multiplayer role-playing game in the 80s – Multi-User Dungeons (MUDs) – also had these features. MUDs which inspired the development and concept of massively multiplayer online games (MMOG) and massively multiplayer online role-playing games (MMORPG) enabled players to interact, socialise, and transact in a persistent digital environment albeit in a text form (Mystakidis, 2022).

In fact, many scholars argue that popular games such as Second Life, World of Warcraft, and the Sims are actually the first iteration of the metaverse – although in a screen-based form (e.g. Lee et al., 2021; Mystakidis, 2022). These games have no bearing or impact on emotional and mental state of the user or player though. The second form, according to Lee et al. (2021), is the digital twins-native continuum where the physical reality exists also in the virtual world and will affect periodical changes to their digital counterparts to reflect these changes. In this form, the connection between the virtual and physical twins is tied by their data (Lee et al., 2021) – which takes the most commonly known form of user/player information or specifically currency. Many developers are trying to push the metaverse in its current form as an economic platform based on blockchain technology, integrating the real world and digital world's economic and social systems. Central to these are two facets of immersive technology, namely VR and AR.

VR immerses users in a simulated three-dimensional (3D) environment, allowing interaction and exploration approximating reality. However, processing limitations in devices like VR headsets, treadmills, and gloves hinder complete realism. According to the Virtual Reality Society (2017), our evolved senses demand synchronised experiences. True immersion requires sensory synchronicity, tactile mastery, and visual impact. Similarly, video games need a comprehensive stimulus package for effective user experience, including aesthetics (Ike et al., 2021; Tan, 2019). Hyper-realistic graphics in VR may soon blur the line between virtual and reality, transforming consumer experiences in digital retailing.

As VR is all about placing the user in an entirely computer-generated environment, AR takes digital images and layers it on the real world around you. According to Rejeb et al. (2023), the characteristics that distinguishes the technology which is AR is the combination of real and virtual elements and how these two elements interact in real time together with an accurate alignment of the digital and real-world objects in question. While modern shopping experiences consist of either an online or physical shopping experience, the future face of retail might be a seamless blend of online and physical experiences albeit with a dash of AR.

These AR experiences may also incorporate personalised algorithms to provide directed customer discounts, advertisements, and recommendations as well as autonomous interactions with the AI itself (Choudhury et al., 2023; Shankar et al., 2021). Automated scanning may make transactions and payments equally seamless and secure, combining the cashless systems that we are now experiencing.

Hence, AR is a powerful tool as it combines VR and modern technology to provide users with an enhanced interactive and visual experience.

While VR relies on hyper-realistic graphics to create a more acceptable retail experience, AR's overlaying of digital information and virtual 3D elements on the real-world environment makes it a more transformative force. Studies have shown that AR technology can add much value in digital retail by providing shoppers with better in-store experiences (Xue et al., 2023). One of the significant value propositions that AR affords is through the concept of enhanced product visualisation. While conventional online shopping often lacks the tactile, try-before-you-buy shopping experiences that physical stores provide, AR can change that by allowing customers to not only virtually try on clothes before making a purchase, but it also may reduce the need to physical fitting rooms and later to combine various articles of clothing from various stores for the consumer to mix and match.

However, the use of AR technology is not limited to online shopping experiences, it can also be deployed as an interactive physical store navigation to help customers locate various products efficiently, calculate discounts on the spot, and view stocks for sizes. It can combine the mobile application versions of large retail shops with the interactive tactile shopping experiences all in one. Interestingly, it may not even require a bulky headgear, a powerful smartphone will suffice – and that opens up the possibility of retailers offering personalised shopping experiences based on individual preferences and retail behaviours by the integration of AI algorithms, customer needs, as well as customer data like size and style.

Some examples of retailers using immersive technologies such as VR, AR, or a mix of both (mixed reality (MR)) are in the use of VFRs. British fast-fashion company, Topshop, developed a VFR where customers can view themselves on screen with a digital version of their clothes superimposed on their physical bodies. This is something that Tommy Hilfiger, American premium lifestyle brand, has also deployed. Nike uses MR in their physical stores to allow customers to experience how Nike shoes are manufactured. Cosmetics giants such as L'Oreal and Sephora are using AR technology to bring the experience of their respective cosmetic products directly to the user, showing them how each of their cosmetic products reflects on the customer's appearance (Aviso, 2023; Tan et al., 2022).

However, as modern consumers navigate more into the online realm, there is a need for secure and transparent transactions in the digital space. While the immersive technologies provide the metaverse with the virtual world where these transactions may take place, the concept of blockchain and Web3 will provide for a secure layer that will allow consumers to own things and to experience a more realistic consumer-like version of the metaverse.

Blockchain Technology

This is a type of decentralised shared and distributed database that stores transactional information such as tangible assets or intangible assets in an immutable format that cannot be manipulated or hacked. It duplicates and distributes these transactions or 'blocks' that are linked via cryptography across a computer network's nodes or 'chains', and its decentralised nature gives it an edge when compared to traditional record keeping which is vulnerable to online fraud and cyberattacks. Walmart Canada's use of blockchain technology is a prime example of utilising distributed ledger technology. The company was facing frequent issues around data discrepancies between its freight carriers and its invoice and payment transactions. Using the power of blockchain's single source of information, Walmart created an automated system to manage its invoices and payments for all its third-party freight carriers with minimum inconsistencies and time delays. Prior to system implementation, over 70% of the freight carriers' invoices were disputed. With the system, less than 1% of invoices have discrepancies (Vitasek et al., 2022). In terms of manpower and time, this has significantly reduced Walmart's operational costs.

In fact, the technology for blockchain is fast growing, and new concepts of utilising this technology from social networks to shared storage solutions are being explored. Blockchain will also enable the metaverse to be a public platform equipped with an open-source ecosystem, allowing retailers and users to create decentralised wallets and exchanges for the use in digital retailing and consumerism (Gadekallu et al., 2022; Yang et al., 2022). Blockchain will revolutionise the immersive experience of the metaverse while providing a secure manner for all manner of transactions and storage of digital assets, finances, and personal information.

The metaverse today adds value to the business-to-consumer (B2C) model, with events like concerts being touted as a metaverse event or buying limited edition non-fungible token (NFT) assets and digital twin products, goods, and services in the market. There are even emerging crypto companies offering decentralised virtual worlds where you can buy, trade, and own your own digital real estate or assets (Chybranov, 2023). The metaverse in this current form is where modern consumerism and digital retailing are moving rapidly towards. The third form is where the digital reality and the physical world will eventually merge and exist primarily in the digital state, where the user's digital identity is the identity that they possess in the physical world. Think of a state where all one's social media accounts, financial accounts, assets, work identity, and all manner of online accounts share one singular digital facsimile of one's self – the identity in which one uses to perform all manner of digital or physical transactions and later interactions.

While digital retailing continues to evolve, the pertinent question to address moving forward is what will people be shopping more for in the distant future? Tangible products or intangible/digital products? According to Catapano et al. (2022), the digital counterparts to actual physical products have become somewhat pervasive in the landscape of consumerism. From digital music to e-books, and even in training materials, the modern world of consumer goods is fast seeing a move towards digital assets. While currently there is an emphasis on differentiation in regard to ownership, the tactile nature, and materiality in the valuation of digital products, that will change in a digital world where the upcoming generation might spend an average of 12 hours or more engrossed in their virtual or digital realms.

152 Brian Kee Mun Wong et al.

As the Web3 and blockchain technology adoption gets more widespread, the resurgence of interest in authenticated and unique digital assets will set the stage for purchase of digital products. A recent study showed that the young Americans aged 18–29 spend time online almost constantly, clocking in an average of seven hours per day (Perrin & Atske, 2021). The study also showed that not only do these young generations of online users spend a vast majority of their time online, but more than 60% of them actually prefer spending time online than in the real world. As these younger generations spend their time online, their retail habits change as well.

In fact, these are the generation that will spend on digital goods and services (Rogers et al., 2023) although currently mostly focused on streaming entertainment and digital services rather than consumer or retail products. However, this generation also do have a strong preference to purchase items via microtransactions for their digital avatars in their preferred video games. Microtransactions are a feature of video games involving the purchase of in-game items like skins, cosmetic features in the game (clothes, character models, and accessories) that do not affect gameplay mechanics, or items (weapons and power-ups) that directly influences gameplay mechanics, using real-world money (Reza et al., 2022). Microtransactions are a crucial part of modern video game revenue stream with free-to-play games with in-app purchases or microtransactions overtaking the traditional premium play models. Free-to-play games are games that cost nothing to purchase or download but rely exclusively on microtransactions as a form for revenue. This is a crucial aspect to consider as society moves towards the metaverse.

Metaverse – The Future of Societal Living

The metaverse refers to the concept of interconnected immersive worlds and realities that merge both physical and digital spaces. As described by the Metaverse Consortium (2021), the metaverse may encompass AR, VR, and MR to move beyond flat two-dimensional (2D) interfaces to more immersive environments, but it is not always expected to be very tech-centred. Instead of isolated virtual experiences, the metaverse is intended to act as a shared online space that seamlessly integrates these technologies. As stated earlier, the metaverse is not a new concept – it is simply a pervasive and massive digital environment that runs parallel to our physical realm. The metaverse is a seamless connection with the real world that can be established, allowing people to have interactive and digital experiences with different entities of these two worlds (Wang et al., 2022).

According to Ning et al. (2023), the concept of the metaverse often revolves around the idea that immersive social experiences appear to be central. The metaverse aims to replicate the depth of in-person connection by combining lifelike representations with persistence across multiple worlds. It thus represents a significant step forward from isolated applications to an integrated ecosystem that brings together technologies, businesses, and individuals. Moreover, as the metaverse evolves, it has the potential to become a critical tool to accelerate the adoption and implementation of circular economy principles in the physical world. By leveraging digital technologies, collaboration, and immersive experiences, the metaverse can actively contribute to sustainable resource management, education, and behaviour change.

To illustrate how the metaverse could drive the adoption of circular economy principles, let's examine a specific potential use case. Through the presence of an embodied avatar, a person could visit a virtual trade fair where innovations in the field of renewable energy are presented. Upon entering the metaverse-based event, the person would be surrounded by exhibits featuring solar panels, wind turbines, and other technologies in a 3D environment. By utilising interactive instructions and visual aids that are only possible in a digital space, participants could learn skills consistent with regenerative models – for example, receiving voice instructions while visually learning how to install rooftop solar panels.

The metaverse overcomes spatial distances and resource constraints, because in the physical world, attending trade fairs or conferences requires enormous time, money, and mobility resources that many people do not have. However, by digitally simulating such events, as mentioned above, without the frictional costs of physical travel or venue constraints, metaverse spaces enable broad, scalable participation worldwide. Consequently, this transformative force can pave the way for a circular and sustainable economy and lead us to a brighter and greener future.

The current state of the metaverse is characterised by ongoing development and exploration. It includes virtual worlds, AR experiences, and online platforms that offer immersive and interactive environments. Companies and platforms in particular are investing in VR and AR technologies to create interconnected virtual spaces. Some real-word applications are Second Life, Roblox, VR Chat, AR Translator, and IKEA Place (Lee et al., 2021), and the landscape of virtual worlds and platforms within the metaverse is constantly evolving with the introduction of new technologies and ideas.

Some potential metaverse applications are immersive social networks. In contrast to traditional 2D scrolling feeds or limited group video calls, immersive social networks in the metaverse, such as Facebook Horizon, enable users to engage with personalised virtual avatars within a shared spatial environment. By facilitating face-to-face interactions between personalised avatars within shared virtual spaces, metaverse social platforms aim to foster deeper social connections. Visual details like body language and spatial context enrich nonverbal cues during conversations or collaborative activities.

Many experts predict that the metaverse will become a ubiquitous platform in the coming decades, and it could grow rapidly as technology and the demand for user convenience advances. What is evident is that the growing digital consumer trends, evolution of retailing especially on digital goods and service, and the adoption of metaverse will now create not only entertainment experiences and advanced social interactions but also entirely new consumer models or retail experiences.

The Retail Metaverse Form

The metaverse constitutes a thoroughly immersive and interactive digital environment, where users may engage with each other and their respective digital devices in real time. Forged through the merging of physical and virtual realities, it frequently aligns with technologies such as VR, AR, and other immersive platforms. This emerging concept holds the promise of fundamentally transforming our interpersonal connections and digital interactions. Within the retail domain, the metaverse offers the potential to revolutionise shopping experiences by crafting personalised journeys attuned to the unique preferences and behaviours of individual customers, as elucidated by Dawson (2022).

The current state of the retail metaverse is still in its early stages. The technologies used to achieve high levels of customer engagement and unique digital assets are not yet mature or at a stage where they can be widely deployed commercially. Thus, most retail metaverse applications are currently experimental proofs of concept rather than full revenue-generating businesses. Although it's still early days, some pioneering retailers such as Gucci, Nike, Louis Vuitton, and Uniqlo and others not listed here have already begun working with video game developers to create engaging shopping experiences in the metaverse (Yoo et al., 2023). For example, Japanese clothing brand Uniqlo collaborated with the popular Nintendo game 'Animal Crossing: New Horizons' in 2020, allowing players to outfit their game characters with Uniqlo clothing by downloading customised designs. The collaboration aimed to use the game's popular features, such as bridge building, flower planting, and virtual social connections, to create a collection that would resonate with fans. The aim was to bring the immersive experience of the game into the real world by offering tangible and digital fashion items (Uniqlo, n.d.).

Xi and Hamari (2021) provide valuable insights into the potential future impact of VR on the way we shop and consume goods. As the retail industry continues to explore the possibilities of VR technology, it is plausible that the concept of the metaverse will play an important role in shaping the future of retail experiences. In the context of retail, the metaverse has the potential to revolutionise the way customers interact with products and brands in virtual environments. According to a 2020 report by Technavio, the COVID-19 pandemic has triggered strong growth in AR and VR technologies. Experts predict that the market will grow at an accelerated annual growth rate of more than 35% until 2024 as the demand for immersive experiences increases worldwide (Xi et al., 2023).

With rapid advances in VR technology, it is becoming increasingly possible to create immersive virtual experiences for customers. The metaverse could create interconnected virtual spaces where customers can explore, interact, and shop in entirely virtual environments. This would blur the boundaries between physical and digital retail experiences, allowing customers to have a more personalised and engaging shopping experience that is not limited by physical space or location. In fact, VR technology is also moving towards multisensory experiences – where it is not merely focused on visuals but sensory experiences. The prevailing theory is that the more realistic the immersive environment, the more engaging the experience is for the users.

For example, a customer could enter a virtual store in the metaverse and browse the products as if they were physically present in the store. Instead of static images, customers can view 3D product models from all angles as their personalised avatars traverse the space. Virtual try on features enhance the tangible experience and allow them to assess fit and style by placing lifelike garments over their selfies right in the store, and tactile experiences can also bring a more realistic experience. As the customer explores the metaverse store, their browsing behaviour provides signals for product recommendations tailored to their current interests. When the customers approach certain clothing items, complementary pieces from that category will be suggested, or if you are interacting with camping items, other relevant gear will be displayed.

These contextual suggestions are dynamic and not generic ads. Retailers hope to offer deeper dimensionality compared to flat websites while offering more convenience than brick-and-mortar retail by seamlessly translating visual and interactive product reviews into the metaverse. In this future paradigm, the metaverse could offer just enough tangible dimensionality to make it feel real, without the same geographic and access limitations of full replication. In general, the concept of the metaverse has the potential to transform the retail industry by creating a seamless and immersive shopping experience that is not limited by physical space or location. The metaverse is expected to become increasingly important in the retail industry as VR technology evolves, offering customers new and innovative ways to interact with products and brands in virtual environments.

Recent researches confirm the promising prospects for the introduction of the metaverse in retail. According to Xi et al. (2023), XR technologies can provide opportunities for highly efficient consumption and hedonistic experiences and will become increasingly important for social and economic development. In addition, Xi et al. (2023) encourage retailers to consider using VR technology to replace online and offline shopping environments. In their view, metaverse stores can offer customers the ability to shop online anytime, anywhere, and immerse themselves in an augmented artificial reality that mimics a physical store. Customers could preview outfits on their video game like avatars or try out furniture in virtual rooms modelled after their real homes. Technology is already enabling us to do this now. Eventually, wearing special glasses and gloves for this MR could be a norm. While physical stores could possibly exist in the real world, more retail experiences will be focused in the virtual space. However, it is not without considerable challenges.

Metaverse in the Rise

As discussed, the metaverse is a stimulating, participatory, and permanent digital landscape in which people can interact with each other and with digital elements in real time. In fact, it is not tied to a specific technology or platform but represents a fundamental shift in the way we perceive and interact with digital content. Among the key features of metaverse include:

Immersion: With technologies such as VR and AR, the metaverse offers an intense sense of presence and participation in the virtual environment.

Interactivity: Users could interact with each other and with digital entities in real time, creating a dynamic and responsive virtual world.

Persistence: The metaverse is a continuous space that persists and evolves, even if the individual user is not actively involved.

Convergence: By removing the boundaries between the physical and digital worlds, the metaverse enables seamless integration and transition between these two realms.

Social interactions: Through the metaverse, users can connect, communicate, and collaborate with each other in shared virtual spaces, fostering social relationships and communities.

Digital economy: Within the metaverse, there is a digital economy where users can create, own, and trade digital goods such as virtual properties, digital fashion items, and other virtual goods.

The metaverse has the potential to transform various industries such as retail, education, and entertainment. Through technological advances, it will open new perspectives for businesses and consumers and reshape the way we interact, learn, work, and shop. It is constantly being expanded and explored. It includes virtual environments, AR experiences, and digital platforms that offer immersive and interactive environments (Wang et al., 2022).

Metaverse in Retail Experience

In retail, the metaverse could transform shopping experiences into immersive, interactive, and personalised encounters. By merging physical and VR, it often integrates technologies such as VR, AR, and immersive platforms. This emerging concept has the potential to fundamentally reshape our digital interactions and interpersonal relationships. The possible applications include:

Virtual malls: The metaverse can host virtual malls where users can engage with different brands and products in a single, immersive space that offers experiences ranging from browsing stores to participating in events such as fashion shows.

Immersive product demonstrations: Retailers can use the metaverse for immersive product demonstrations that allow customers to interact with products in a realistic way. In a furniture store, for example, customers could virtually place and rearrange furniture in a simulated room.

Virtual try on and fitting: Customers can virtually try on products such as clothing and accessories before purchasing and personalise them using customisation options.

Social shopping experiences: The metaverse can enable social shopping, where users shop together in a virtual environment, including features such as group discounts and shared wish lists.

Gamification and rewards: Retailers can create gamified shopping experiences in the metaverse by offering challenges and rewards to motivate customers, such as virtual treasure hunts for discounts.

Seamless omnichannel integration: The metaverse can connect online and offline shopping experiences and offer customers a consistent experience across different channels.

The metaverse has the potential to revolutionise the retail landscape by tailoring personalised experiences to customers' individual preferences and behaviours (Dawson, 2022). While the retail metaverse is still in its early stages, retailers such as Gucci, Nike, and Louis Vuitton are already working with video game developers to create engaging shopping experiences in the metaverse (Yoo et al., 2023). Uniqlo, for example, has partnered with the game 'Animal Crossing: New Horizons,' allowing players to dress their characters in Uniqlo clothing (Uniqlo, n.d.).

Precautions of Modern Consumerism in the Metaverse Setting

As mentioned earlier, in a rapidly expanding landscape of the metaverse, consumers will find themselves traversing a digital frontier that transcends traditional boundaries. However, this immersive digital realm introduces a myriad of considerations, compelling users to exercise vigilance across various dimensions.

Digital security concerns: Dwivedi et al. (2022) underscore the critical aspect of digital security in the metaverse setting. The ownership and rights associated with virtual assets often exist in a legally ambiguous space, demanding users to comprehend complex platform terms. The metaverse's immersive nature amplifies the risks of identity theft and cybersecurity threats, necessitating heightened caution and proactive measures to safeguard personal information. For instance, instances of identity theft within virtual environments emphasise the urgency of robust security measures to protect user identities and digital assets.

Legal ambiguity surrounding virtual assets: Ownership and rights pertaining to virtual assets, as highlighted by Dwivedi et al. (2022), are frequently legally ambiguous. Users must acquaint themselves with platform terms to navigate this complexity effectively. Legal frameworks governing virtual assets are still evolving, emphasising the need for users to stay informed and assertive in understanding their rights. Disputes over virtual property, such as virtual real estate or in-game items, underscore the importance of users being legally literate in the metaverse to protect their digital investments.

Privacy and financial risks: Bansod and Ragha (2022) shed light on privacy concerns, while Dwivedi et al. (2022) address financial risks associated with virtual transactions. The metaverse's extensive data collection gives rise to heightened privacy concerns, necessitating user cognisance. Users must be aware of potential financial risks linked to virtual transactions and the use of cryptocurrencies. This requires a commitment to awareness and informed decision-making to navigate these risks effectively. Instances of virtual theft and fraudulent activities in virtual economies underscore the need for financial vigilance.

Considerations for platform reliability, regulation, and ethics: Ghermandi et al. (2023) and Kuhn et al. (2023) contribute insights into platform reliability, regulatory developments, and ethical considerations. Users must evaluate platform reliability, stay informed about regulatory changes, and address social and ethical considerations. Staying informed about regulatory developments is crucial to understanding the evolving legal landscape of the metaverse. Social and ethical considerations, encompassing issues like digital inequality and the environmental impact of virtual activities, extend beyond individual safety to broader societal responsibilities in the metaverse. This involves actively participating in shaping ethical norms and advocating for sustainable practices within virtual spaces.

In essence, consumer precautions within the metaverse transcend routine digital interactions, necessitating a nuanced understanding of security, ownership, privacy, financial transactions, content consumption, mental health considerations, platform reliability, regulatory landscapes, and ethical implications.

The metaverse, while promising unprecedented experiences, requires an informed and vigilant consumer approach. Users must actively navigate the multifaceted challenges and opportunities presented by this evolving digital frontier, ensuring a secure, ethical, and rewarding metaverse engagement.

Case Study – Digital Retailing: The Metaverse Bound in DressX

The metaverse, accessible through diverse technologies like VR or AR, represents a digital realm where individuals can engage in communication and collaboration. Corporations are actively seeking to exploit this trend, recognising the potential for business opportunities within the metaverse. Mirroring this trend, with teens and young adults spending more than eight hours a day on digital devices, luxury brands have recognised the need to evolve for these digital-savvy customers (Williams, 2021).

Companies such as Gucci, Burberry, Ralph Lauren, and Louis Vuitton are increasingly implementing new technologies into their customer experiences and offerings. AI now enables more seamless interactions with the brand, while NFTs allow for certified authenticity when selling unique digital artworks. As younger demographics demand digital connectivity, luxury retailers must continue to integrate innovative platforms such as VFRs and blockchain-enabled merchandise into their business models. The survival of brands in the coming decade depends on appealing to the next generation of consumers who live their lives through screens (Chawla et al., 2024; Joy et al., 2022; Verma & Tandon, 2022).

While various metaverse implementations for retail in different industries have been studied in the academic literature, we opted to select the fashion industry for a more detailed analysis. In particular, we will discuss the findings from a recent case study that explored how immersive technologies could reshape relationships along the value chain in the fashion industry. By allowing customers to interact via personalised avatars rather than as anonymous website visitors, VFRs and contextual recommendations in persistent 3D stores aim to deliver more resonant brand experiences.

As highlighted by Periyasami and Periyasamy (2022), metaverse and immersive technologies have enormous potential to transform customer relationships across the fashion retail value chain. Through photorealistic avatars, VFRs, and personalised 3D stores, brands can enable more intimate and exciting shopping experiences that are not limited by physical constraints. DressX, for example, offers purely digital clothing for AR avatars with interactive customisation and global fitting options that go far beyond traditional e-commerce.

DressX (n.d.) is a pioneer in the field of immersive and sustainable digital fashion. As described on its website (https://dressx.com), DressX, founded in 2019, is one of the first native brands of the metaverse to offer exclusively virtual clothing for personalised avatars. DressX's online store and mobile AR apps allow users worldwide to browse and try on over 400 digital clothing and accessory designs. Users can try on the garments on customisable mannequins that exactly match their body measurements and skin tone. For more information about DressX's innovative approach, visit the company's official website.

By minting garments exclusively in the form of blockchain-verified NFTs, DressX avoids material waste while maintaining proof of authenticity and sole ownership. Customers participating in the emerging virtual fashion economy can responsibly trade or resell limited edition designer goods, similar to limited physical editions. Strategic partnerships occasionally bridge the gap between the digital and physical worlds. The selected archetypal NFTs (which refer to particularly iconic or representative DressX designs that are only available digitally and embody their virtual couture vision) can enable the ethical production of exclusive physical versions for owners who wish to transform these rare digital artefacts into tangible, bespoke garments.

This ground-breaking, blended model provides inclusive virtual access that would otherwise not be possible, democratising designer fashion regardless of geography or means. DressX uses technology to simultaneously promote sustainability and freedom of self-expression. The example of DressX shows how the transformation of retail combined with a participatory community and decentralised ownership can transform relationships and access. When creation merges with community-driven distribution in a responsible way, a balance emerges.

To date, DressX has implemented foundational metaverse features including blockchain-verified digital ownership, AR visualisation and sampling, avatar fashion customisation, and community-driven circular economy. These are innovatively aligned with the emerging virtual fashion paradigm through the trading of digitally scarce NFTs for garments. It has implemented basic metaverse features such as blockchain-verified digital ownership, AR visualisation, avatar fashion customisation and a community-driven circular economy. By offering digital clothing to personalised avatars and enabling virtual try on experiences, DressX demonstrates an immersive shopping experience beyond physical constraints.

Blockchain technology and NFTs enable DressX to ensure a secure digital ownership and promote a thriving digital economy within the metaverse. By minting garments as unique NFTs, DressX guarantees the authenticity and rarity of digital fashion items and enables users to securely own and trade their virtual possessions. In addition, DressX encourages social interactions by allowing users to express themselves through personalised avatars and interact with others in virtual environments. This reflects the metaverse's goal of creating shared, interactive spaces where users can meaningfully interact with each other and with digital content.

In fact, DressX highlights the potential for seamless integration between physical and virtual worlds, a crucial aspect of the metaverse. By bridging the gap between digital and physical fashion through strategic partnerships and the creation of physical versions of iconic digital designs, it illustrates how the metaverse can blur the boundaries between online and offline experiences. As the metaverse evolves, initiatives like DressX offer a glimpse into the future of retail, where immersive technologies, digital ownership, and social interactions come together to redefine how consumers engage with brands and products. By embracing the principles of the metaverse, retailers can be at the forefront of this transformation, unlocking new growth opportunities and driving innovation.

To further enhance the DressX ecosystem, decentralised identity persistence, enhanced avatar interoperability, integration with gaming metaverse environments, and responsive, sensor-driven clothing could be considered for future development. As concrete 3D metaverse worlds move towards a cross-platform alignment driven by user-independent avatars, wearable identities, inventories, and tokens, DressX needs to secure its position at the infrastructure crossroads. Although DressX is ahead of traditional brands, the company risks being marginalised if it relies solely on its existing Web 2.0 foundation. The clothing itself conveys a vision – but a thorough technological implementation means reaching a scale that is best suited to making an impact.

DressX's ground-breaking model is just one early example of how brands are leveraging the emerging vision of the metaverse for previously unrealised digital experience formats, assets, and community-driven economies. And if the dynamics of the model are similar to the paths that pioneers often take when pushing the boundaries of the virtual world before mass adoption, then exponential global development is probably still a long way off.

As augmented and virtual worlds become commonplace places of collaboration in the coming decade, traditional retailers are now at a crossroads where they must act rather than hesitate. The digital hesitation cemented in the 2010s has done little to prepare for the paradigm shift; consumer hardware, connectivity, and cultural readiness now herald unprecedented environments regardless. By studying innovators who are succeeding even in the face of initial technological limitations and ambiguity, leaders can develop prudent transition plans that are attuned to the realities to come. In any case, the metaverse's early success at the virtual forefront of retail is rarely due to perfect timing of market windows. Rather, progress is due to the brave who step forward before the uncertainty subsides to listen and adapt carefully as structures are built.

The fashion value chain case study shows how the metaverse has the potential to transform retail across multiple industries, including fashion, gaming, entertainment, and education. This transformation enables personalised and immersive customer interactions that transcend physical boundaries and, when leveraged strategically, offer new opportunities for growth and innovation. Leading brands that pioneer the development of complex virtual worlds and foster engaged customer communities in these environments can establish themselves as industry leaders as the metaverse evolves. Their success will depend on visionary strategies that combine innovative environments with value delivery, ensuring that customer experiences not only stand out for their novelty but also thrive through meaningful connections and fair relationships.

In addition to DressX, numerous retailers are also exploring metaverse technologies to create engaging and interactive shopping experiences. Nike, for example, has launched 'Nikeland,' a virtual realm on the popular gaming platform Roblox (2023), where users can customise avatars, participate in activities, and virtually try on Nike products (Temperino, 2023). Similarly, luxury brand Gucci hosted a virtual fashion show called 'Gucci Garden' on Roblox, where users had the opportunity to explore themed spaces, view digital renditions of Gucci items, and purchase exclusive virtual merchandise for their avatars.

Conclusion

The rise of consumerism instigates extensive regulatory measures, integrating them into business practices. Conversely, developing countries exhibit lower corporate responsiveness due to limited consumer influence. Digital retail undergoes a transformative revolution, emphasising convenience, personalisation, and emotional connections, fuelled by major tech advancements like AR and emotional resonance. The adaptation of online shopping, mobile commerce, data analytics, technology, user reviews, and contactless payments reflects a responsive adjustment to modern consumerism, enabling businesses to create unique customer experiences in the digital retail landscape. The retail industry undergoes a seismic shift propelled by technological advancements and accelerated by the COVID-19 pandemic. Post-pandemic, online retail is expected to claim 25% of global profits by 2027, driven by key technologies such as AI, XR immersive devices (VR/AR/MR) and experiences (metaverse), and blockchain-infused platforms (Web3). AI enhances customer experiences, VR creates immersive shopping, AR blends online and physical shopping, and blockchain ensures secure transactions, and the metaverse creates a persistent digital world and shopping experience.

Blending into the metaverse, the retail industry can be further revolutionised with personalisation and boundary-free shopping experiences. Early applications are experimental, with pioneers like Gucci and Uniqlo collaborating with video game developers. As immersive technologies advances, interconnected virtual spaces may seamlessly blend physical and digital retail, providing immersive, personalised shopping. Despite costs and learning curves, the metaverse's future role in reshaping shopping is anticipated. In the expansive metaverse, users face complex considerations. Digital security is paramount due to identity theft and cybersecurity threats. Legal ambiguity surrounds virtual assets, demanding user comprehension of platform terms. Privacy, financial risks, and ethical considerations necessitate user awareness. Platform reliability evaluation, staying informed on regulations, and addressing societal responsibilities are crucial. The metaverse requires vigilant, informed consumer engagement to navigate challenges and capitalise on opportunities in this evolving digital landscape.

References

Amin, N., & Mohd Nor, R. (2013). Online shopping in Malaysia: Legal protection for E-consumers. *European Journal of Business and Management*, 5(24), 79–86.

Anica-Popa, I., Anica-Popa, L., Rădulescu, C., & Vrîncianu, M. (2021). The integration of artificial intelligence in retail: benefits, challenges and a dedicated conceptual framework. *Amfiteatru Economic*, 23(56), 120–136.

162 Brian Kee Mun Wong et al.

Appel, G., Grewal, L., Hadi, R. & Stephen, A. T. (2020). The future of social media in marketing. *Journal of the Academy of Marketing Science, 48*(1), 79–95.

Aviso, A. (2023). *Virtual reality (VR) in retail: guide with examples.* Retrieved April 1, 2023, from https://fitsmallbusiness.com/virtual-reality-in-retail/

Bansod, S., & Ragha, L. (2022). Challenges in making blockchain privacy compliant for the digital world: some measures. *Sādhanā, 47*, 168. https://doi.org/10.1007/s12046-022-01931-1

Barker, A.T. (1987). Consumerism in New Zealand. *International Marketing Review, 4*(3), 63–74. https://doi.org/10.1108/eb008337

Barksdale, H. C., & Perreault, W. D. (1980). Can consumers be satisfied? *MSU Business Topics, 28*(Spring), 19–30.

Bezovski, Z. (2016). The future of the mobile payment as electronic payment system. *European Journal of Business and Management, 8*(8), 127–132.

Bischof, S. F., Boettger, T. M., & Rudolph, T. (2020). Curated subscription commerce: A theoretical conceptualization. *Journal of Retailing and Consumer Services, 54*, 101822. https://doi.org/10.1016/j.jretconser.2019.04.019

Bisschop, L., Hendlin, Y., & Jaspers, J. (2022). Designed to break: planned obsolescence as corporate environmental crime. *Crime, Law and Social Change, 78*(3), 271–293.

Cakir, G., Bezbradica, M., & Helfert, M. (2019). The shift from financial to non-financial measures during transition into digital retail–a systematic literature review. In W. Abramowicz & R. Corchuelo (Eds.), *Business information systems: 22nd international conference*, BIS 2019, Seville, Spain, June 26–28, 2019, Proceedings, Part I 22 (pp. 189–200). Springer International Publishing.

Campbell, C. (2018). The puzzle of modern consumerism. In J. C. Alexander, R. Eyerman, D. Inglis & P. Smith (Eds.), *The romantic ethic and the spirit of modern consumerism. Cultural sociology.* Palgrave Macmillan. https://doi.org/10.1007/978-3-319-79066-4_3

Cano, J. A., Londoño-Pineda, A. A., Campo, E. A., & Fernández, S. A. (2023). Sustainable business models of e-marketplaces: An analysis from the consumer perspective. *Journal of Open Innovation: Technology, Market, and Complexity, 9*(3), 100121. https://doi.org/10.1016/j.joitmc.2023.100121

Catapano, R., Shennib, F., & Levav, J. (2022). Preference reversals between digital and physical goods. *Journal of Marketing Research, 59*(2), 353–373.

Chawla, U., Verma, B., & Mittal, A. (2024). Resistance to O2O technology platform adoption among small retailers: The influence of visibility and discoverability. *Technology in Society, 76*(C), 102482.

Chen, T., Samaranayake, P., Cen, X., Qi, M., & Lan, Y. C. (2022). The impact of online reviews on consumers' purchasing decisions: evidence from an eye-tracking study. *Frontiers in Psychology, 13*, 865702.

Chiarelli, B. (2014). Consumerism: a general introduction. *Global Bioethics, 22*(1–4), 1–1. https://doi.org/10.1080/11287462.2009.10800679

Choudhury, R. R., Phatak, M., & Joshi, I. (2023). Artificial intelligence in retail: opportunities and challenges for the future. *European Economic Letters (EEL), 13*(4), 921–936.

Chybranov, G. (2023). *The current state of the metaverse and its limitations.* Retrieved December 18, 2023, from https://www.softserveinc.com/en-us/blog/the-current-state-of-the-metaverse#:~:text=the%20current%20state%20of%20the%20metaverse%20is%20characterised%20by%20a,minecraft%2c%20roblox%2c%20and%20fortnite

Coppola, D. (2023). *E-commerce as share of total retail sales worldwide 2015-2027.* Statistica. Retrieved December 9, 2023, from https://www.statista.com/statistics/534123/e-commerce-share-of-retail-sales-worldwide/

Craig-Lees, M., & Hill, C. (2002). Understanding voluntary simplifiers. *Psychology & Marketing, 19*(2), 187–210. https://doi.org/10.1002/mar.10009

Dawson, A. (2022). Data-driven consumer engagement, virtual immersive shopping experiences, and blockchain-based digital assets in the retail metaverse. *Journal of Self-Governance and Management Economics*, *10*(2), 52–66. https://doi.org/10.22381/jsme10220224

Dekker, B., & Okano-Heijmans, M. (2020). *Europe's digital decade? Navigating the global battle for digital supremacy*. Clingendael Netherlands Institute of International Relations. https://www.clingendael.org/publication/europes-digital-decade

DressX. (n.d.). *DressX metaverse. DressX*. Retrieved January 7, 2024, from https://dressx.com/collections/dressx-metaverse

Dwivedi, Y. K., Hughes, L., Baabdullah, A. M., Ribeiro-Navarrete, S., Giannakis, M., Al-Debei, M. M., Dennehy, D., Metri, B., Buhalis, D., Cheung, C. M. K., Conboy, K., Doyle. R., Dubey, R., Dutot, V., Felix, R., Goyal, D. P., Gustafsson, A., Hinsch, C., Jebabli, I., ... Wamba, S. F. (2022). Metaverse beyond the hype: Multidisciplinary perspectives on emerging challenges, opportunities, and agenda for research, practice and policy. *International Journal of Information Management*, *66*, 102542. https://doi.org/10.1016/j.ijinfomgt.2022.102542

Dwivedi, Y. K., Ismagilova, E., Hughes, D. L., Carlson, J., Filieri, R., Jacobson, J., Jain, V., Karjaluoto, H., Kefi, H., Krishen, A. S, Kumar, V., Rahman, M. M., Raman, R., Rauschnabel, P. A., Rowley, J., Salo, J., Tran, G. A., & Wang, Y. (2021). Setting the future of digital and social media marketing research: Perspectives and research propositions. *International Journal of Information Management*, *59*, 102168. https://doi.org/10.1016/j.ijinfomgt.2020.102168

Gadekallu, T. R., Huynh-The, T., Wang, W., Yenduri, G., Ranaweera, P., Pham, Q. V., .. & Liyanage, M. (2022). *Blockchain for the metaverse: A review*. arXiv preprint arXiv:2203.09738.

Ghermandi, A., Langemeyer, J., Van Berkel, D., Calcagni, F., Depietri, Y., Vigl, L. E., Fox, N., Havinga, I., Jager, H., Kaiser, N., Karasov, O., McPhearson, T., Podschun, S., Ruiz-Frau, A., Sinclair, M., Venohr, M., & Wood, S. A. (2023). Social media data for environmental sustainability: A critical review of opportunities, threats, and ethical use. *One Earth*, *6*(3), 236–250.

Giray, L. (2022). Meet the centennials: Understanding the generation Z students. *International Journal of Sociologies and Anthropologies Science Reviews*, *2*(4), 9–18.

Goswami, D., & Verma, B. (2024). The intersection of ethics and big data: addressing ethical concerns in digital age of artificial intelligence. In B. Verma, B. Singla & A. Mittal (Eds.), *Digital technologies, ethics, and decentralization in the digital era* (pp. 269–285). IGI Global.

Hansen, R., & Sia, S. K. (2015). Hummel's digital transformation toward omnichannel retailing: key lessons learned. *MIS Quarterly Executive*, *14*(2), 51–66.

Ike, T. C., Hoe, T. W., & Yatim, M. H. M. (2021). Designing elements for immersive user experience in educational games using the entertainment game development approach. *Review of International Geographical Education Online*, *11*(4), 738–747.

Jain, S., & Werth, D. (2019). Current state of mixed reality technology for digital retail: a literature review. In F. F. Nah & K. Siau (Eds.), *HCI in business, government and organizations. ecommerce and consumer behavior: 6th international conference*, HCIBGO 2019, Proceedings, Part I 21 (pp. 22–37). Springer International Publishing.

Joy, A., Zhu, Y., Peña, C., & Brouard, M. (2022). Digital future of luxury brands: Metaverse, digital fashion, and non-fungible tokens. *Journal of Strategic Marketing*, *31*(3), 337–343. Special Issue: Luxury, Entrepreneurship, and Innovation, Part I. https://doi.org/10.1002/jsc.2502

Kaynak, E. (1985). Some thoughts on consumerism in developed and less developed countries. *International Marketing Review*, *2*(2), 15–30. https://doi.org/10.1108/eb008273

Koppens, R. (2021). *E-commerce retail & augmented reality. An exploratory study about virtual fitting room technologies and online customer experiences.* Master dissertation, Erasmus University. Erasmus University Thesis Repository. https://thesis.eur.nl/pub/60663

Kuhn, C., Khoo, S.-M., Czerniewicz, L., Lilley, W., et al. (2023). Understanding digital inequality: a theoretical kaleidoscope. *Postdigital Science and Education, 5*(3), 894–932.

Lee, L. H., Braud, T., Zhou, P., Wang, L., Xu, D., Lin, Z., Kumar, A., Bermejo, C., & Hui, P. (2021). *All one needs to know about metaverse: A complete survey on technological singularity, virtual ecosystem, and research agenda.* arXiv preprint arXiv:2110.05352.

Metaverse Consortium. (2021). *The metaverse and how we'll build it together.* Connect 2021 [Video]. YouTube. https://www.youtube.com/watch?v=Uvufun6xer8

Mystakidis, S. (2022). *Metaverse. Encyclopedia, 2*(1), 486–497.

Ning, H., Wang, H., Lin, Y., Wang, W., Dhelim, S., Farha, F., Ding, J., & Daneshmand, M. (2023). A survey on the metaverse: The state-of-the-art, technologies, applications, and challenges. *IEEE Internet of Things Journal, 10*(16), 14671–14688. https://doi.org/10.1109/JIOT.2023.3278329

Pelet, J.-É., & Taieb, B. (2022). Context-aware optimization of mobile commerce website interfaces from the consumers' perspective: Effects on behavioral intentions. *Computers in Human Behavior Reports, 7*, 100225. https://doi.org/10.1016/j.chbr.2022.100225

Pennell, S. (1999). Consumption and consumerism in early modern England. *The Historical Journal, 42*(2), 549–564.

Periyasami, S., & Periyasamy, A. P. (2022). Metaverse as future promising platform business model: Case study on fashion value chain. *Businesses, 2*(4), 527–545. https://doi.org/10.3390/businesses2040033

Perrin, A., & Atska, S. (2021). *About three-in-ten U.S. adults say they are 'almost constantly' online.* Pew Research Centre. Retrieved December 18, 2023, from https://www.pewresearch.org/short-reads/2021/03/26/about-three-in-ten-u-s-adults-say-they-are-almost-constantly-online/

Rajan Varadarajan, P., Bharadwaj, S. G., & Thirunarayana, P. N. (1992). Attitudes towards marketing practices, consumerism and government regulations: a study of managers and consumers in an industializing country. *Journal of International Consumer Marketing, 4*(1–2), 121–158. https://doi.org/10.1300/J046v04n01_06

Rajan Varadarajan, P., & Thirunarayana, P. N. (1990). Consumers' attitudes towards marketing practices, consumerism and government regulations: cross-national perspectives. *European Journal of Marketing, 24*(6), 6–23. https://doi.org/10.1108/03090569010137934

Reddy, A. C., & Campbell, D. P. (1994). *Marketing's role in economic development.* Bloomsbury Academic.

Reinartz, W., Wiegand, N., & Imschloss, M. (2019). The impact of digital transformation on the retailing value chain. *International Journal of Research in Marketing, 36*(3), 350–366.

Rejeb, A., Rejeb, K., & Treiblmaier, H. (2023). How augmented reality impacts retail marketing: A state-of-the-art review from a consumer perspective. *Journal of Strategic Marketing, 31*(3), 718–748.

Renouard, J. (2023). *Retail statistics: brick and mortar stores vs the rise of ecommerce.* Retrieved December 11, 2023, from https://www.websitebuilderexpert.com/building-online-stores/retail-statistics/

Retail News Asia. (2020). *Digitalization key to helping Asian retailers emerge from Covid-19.* Retail News Asia. Retrieved December 9, 2023, from https://www.retailnews.asia/digitalization-key-to-helping-asian-retailers-emerge-from-covid-19/

Reza, A., Chu, S., Nedd, A., & Gardner, D. (2022). Having skin in the game: How players purchase representation in games. *Convergence, 28*(6), 1621–1642.

Roblox. (2023). *NIKELAND* [Virtual world]. https://www.roblox.com/games/7462526249/NIKELAND

Rogers, S., Lobaugh, K., & Waelter, A. (2023). *The rise of digital goods and services: Opportunity over threat.* Deloitte Insights. Retrieved December 18, 2023, from https://www2.deloitte.com/us/en/insights/industry/retail-distribution/consumer-behavior-trends-state-of-the-consumer-tracker/the-rise-of-digital-services.html

Segal, T. (2023). *5 Cs of credit: What they are, how they're used, and which is most important.* Investopedia. Retrieved December 16, 2023, from https://www.investopedia.com/terms/f/five-c-credit.asp.

Shankar, V., Kalyanam, K., Setia, P., Golmohammadi, A., Tirunillai, S., Douglass, T., Hennessey, J., Bull, J. S., & Waddoups, R. (2021). How technology is changing retail. *Journal of Retailing, 97*(1), 13–27.

Söderholm, P. (2020). The green economy transition: the challenges of technological change for sustainability. *Sustainable Earth, 3,* 6. https://doi.org/10.1186/s42055-020-00029-y

Stearns, P. N. (2009). Consumerism. In J. Peil & I. v. Staveren (Eds.), *Handbook of economics and ethics* (pp. 62–76). Edward Elgar Publishing. https://doi.org/10.4337/9781848449305.00016

Steiner, G. A., & Steiner, J. F. (1997). *Business, government and society – A managerial perspective.* McGraw-Hill.

Tan, C. I. (2019). Linking the elements of learning, assessment, and play experience in a validation framework. In W. H. Tan (Ed.), *Design, motivation, and frameworks in game-based learning* (pp. 93–122). IGI Global.

Tan, C. I., & Wong, C. Y. (2016). Validating the efficacy of serious games for teaching and learning. In L. Elbæk, G. Majgaard, A. Valente & S. Khalid (Eds.), *European conference on games based learning* (p. 658). Academic Conferences International Limited.

Tan, Y. C., Chandukala, S. R., & Reddy, S. K. (2022). Augmented reality in retail and its impact on sales. *Journal of Marketing, 86*(1), 48–66.

Taylor, H. (2016). *Lowe's introduces LoweBot, a new autonomous in-store robot.* CNBC. Retrieved April 1, 2024, from https://www.cnbc.com/2016/08/30/lowes-introduces-lowebot-a-new-autonomous-in-store-robot.html

Temperino, E. (2023). The perks of being digital. Nikeland: A case study. In N. Sabatini, T. Sádaba, A. Tosi, V. Neri & L. Cantoni (Eds.), *International conference on fashion communication: between tradition and future digital developments* (pp. 88–95). Springer Nature Switzerland.

Trentmann, F. (2004). Beyond consumerism: New historical perspectives on consumption. *Journal of Contemporary History, 39*(3), 373–401. https://doi.org/10.1177/0022009404044446

Tucci, L. (2023). *What is the metaverse? An explanation and in-depth guide.* TechTarget. Retrieved December 18, 2023, from https://www.techtarget.com/whatis/feature/The-metaverse-explained-Everything-you-need-to-know#:~:text=The%20metaverse%20is%20a%20vision,not%20in%20the%20physical%20world

Uniqlo. (n.d.). *UT magazine fall/winter 2022.* Retrieved January 6, 2024, from https://www.uniqlo.com/jp/en/contents/feature/ut-magazine/s82/

Verhoef, P. C., Lemon, K. N., Parasuraman, A., Roggeveen, A., Tsiros, M., & Schlesinger, L. A. (2009). Customer experience creation: Determinants, dynamics and management strategies. *Journal of Retailing, 85*(1), 31–41. http://doi.org/10.1016/j.jretai.2008.11.001

Verma, B., & Tandon, U. (2022). Modelling barriers to wearable technologies in Indian context: validating the moderating role of technology literacy. *Global Knowledge, Memory and Communication, 73*(6/7), 984–1004.

Virtual Reality Society. (2017). *What is virtual reality?* Retrieved December 18, 2023, from https://www.vrs.org.uk/virtual-reality/what-is-virtual-reality.html.

Vitasek, K., Bayliss, J., Owen, L., & Srivastava, N. (2022). How Walmart Canada uses blockchain to solve supply-chain challenges. *Harvard Business Review*. Retrieved April 1, 2023, from https://hbr.org/2022/01/how-walmart-canada-uses-blockchain-to-solve-supply-chain-challenges

Wang, Y., Siau, K. L., & Wang, L. (2022). Metaverse and human-computer interaction: A technology framework for 3D virtual worlds. In J. Y. C. Chen, G. Fragomeni, H. Degen & S. Ntoa (Eds.), *International conference on human-computer interaction* (pp. 213–221). Springer Nature. https://doi.org/10.1007/978-3-031-21707-4_16.

Williams, R. (2021). *Gucci's Robert Triefus on testing luxury's allure in the metaverse*. Business of Fashion. https://www.businessoffashion.com/articles/luxury/the-state-of-fashion-2022-bof-mckinsey-gucci-robert-triefus-metaverse-virtual-nft-gaming/

Xi, N., Chen, J., Gama, F., Riar, M., & Hamari, J. (2023). The challenges of entering the metaverse: An experiment on the effect of extended reality on workload. *Information Systems Frontiers*, *25*(2), 659–680. https://doi.org/10.1007/s10796-022-10244-x

Xi, N., & Hamari, J. (2021). Shopping in virtual reality: A literature review and future agenda. *Journal of Business Research*, *134*, 37–58. https://doi.org/10.1016/j.jbusres.2021.04.075

Xue, L., Parker, C. J., & Hart, C. A. (2023). How augmented reality can enhance fashion retail: a UX design perspective. *International Journal of Retail & Distribution Management*, *51*(1), 59–80.

Yang, Q., Zhao, Y., Huang, H., Xiong, Z., Kang, J., & Zheng, Z. (2022). Fusing blockchain and AI with metaverse: A survey. *IEEE Open Journal of the Computer Society*, *3*, 122–136. https://doi.org/10.1109/OJCS.2022.3188249

Yoo, J. (2023). The effects of augmented reality on consumer responses in mobile shopping: The moderating role of task complexity. *Heliyon*, *9*(3), e13775.

Yoo, K., Welden, R., Hewett, K., & Haenlein, M. (2023). The merchants of meta: A research agenda to understand the future of retailing in the metaverse. *Journal of Retailing*, *99*(2), 173–192. https://doi.org/10.1016/j.jretai.2023.02.002

Zhang, T., Wang, W. Y. C., Cao, L., & Wang, Y. (2019). The role of virtual try-on technology in online purchase decision from consumers' aspect. *Internet Research*, *29*(3), 529–551.

Chapter 9

Ethical AI for Retail: A Bibliometric Roadmap to Building Trust and Transparency

Divya Goswami and Balraj Verma

Chitkara Business School, Chitkara University, Punjab, India

Abstract

Using VOSviewer software, this research delves into the various implications of ethical artificial intelligence (AI) within the retail industry. We explored the latest research trends using bibliometric analysis unveiling the journals, organisations, sources, articles, and documents that topped the chart. To shed light on the critical areas, we leveraged a citation analysis approach to explore the numerous trending research areas that were associated with fostering trust and transparency in AI-based retail applications. The research recognised the most influential areas by investigating the highly cited works. This research insight works as a guiding roadmap to navigate the complexities related to the ethical use of AI and direct towards fostering trust.

Keywords: Retailers; artificial intelligence (AI); ethical responsibilities; trust; retail

1. Introduction

There has been an unparallel transformation in the subsistence of the people with the development of AI (De Silva et al., 2020). AI is a technology that is based on algorithms that can give suggestions, do predictions using robotic automation processes (Chen & Asch, 2017; Davenport & Kalakota, 2019). This algorithm-based

---

Augmenting Retail Reality: Blockchain, AR, VR, and the Internet of Things, Part A, 167–182
Copyright © 2025 by Divya Goswami and Balraj Verma
Published under exclusive licence by Emerald Publishing Limited
doi:10.1108/978-1-83608-634-520241023

technology is driving a significant change in the retail industry. Furthermore, AI has the possible power to transform the numerous retail operations, from giving recommendations to personalised marketing (e.g. Oosthuizen et al., 2021). But, the question is 'how ethically this technology functions'. In today's digital retail environment, a significant revolution is taking place, focusing on convenience, personalised experiences, and emotional connects. The positive impacts of AI have already been experienced across the varied array of industries (Dwivedi et al., 2021). The distinguished studies by various researchers have confirmed that AI can perform repetitive tasks (Ribeiro et al., 2021), complex decision-making, and real-time predictions more accurately than the human in numerous businesses (Javaid et al., 2022; Ng et al., 2021). Nowadays, people are using these natural language services (AI) that are capable of grasping the lingo and different languages used in numerous industries (Wu & Monfort, 2023). Some people used these emerging artificial technologies to solve complex decision-making process or to automate business processes in a supple way across the hybrid cloud (Weber, 2023). Thus, this signifies the upsurge in the usage of artificial technologies by numerous persons to increase their value of work and better decision-making.

There are abundant of research articles in which the researchers have discussed about the increased use of AI (Pai & Chandra, 2022). Moreover, these abundant studies discuss only about the strengths and weaknesses of the natural language intelligence, but very few studies consider the responsible factors that an AI must cover relating to the stakeholders including the government, the investors, civil societies, academicians, and others (John-Mathews et al., 2022). However, the deployment of AI in retail also raises critical ethical concerns. To ensure the responsible and ethical adoption in retail, it is essential to build trust and transparency with consumers. Research indicates that trust and transparency are associated (Rawlins, 2008) and is a crucial asset in effectively establishing or re-establishing relationships (Bandsuch et al., 2008).

According to Huang (2001), trust has the potential to enhance the likelihood of stakeholders maintain their connections with organisations following a significant crisis. Scholars propose that in order to build trust, an organisation should be viewed as competent, dependable, and possessing veracity (Garbarino & Johnson, 1999). Therefore, a holistic and system approach that acts as a prerequisite for the businessmen, investors, societies, and various stakeholders needs to develop and deploy AI systems.

Several international as well as government organisations are looking forward with the strong commitment to safeguard the interest of not only the investors but also the business organisations. The use of AI requires various security measures concerned with data privacy, security, and ethics. Furthermore, the ethical application of AI in financial services is crucial and raises various concerns. Hence, to ensure the responsible and ethical adoption of AI in retail, it is essential to build trust and transparency with consumers.

This chapter presents a bibliometric roadmap to ethical AI in retail. Bibliometrics is a subject of information science and library science that employs quantitative approaches to assess academic publications. A bibliometric roadmap can help to identify key research areas, emerging trends, and influential studies in a particular field.

2. Theoretical Background

Ethics in academics is a subset of psychology that generally answers the questions such as 'What is a bad action?', 'What is a good action?', 'What is the value of human life?', 'What is justice?' (AI, 2019). Ethical considerations in AI technology have garnered significant attention due to increasing privacy and security concerns in retail services. Discussions on ethics are general and wide-ranging, but they must be directed towards specific technologies in order to be practically significant. In line with this, recent years have witnessed a number of systematic evaluations on AI literature across various disciplinary streams like business strategy, sustainability, decision-making, digital marketing, retailing, social media, internet of things, blockchain, education, and learning. The users are increasingly accepting AI-powered technology including digital assistants (Martin, 2019), and industries in numerous sectors, including retail, are facing challenges due to the growth of AI. Furthermore, the emerging technologies, innovative models, and the power of big data analytics are highlighting a strong need to comprehend the crucial elements of the retailing ecosystem and its future direction.

The users have mixed reviews in context with the use of AI-based technology in retail because of several ethical difficulties surrounding its development and application (Du & Xie, 2021). Digital ethics can be defined as 'the systems of values and moral principles for the conduct of electronic interactions' according to Buytendijk (2019). In the realm of AI utilisation, these automated connections encompass both human–machine and machine–machine interactions.

The ethical considerations surrounding AI in numerous industries have increasingly captured the attention of both academic and commercial communities over the past era. Many officialdoms and businesses are now hiring AI ethicists to adhere to ethical standards. For instance, Google has developed a set of ethical principles for AI use, which are available at https://ai.google/principles. These concerns, particularly regarding AI's role in different areas may be healthcare, education, services, or any other, have sparked significant interest in AI ethics. Nowadays, there is an increasing interest in researching the ethics of AI. Qualitative assessments of prior studies, such as those undertaken by (Lillywhite & Wolbring, 2019). In this research, we intend to discover answers to the following questions:

1. Which nations, organisations, sources, and papers are most influential in the subject of ethical AI in retail?
2. What gaps exist in the literature, and what are the future research directions?

3. Methodology of Research

In this research, we gathered data from the Scopus database on 15 March 2024, without limiting our analysis to a specific time period. We conducted a search using these keywords: 'ethic' OR 'ethical' AND 'artificial intelligence' OR 'AI' AND 'retail'. We intentionally considered AI in our survey, leaving words like ML, deep learning, and others in order to keep it focused. While AI includes both virtual and physical ethics, the ethics of machine learning and deep learning are largely epistemological and relate to virtual ethics. Our search was conducted in the 'Title, Abstract, or Keywords' section, and we narrowed our study to topics in Business, Management and Accounting, Economics, Econometrics, and Humanities. We included only those articles that were published and written in the English language.

In this stage, we identified 1,387 documents, limited to specific subjects (425 papers) and only articles published (189 papers) in the English language to arrive at 184 papers. Next, we manually screened the abstracts to assess relevancy, eliminate duplicates, and remove reviews, resulting in a total 100 documents.

The authors worked together to develop and agree on the specific search parameters. Furthermore, they meticulously extracted the necessary information from the recognised sources. Various types of string were created, eventually making significant contributions to intellectual research ('ai' OR 'artificial intelligence' OR 'ethical ai' OR 'responsible ai') AND ('retail').

This investigation analysed studies on AI ethics in retail using bibliometrics, using VOSviewer software. Researchers from various fields have utilised bibliometric analysis to grasp the knowledge framework of a field and pinpoint key facets (Saheb & Saheb, 2019). In this research, we have used citation analysis using VOSviewer software over the bibliometric approaches. All the three visualisations were utilised, Density visualisation, network visualisation, and overlay visualisation based on various nodes and edges. Network visualisation is based on nodes and edges. Nodes, including nations, keywords, institutions, and edges, represent connections between nodes.

4. Data Analysis

According to Donthu et al. (2021), bibliometric analysis is used to analyse academic literature based on various sub-analysis such as citation analysis, keyword co-occurrence analysis, etc. The bibliometric analysis is a statistical method that utilises techniques to assess the recent trends of scholarly articles particularly by examining citation statistics (Moed, 2005). This research paper employs VOSviewer software to identify the emerging fields and to delve into the evolution of research documents and themes over time (Van Eck & Waltman, 2010). The complete dataset was extracted from Scopus database, to get valuable insights into research trends, most influential authors, institutions, and countries that are unveiling the crucial aspects of ethical AI. The tables were formed using a bottom-up approach, keeping the article, source, document, country, and author at the first place in the table according to the number of citations and link strength. The VOSviewer software was further used to create visualisations to get a clearer picture highlighting the most prominent areas of research and their interconnections.

The data taken from the Scopus database on ethics and AI were further scrutinised in order to present the complete intellectual structure using citation analysis and assessing the performance. Table 9.1 and Fig. 9.1 provide detailed information about the published document trends based on the data extracted from Scopus. Of the total documents, 63 meet the threshold. For these documents, the number of citation links was calculated. The document with the larger number of links was selected. Table 9.1 and Fig. 9.1 show that Dwivedi (2021) has most of the citations of any research document on the list, at 960. This is followed by a paper by Carneiro (2017) with 176 and Pillai and Sivathanu (2020) with

Table 9.1. Citation of Documents.

S. No.	Document	Citations
1	Dwivedi (2021)	960
2	Carneiro (2017)	176
3	Pillai and Sivathanu (2020)	167
4	Cubric (2020)	122
5	De Bellis (2020)	115
6	Hübner (2012)	113
7	Moriuchi (2021)	82
8	Chopra (2019)	69
9	Sung (2021)	67
10	Aw (2022)	63

Source: Authors' compilation.

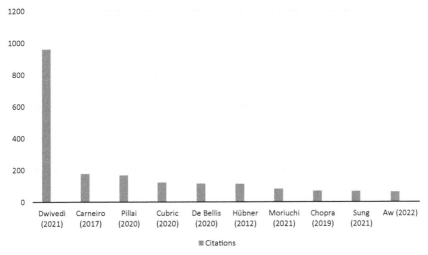

Fig. 9.1. Citations of Documents. *Source*: Authors' representation.

167 citations. VOSviewer (Fig. 9.2) was used to analyse the citation networks of the top documents retrieved from Scopus database. This helped in visualising the relationships between these highly influential documents and identifying emerging research topics.

Table 9.2 identified the papers of the sources that have served the cornerstone of knowledge in the domain. The sources were retrieved from the Scopus database. The different sources were interconnected with multiple disciplines. This provided insights to the potential areas for developing research frontiers. The detailed information is provided in Table 9.2 and Fig. 9.3. The minimum

Fig. 9.2. Citation Network of Documents. *Source*: Authors' representation.

Table 9.2. Citation Analysis of Sources.

S. No.	Source	Documents	Citations
1	Big Data and Cognitive Computing	2	1,048
2	International Journal of Information Management	2	328
3	International Journal of Production Research	2	140
4	International Journal of Recent Technology and Engineering	2	130
5	International Journal of Retail and Distribution Management	2	125
6	International Journal of System Assurance Engineering and Management	2	120
7	International Review of Retail, Distribution and Consumer Research	2	100
8	Journal of Business Research	2	46
9	Journal of Financial Services Marketing	2	45
10	Journal of Retailing	2	41

Source: Authors' compilation.

Ethical AI: Building Trust and Transparency 173

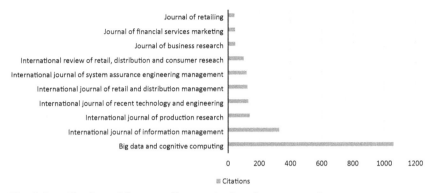

Fig. 9.3. Citation of Sources. *Source*: Authors' representation.

Table 9.3. Citation of Authors.

S. No.	Authors	Documents	Citations	Total Link Strength
1	Carneiro, Nuno	1	176	0
2	Costa, Miguel	1	176	0
3	Figueira, Goncalo	1	176	0
4	Dwivedi, Yogesh K.	1	167	1
5	Pillai, Rajasshrie	1	167	1
6	Sivathanu, Brijesh	1	167	1
7	Cubric, Marjia	1	122	0
8	De Bellis, Emanuel	1	115	13
9	Venkataramani Johar, Gita	1	115	13
10	Hubner, Alexander	1	113	0

Source: Authors' compilation.

number of documents of a source was taken as 2, and out of the total documents, 14 sources were selected. The journal *Big Data and Cognitive Computing* leads the rankings with the highest number of citations, totalling 1,048. In contrast, the *International Journal of Information Management* has a respectable number of citations, with a total of 328, placing it second among the selected sources.

Furthermore, the *International Journal of Production Research* took the third place with 140 citations. This analysis provides insights into the potential for cross-fertilisation of ideas and the development of new research frontiers.

Table 9.3 and Figs. 9.4 and 9.5 enlist the sources list of top 10 authors, demonstrating a strong understanding of the topic. Citations show that the work is grounded in research and that authors are not simply making the claims.

VOSviewer was used to visualise the relationship between different bibliographic elements utilising density visualisation (Fig. 9.6). This helped in identifying the frequently cited author clusters around this specific topic on ethics and AI.

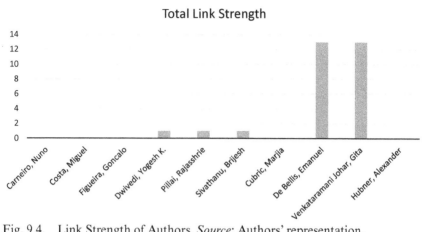

Fig. 9.4. Link Strength of Authors. *Source*: Authors' representation.

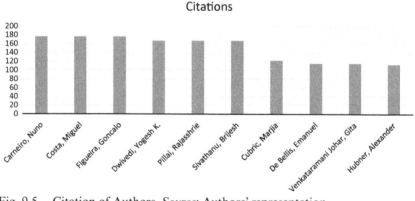

Fig. 9.5. Citation of Authors. *Source*: Authors' representation.

Among the list, Carneiro, Costa, and Figueria with 176 citations topped the charts. Additionally, De bellis and Venkataramani Johar with 115 citations held the highest link strength of 13. However, the surge in authorship and cooperation may stimulate additional interest in this area. However, the surge in authorship and cooperation may stimulate additional interest in this area. Density visualisation of author citation is a useful tool to analyse publication trends and identify influential researchers in a particular field. In this type of visualisation, authors are positioned on a two-dimensional plane, and the density of data points around an author represents their citation count. This visualisation (Fig. 9.6) was helpful for spotting emerging areas of research as well as for tracking the impact of individual researchers.

Table 9.4 was constructed to determine the countries that have had the most influence on the discipline of responsible AI. The curated database includes a minimum number of documents and a minimum number of citations, i.e. 1.

Ethical AI: Building Trust and Transparency 175

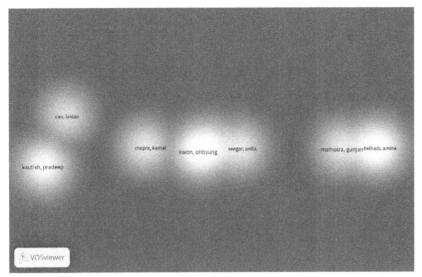

Fig. 9.6. Density Visualisation of Citation of Authors. *Source*: Authors' representation.

Table 9.4. Citation of Countries.

S. No	Country	Documents	Citations	Total Link Strength
1	United Kingdom	13	1,578	11
2	India	24	1,493	29
3	Netherlands	2	1,027	2
4	Denmark	5	1,017	6
5	United States	21	511	20
6	Germany	8	240	4
7	Portugal	2	176	0
8	South Korea	7	146	6
9	Switzerland	1	115	11
10	China	7	107	1

Source: Authors' compilation.

For each of the 41 countries, the total link strength of the citation links with the other countries was also calculated using VOSviewer software. The countries with highest citation and total link strength were identified and presented using a bar chart (Figs. 9.7 and 9.8). The United Kingdom has the top position in terms of the geographic distribution of literary works. It ranks first among the top 10 nations with 13 documents and 1,578 citations and link strength in total. India placed at the second position with 24 documents, 1,493 citations, and with

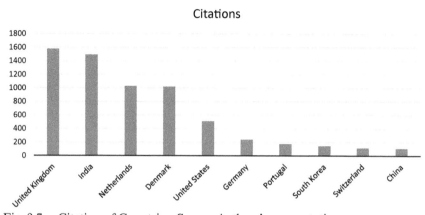

Fig. 9.7. Citation of Countries. *Source*: Authors' representation.

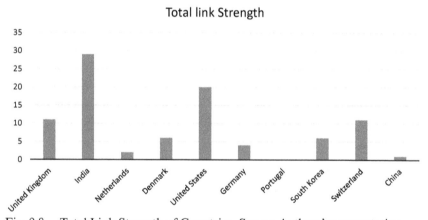

Fig. 9.8. Total Link Strength of Countries. *Source*: Authors' representation.

a total link strength of 29. These nations are leading the way in the creation of knowledge regarding the ethical principles to be followed using AI-based technologies in any sector, may be businesses or finances.

Additionally, Fig. 9.9 presents the overlay visualisation of citation of countries. This visualisation highlights the countries focusing on ethical AI. In Fig. 9.9, the circle sizes represent the country's citation impact in the field of ethical AI. The thickness or intensity of the lines connecting the countries can represent the strength of their collaboration, based on the number of co-authored research papers. Hence, this reveals the countries that are most closely collaborating on ethical AI.

Table 9.5 analysed citations data for organisations which has the most influence on the discipline of ethical AI. The organisations with highest citation and total link strength were identified and presented using a bar chart, i.e. the Faculty of Engineering at the University of Portugal and the Mathematical Institute at the

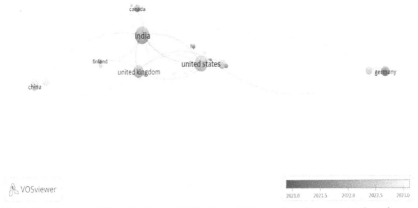

Fig. 9.9. Overlay Visualisation of Citation of Countries. *Source*: Authors' representation.

Table 9.5. Citation of Organisations.

S. No.	Organisation	Documents	Citations	Total Link Strength
1	Faculty of engineering of the University of Portugal	1	176	0
2	Mathematical Institute, University of Oxford	1	176	0
3	Emerging Market Research Centre, Swansea University, Wales	1	167	1
4	Pune Institute of Business Management, Pune	1	167	1
5	Sri Balaji University, Pune	1	167	1
6	Hertfordshire Business School, University of Hertfordshire, UK	1	122	0
7	Institute of Customer Insight, Switzerland	1	115	12
8	Columbia Business School, USA	1	115	12
9	Catholic University, Germany	1	113	0
10	E. Philip Saunders College of Business, USA	1	82	0

Source: Authors' compilation.

University of Oxford (Figs. 9.10 and 9.11). The curated database discovered the minimum number of documents, i.e. 1. For each of these organisations, the total link strength of the citation links with the other organisations was also calculated using VOSviewer software. The organisations with highest citation and total link

178   Divya Goswami and Balraj Verma

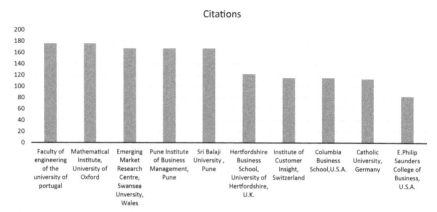

Fig. 9.10.   Citations of Organisations. *Source*: Authors' representation.

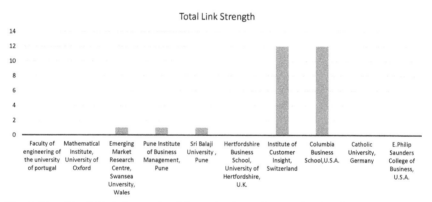

Fig. 9.11.   Total Link Strength of Organisations. *Source*: Authors' representation.

strength were identified and presented using a bar chart (Figs. 9.10 and 9.11). Network visualisation of citations of organisations is also presented in Fig. 9.12.

VOSviewer broadens the range of study and improves comprehension of a typical pattern (Ding & Yang, 2022). Essentially, VOSviewer effectively contrasts past and current behaviours, illuminating the advances in several study domains. To obtain more insights, VOSviewer was utilised to evaluate organisations according to their citation counts. Of the 233 organisations, 192 meet the thresholds. The distribution of the literary works is given in Table 9.5 and Fig. 9.12. Citations to highly referenced organisations are included. With a total of 176 citations, Faculty of Engineering of the University of Portugal and Mathematical Institute, University of Oxford, topped the chart. On the other hand, Emerging Market Research Centre, Swansea University, Wales; Pune Institute of Business Management, Pune; and Sri Balaji University, Pune, with 167 citations stood at the second place. Additionally, Fig. 9.12 presents the overlay visualisation of citation of organisations.

Ethical AI: Building Trust and Transparency   179

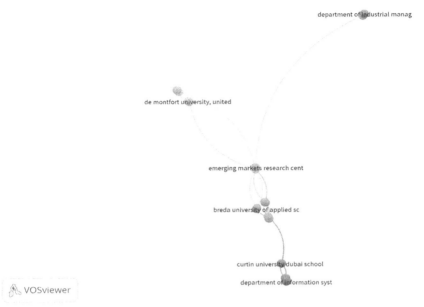

Fig. 9.12. Network Visualisation of Citation of Organisations. *Source*: Authors' representation.

5. Future Challenges for Responsible AI

- *Regulatory Complexity* – As AI applications become more pervasive in e-commerce and financial services, navigating the evolving regulatory landscape poses challenges. Organisations must stay abreast of changing regulations, standards, and guidelines to ensure compliance and mitigate legal risks (Chen et al., 2021).
- *Algorithmic Responsibility and Accountability* – To ensure accountability for AI is itself a challenge. Establishing mechanisms for auditing, monitoring, and recourse in cases of algorithmic errors or biases is essential to uphold fairness, transparency, and user trust.
- *Ethical Dilemmas* – Balancing personalisation with privacy is a very complex ethical problem or dilemma for raising AI technologies. Addressing these dilemmas requires needful consideration of ethical principles, stakeholders interests, and societal impact (Floridi et al., 2018).
- *AI Adoption Risks* – Rapid adoption of AI without proper safeguards can lead to unintended consequences, including privacy breaches, algorithmic biases, and systematic risks. Organisation must conduct robust risk assessments and implement responsible AI practices to mitigate potential harms.

6. Conclusion

There is an upsurge in the use of AI technologies, stimulating debates on the influences, assistances, jeopardies, and risks brought by these technologies in

180 *Divya Goswami and Balraj Verma*

the society. In this study, there is an emphasis on the critical role of transparency and accountability in AI systems. According to Manohar et al. (2020), Goyal et al. (2019) & Floridi et al. (2018), there is an utmost need of prioritising ethical considerations in the development and deployment of AI technologies within e-commerce and financial service sectors. It highlights the need to ensure fairness, transparency, accountability, integrity, and security in the AI ecosystems. This chapter discusses the key insights and recommendations regarding responsible AI to address complex ethical, legal, and technical issues. Furthermore, this chapter includes the highly cited papers in this domain. The study suggests that collaborations between experts from diverse disciplines, including AI, ethics, law, and social sciences, are very vital and crucial for developing holistic solutions to responsible AI technologies. The main agenda is to create policy frameworks that balance economic progress with the safety of human rights, privacy, and security that will help build trust between public, industry, and organisations, ensuring positive outcomes and social well-being.

References

AI, H. (2019). High-level expert group on artificial intelligence. *Ethics guidelines for trustworthy AI*, 6.

Aw, E. C. X., Tan, G. W. H., Cham, T. H., Raman, R., & Ooi, K. B. (2022). Alexa, what's on my shopping list? Transforming customer experience with digital voice assistants. *Technological Forecasting and Social Change, 180*, 121711.

Bandsuch, M. R., Pate, L. E., & Thies, J. (2008). Rebuilding stakeholder trust in business: An examination of principle-centered leadership and organizational transparency in corporate governance. *Business and Society Review, 113*(1), 99–127.

Buytendijk, F., Hare, J., & Jones, L. C. (2019). *Digital ethics by design: A framework for better digital business*. URL: https://www. gartner. com/en/documents/3953794/digital-ethics-by-design-aframework-for-a-better-digita.

Carneiro, D., Pinheiro, A. P., & Novais, P. (2017). Context acquisition in auditory emotional recognition studies. *Journal of Ambient Intelligence and Humanized Computing, 8*, 191–203.

Chen, J. H., & Asch, S. M. (2017). Machine learning and prediction in medicine – Beyond the peak of inflated expectations. *The New England journal of medicine, 376*(26), 2507.

Chen, J. H., Li, K., Zhang, Z., Li, K., & Yu, P. S. (2021). A survey on applications of artificial intelligence in fighting against COVID-19. *ACM Computing Surveys (CSUR), 54*(8), 1–32.

Chopra, K. (2019). Indian shopper motivation to use artificial intelligence: Generating Vroom's expectancy theory of motivation using grounded theory approach. *International Journal of Retail & Distribution Management, 47*(3), 331–347.

Cubric, M. (2020). Drivers, barriers and social considerations for AI adoption in business and management: A tertiary study. *Technology in Society, 62*, 101257.

Davenport, T., & Kalakota, R. (2019). The potential for artificial intelligence in healthcare. *Future Healthcare Journal, 6*(2), 94.

De Bellis, E., & Johar, G. V. (2020). Autonomous shopping systems: Identifying and overcoming barriers to consumer adoption. *Journal of Retailing, 96*(1), 74–87.

De Silva, D., Sierla, S., Alahakoon, D., Osipov, E., Yu, X., & Vyatkin, V. (2020). Toward intelligent industrial informatics: A review of current developments and future directions of artificial intelligence in industrial applications. *IEEE Industrial Electronics Magazine, 14*(2), 57–72.

Ding, X., & Yang, Z. (2022). Knowledge mapping of platform research: A visual analysis using VOSviewer and CiteSpace. *Electronic Commerce Research, 11*(10), 1–23.

Donthu, N., Kumar, S., Mukherjee, D., Pandey, N., & Lim, W. M. (2021). How to conduct a bibliometric analysis: An overview and guidelines. *Journal of Business Research, 133*, 285–296.

Du, S., & Xie, C. (2021). Paradoxes of artificial intelligence in consumer markets: Ethical challenges and opportunities. *Journal of Business Research, 129*, 961–974.

Dwivedi, Y. K., Ismagilova, E., Hughes, D. L., Carlson, J., Filieri, R., Jacobson, J., Jain, V., Karjaluoto, H., Kefi, H., Krishen, A. S., Kumar, V., Rahman, M. M., Raman, R., Rauschnabel, P. A., Rowley, J., Salo, J., Tran, G. A., & Wang, Y. (2021). Setting the future of digital and social media marketing research: Perspectives and research propositions. *International Journal of Information Management, 59*, 102168.

Floridi, L. (2018). Soft ethics and the governance of the digital. *Philosophy & Technology, 31*, 1–8.

Garbarino, E., & Johnson, M. S. (1999). The different roles of satisfaction, trust, and commitment in customer relationships. *Journal of Marketing, 63*(2), 70–87.

Goyal, J., Singh, M., Singh, R., & Aggarwal, A. (2019). Efficiency and technology gaps in Indian banking sector: Application of meta-frontier directional distance function DEA approach. *The Journal of Finance and Data Science, 5*(3), 156–172.

Huang, Y. H. (2001). Values of public relations: Effects on organization-public relationships mediating conflict resolution. *Journal of Public Relations Research, 13*(4), 265–301.

Hübner, A. H., & Kuhn, H. (2012). Retail category management: State-of-the-art review of quantitative research and software applications in assortment and shelf space management. *Omega, 40*(2), 199–209.

Javaid, M., Haleem, A., Singh, R. P., & Suman, R. (2022). Artificial intelligence applications for industry 4.0: A literature-based study. *Journal of Industrial Integration and Management, 7*(1), 83–111.

John-Mathews, J. M., Cardon, D., & Balagué, C. (2022). From reality to world. A critical perspective on AI fairness. *Journal of Business Ethics, 178*(4), 945–959.

Lillywhite, A., & Wolbring, G. (2019). Coverage of ethics within the artificial intelligence and machine learning academic literature: The case of disabled people. *Assistive Technology, 33*, 129–135. https://doi.org/10.1080/10400435.2019.1593259

Martin, S. M. (2019). *Artificial intelligence, mixed reality, and the redefinition of the classroom.* Rowman & Littlefield

Manohar, S., Mittal, A., & Marwah, S. (2020). Service innovation, corporate reputation and word-of-mouth in the banking sector: A test on multigroup-moderated mediation effect. *Benchmarking: An International Journal, 27*(1), 406–429.

Moed, H. F. (2005). Statistical relationships between downloads and citations at the level of individual documents within a single journal. *Journal of the American Society for Information Science and Technology, 56*(10), 1088–1097.

Moriuchi, E. (2021). An empirical study on anthropomorphism and engagement with disembodied AIs and consumers' re-use behavior. *Psychology & Marketing, 38*(1), 21–42.

Ng, D. T. K., Leung, J. K. L., Su, J., Ng, R. C. W., & Chu, S. K. W. (2023). Teachers' AI digital competencies and twenty-first century skills in the post-pandemic world. *Educational Technology Research and Development, 71*(1), 137–161.

Oosthuizen, K., Botha, E., Robertson, J., & Montecchi, M. (2021). Artificial intelligence in retail: The AI-enabled value chain. *Australasian Marketing Journal, 29*(3), 264–273.

Pai, V., & Chandra, S. (2022). Exploring factors influencing organizational adoption of artificial intelligence (AI) in corporate social responsibility (CSR) initiatives. *Pacific Asia Journal of the Association for Information Systems, 14*(5), 4.

Pillai, R., & Sivathanu, B. (2020). Adoption of artificial intelligence (AI) for talent acquisition in IT/ITeS organizations. *Benchmarking: An International Journal, 27*(9), 2599–2629.

Rawlins, B. (2008). Give the emperor a mirror: Toward developing a stakeholder measurement of organizational transparency. *Journal of Public Relations Research, 21*(1), 71–99.

Ribeiro, J., Lima, R., Eckhardt, T., & Paiva, S. (2021). Robotic process automation and artificial intelligence in industry 4.0–a literature review. *Procedia Computer Science, 181*, 51–58.

Saheb, T., & Saheb, M. (2019). Analyzing and visualizing knowledge structures of health informatics from 1974 to 2018: A bibliometric and social network analysis. *Healthcare Informatics Research, 25*, 61–72. https://doi.org/10.4258/hir.2019.25.2.61

Sung, E. C., Bae, S., Han, D. I. D., & Kwon, O. (2021). Consumer engagement via interactive artificial intelligence and mixed reality. *International Journal of Information Management, 60*, 102382.

Van Eck, N., & Waltman, L. (2010). Software survey: VOSviewer, a computer program for bibliometric mapping. *Scientometrics, 84*(2), 523–538.

Weber, P. (2023). Unrealistic optimism regarding artificial intelligence opportunities in human resource management. *International Journal of Knowledge Management (IJKM), 19*(1), 1–19.

Wu, C. W., & Monfort, A. (2023). Role of artificial intelligence in marketing strategies and performance. *Psychology & Marketing, 40*(3), 484–496.

Chapter 10

Ethical and Social Consequences of Accelerated Technology Adoption

Anuja Shukla[a] and Poornima Jirli[b]

[a]*Jaipuria Institute of Management, Noida*
[b]*Swiss School of Business Management, Geneva, Switzerland*

Abstract

This study examines the ethical and social consequences of the accelerated adoption of new technologies. An empirical approach is employed to explore the impacts of rapid technological integration on societal norms, ethical considerations, and individual behaviours. Responses from 305 participants are analysed using partial least squares structural equation modelling (PLS-SEM), focusing on perceived usefulness, ease of use, relative advantage, personal innovativeness, and fear of missing out (FOMO). The findings unveil intricate interactions between technological advancements and ethical–social dynamics, underscoring challenges and opportunities. This study offers critical insights for policymakers, technology developers, and society at large, aiming to encourage a more ethically informed and socially conscious approach to technology adoption.

Keywords: Technology adoption; ethical implications; social impact; accelerated integration; perceived usefulness; ease of use; relative advantage; personal innovativeness; fear of missing out; technology diffusion; PLS-SEM

1. Introduction

A significant shift in both individual and organisational growth has been brought about by the adoption of technology, particularly artificial intelligence (AI), in modern times, with an impact on sectors ranging from commerce to healthcare (Castells,

---

Augmenting Retail Reality: Blockchain, AR, VR, and the Internet of Things, Part A, 183–209
Copyright © 2025 by Anuja Shukla and Poornima Jirli
Published under exclusive licence by Emerald Publishing Limited
doi:10.1108/978-1-83608-634-520241025

2009; Statista, 2023). AI is expected to reach $207 billion by 2023, which highlights its transformative potential. However, the rapid adoption of generative AI technologies such as ChatGPT has led to a number of ethical and social dilemmas (Dignum, 2018; Hurlburt, 2023; Schlagwein & Willcocks, 2023; UNESCO, 2023). Despite their utility, these technologies raise substantial concerns, particularly their potential to mirror and perpetuate societal biases, and hence need to be carefully examined.

As AI technologies are rapidly integrating, ethical considerations must be taken into account when developing and using them, reflecting the challenges posed by early media diffusion influenced by socioeconomics and infrastructure availability (Chaffee & Metzger, 2001). While the internet and smartphones have democratised technology access, inequalities persist, highlighting a digital divide that leaves many segments of the global population at a disadvantage due to multiple barriers (Warschauer, 2004).

A critical evaluation of the ethical and social consequences of accelerating adoption rates of technology is undertaken in this study. This study seeks to uncover complex social changes and ethical challenges arising from technological integration by exploring the nuances of technological integration. These changes include shifts in trust dynamics, information overload, and a redefinition of human identity (Danaher, 2020; Danaher & Sætra, 2022; Horwich, 2006; Lee & See, 2004). Technology is reshaping societal norms and ethical frameworks in the context of these aspects. An understanding of these aspects is crucial to crafting a holistic perspective on how technology is impacting society.

2. Literature Review

The credit for understanding the adoption of technology historically is attributed to the theory of diffusion of innovation (DOI) by Everett M. Rogers (1962), which explains how new ideas and technologies spread within a social system (Davis, 1989). Over the years, this theory has been applied across various fields to study the adoption of new technologies.

Initially proposed in 1962, Rogers' DOI theory aims to elucidate how new ideas, practices, or technologies are spread and eventually integrated into social systems (Rogers, 1962). The theory highlights the significance of communication channels, social networks, and adopter categories in adoption (Davis, 1989). Additionally, several factors contribute to adoption, including relative advantage, compatibility, complexity, trialability, and observability (Davis, 1989). In 1962, sociologist Everett Rogers consolidated these studies into a series of generalisations forming the foundation of the current diffusion model, utilised globally in industrialised and developing countries. The diffusion process is often represented by 'bell-shaped' curves (Rogers, 1962).

In the diffusion curve, five segments represent distinct groups within a social system: innovators, early adopters, early majority, late majority, and laggards (Rogers, 1962). It is noted that innovators are characterised by high education levels, a propensity for risk-taking, access to funding, specialised skills for understanding and applying technical knowledge, and exposure to diverse information sources. The DOI within a social system is a temporal process (Rogers, 1962). Drawing upon Lazarsfeld and Menzel's (1963) theories, Rogers highlights the importance of personal influence over media influence in this process. The diffusion process is significantly shaped by private information and media influences, yet it is inseparable from the social environment in which it occurs. Factors such as prevailing social norms, the role of opinion leaders, and the presence of change agents and aides critically influence the rate of diffusion of an innovation (Sætra, 2023). Initially formulated in the early 20th century, the diffusion model originated from the industrialised Western world, reflecting its specific social, cultural, economic, and communicational contexts. Given the rapid technology adoption rates in contemporary times, there is a recognised need to reassess the Rogers diffusion model.

The adoption and usage of technology have been extensively researched across various contexts, including individual users (Thong et al., 2006), groups (Sarker et al., 2005; Sia et al., 2002), organisations (Sia et al., 2004; Thong, 1999), and multiple levels (Magni et al., 2012; Maruping & Magni, 2012; Yen et al., 2015). Transparency and ethical considerations play a critical role in AI adoption in industries like supply chain. Common ethical language is important among stakeholders (Manning et al., 2022). A significant increase in the diffusion of new digital technologies has been observed over the past decade (McKinsey, 2023; OECD, 2020). The emergence of these technologies is anticipated to lead to the decline of several sectors and firms, altering their organisational structures, competitive strategies, and customer interactions (Agrawal et al., 2018; DeStefano et al., 2020; Iansiti & Lakhani, 2020). There are substantial investments due to interest across industries in rapid adoption of the generative AI and other technologies in the recent years (Chui et al., 2023). Substantial improvements in task performance have been demonstrated in natural language processing models like GPT-3 (Brown, 2020). This convergence of complementary digital technologies is often called 'Industry 4.0' (Bradford & Florin, 2003). The literature identifies nine technologies as next-generation disruptive technologies (NGDTs), including IoT, mobile devices, big data, cloud computing, AI, blockchain, virtual/augmented reality, robotics, and three-dimensional (3D) printing (OECD, 2020). In the latter half of the 20th century, digital technologies have progressively replaced analogue technologies. NGDTs enable more effective generation and utilisation of data, thus facilitating process automation and aiding firms in making more accurate decisions (Agrawal et al., 2018; Cho et al., 2023). Despite widespread study, most current research examines these NGDTs in isolation (DeStefano et al., 2020; Goswami & Verma, 2024).

It has been observed that certain firms exhibit a higher propensity for technology adoption compared to others, according to firm-level data (Cho et al., 2023). This tendency is particularly notable with traditional digital technologies, which are biased towards more prominent firms. Larger firms possessing more knowledge-based capital and accumulated technology find it easier to adopt emerging technologies (Agrawal et al., 2018). Large firms' adoption of modern technologies may have initiated dynamics that benefit a select group of leading frontier firms, thereby exacerbating disparities across businesses (Brynjolfsson & McAfee, 2014). Additionally, enterprise resource planning (ERP) software is advantageous for large multinational corporations, enabling them to efficiently coordinate and capitalise on extensive production networks (Cho et al., 2023; OECD, 2020; Verma et al., 2024).

It is theorised that younger firms, often equipped with newer assets, are more likely to be compatible with recent technologies (Cho et al., 2023). Young firms experiencing rapid growth are more likely to own a website (Agrawal et al., 2018; Castells, 2009). Additionally, these firms adopt certain types of hardware more readily than their older counterparts (DeStefano et al., 2020). Furthermore, young firms have the potential to adopt emerging technologies even while they are still relatively small (Bradford & Florin, 2003; Cho et al., 2023).

Frontier digital technologies are increasingly being diffused as firms become more reliant on assets such as data, highlighting the significance of intangible investments in these technologies (DeStefano et al., 2020). Lopez-Acevedo and Griffith (2002) have noted that foreign-owned firms typically exhibit higher productivity and more effective use of technology (DeStefano et al., 2020). Multinational corporations, maintaining stringent productivity and production standards, are often inclined to share new technologies readily (Iansiti & Lakhani, 2020; Thong et al., 2006).

Bedué and Fritzsche (2022) state that AI represents one of the most rapidly advancing areas in the field of technology, encompassing a diverse array of applications in sectors such as finance, healthcare, the internet, and marketing. Due to its profound impact on society, organisations, and individuals, AI has been a subject of extensive discussion across various research domains (Agrawal et al., 2018). Within information systems, scholars have shown a particular interest in examining the acceptance and adoption of AI technologies (Brynjolfsson & McAfee, 2014).

The utilisation of AI technologies presents several potential benefits, yet the extent of AI's capabilities has not been fully realised in current implementations (Bedué & Fritzsche, 2022). Adopting AI at an individual level is influenced by various factors, including trust, social influence, hedonic motivation, and effort expectations (Agarwal & Prasad, 1998). Additionally, the broader socioeconomic context significantly shapes AI adoption, distinguishing it from other technological advancements (Agrawal et al., 2018; Castells, 2009). Despite acknowledging the potential and functionalities of AI, industry decision-makers face uncertainties regarding its future applications (Bengio, 2017), and there is a reliance on trustworthy sources for information about the risks and benefits associated with AI (Alutaybi et al., 2020).

In AI, generative AI, a specialised subfield, has been developed to automate the creation of textual, visual, and musical content. This is achieved by utilising deep learning techniques to generate new outputs informed by patterns identified in training data (Goodfellow et al., 2016). Over the past decade, there has been a significant advancement in generative AI technology, exemplified by sophisticated models such as GPT-4 from OpenAI.

According to the DOI theory, the adoption of generative AI has progressed beyond the initial stage of 'innovators', typically comprising tech enthusiasts and AI researchers. It has entered the 'early adopters' phase. In this phase, business organisations increasingly implement generative AI for diverse purposes, such as content creation, chatbot development, and data analysis (Perez, 2022). Many

Ethical and Social Consequences of Accelerated Technology   **187**

potential adopters are currently positioned in the 'early majority' stage, awaiting further proof of the technology's effectiveness. Challenges like discrimination in AI applications, misuse of AI technologies, and concerns about AI ethics and regulatory aspects are some obstacles impeding its broader acceptance (Bengio, 2017).

Recognised as an innovative breakthrough, generative AI is distinguished by its unique attributes, notably its unpredictability and capability to produce novel outcomes (Bengio, 2017). The role of communication channels in disseminating information about advanced AI has been emphasised in numerous studies. Online platforms such as Medium, arXiv, and Github have played a pivotal role in enhancing awareness of generative AI within technology communities and business sectors (Santos, 2020).

The broader implementation of generative AI is currently nascent, with expectations of increased acceptance as technology develops and its societal advantages become more evident (Wirtz et al., 2019). The social ecosystem encompassing the diffusion of generative AI comprises various stakeholders, including developers, researchers, business entities, and end-users. These actors exhibit varying degrees of readiness for adopting advanced AI. Within this social framework, policymakers play a crucial role in either facilitating or hindering the dissemination of this technology through their regulatory actions (Scherer, 2020).

Recent technological advancements, particularly in digital platforms and AI-based services, have notably accelerated adoption rates. The generative AI model, ChatGPT, exemplified this trend by attracting one million users within just five days of its launch in 2022. This rapid user acquisition contrasts with older platforms like Instagram, which took around 2.5 months to reach the same user milestone after its 2010 launch. Furthermore, traditional media platforms such as Facebook and Twitter took even longer to gather a similar number of users (Exploding Topics, 2023; *The Guardian*, 2023).

This trend of swift growth is also evident in the rise of social media platforms. By 2021, YouTube reported over 2 billion monthly active users, while Instagram had over one billion. The transformation in communication, information sharing, and consumption facilitated by these platforms has significantly contributed to their rapid adoption (Statista, 2021b).

The quick expansion and user engagement with OpenAI further underscores the accelerated adoption of AI technologies (SimilarWeb, 2023). In this rapidly evolving landscape, factors like perceived usefulness, ease of use, relative advantage, personal innovativeness, and the FOMO are increasingly influential in the diffusion of new technologies.

3. The Growing Economic Footprint of AI

The economic footprint of AI is expanding rapidly, as evidenced by critical insights from the global AI market (Statista, 2023). In 2023, the market will reach an impressive $207 billion, signifying AI's substantial influence on the global economy and its pivotal role in driving innovation across various sectors. This remarkable market valuation reflects the widespread integration of AI technologies into business operations, healthcare, finance, and consumer applications, underscoring the importance of understanding the factors influencing the adoption of such transformative technologies (Statista, 2023).

Financial commitments towards chatbot and conversational AI startups are strong indicators of the sector's significance and potential. As of 2023, leading startups in this domain have garnered impressive funding, reflecting investor confidence in their technological advancements and market potential. For instance, ASAPP leads with funding of $380 million, followed by Observe.ai at $214 million and Ada at $191 million, among others. The funding these companies have received is a testament to their business models and broader investment trends within the AI industry.

Such funding highlights the competitive edge and innovative strides that these startups are making. With significant financial backing, these companies are well-positioned to advance the development and integration of AI technologies in various customer service applications, signalling a transformative shift in how businesses interact with their clients.

In the context of technology adoption, these investments are a prelude to the broader acceptance and integration of conversational AI technologies into the mainstream market. The support from venture capital and other investment forms underscores the anticipated role of chatbots and AI in enhancing operational efficiencies and customer experiences across sectors.

Furthermore, investment in AI startups remains robust, with global funding reaching $12.1 billion in the second quarter of 2022 alone (Statista, 2023). This substantial investment underscores AI startups' vitality and growth potential and reflects investor confidence in AI as a leading sector for technological advancement and economic opportunity (Statista, 2023).

The global explainable artificial intelligence (XAI) market is experiencing significant growth, valued at $5.1 billion in 2022, with projections indicating a rise to over $24 billion by 2030 (Thormundsson, 2023).

3.1 Ethics

In discussing AI ethics, the UNESCO report (2023) brings attention to the ethical intricacies within AI, notably its ability to amplify societal biases, as illustrated by gender disparities in search engine outcomes. The report raises concerns about the integration of AI in judicial systems, highlighting the potential lack of transparency and intrinsic biases that could undermine fairness and human rights (UNESCO, 2023). UNESCO advocates for stringent ethical frameworks to address the profound societal effects of AI (UNESCO, 2023). Hurlburt (2023) offers a critical perspective on AI, noting its lack of accurate intelligence attributes such as consciousness and free will, which raises questions about its ethical decision-making capabilities (Hurlburt, 2023). He identifies shortcomings in large language models like Generative Pre-trained Transformer (GPT), particularly

Ethical and Social Consequences of Accelerated Technology **189**

their failure to meet Findable, Accessible, Interoperable, and Reusable (FAIR) data principles, leading to possible misinformation (Hurlburt, 2023). Hurlburt also discusses the ethical complications in AI-driven content moderation, emphasising the difficulty of eliminating bias and the impact on content moderators, as well as the equity issues within the generative AI field due to high operational costs that could lead to business-induced biases (Hurlburt, 2023). Schlagwein and Willcocks (2023) explore the ethical biases embedded in AI systems, especially in generative models like ChatGPT, which often reflect the biases in their training data. This can significantly affect AI-generated content and decisions, reinforcing existing societal prejudices (Schlagwein & Willcocks, 2023). To address these challenges, Srinivasan and Parikh (2021) suggest employing generative artworks as pedagogical tools to bridge the communication gaps in AI ethics. They propose that such artworks could depict a variety of ethical viewpoints, visualise hypothetical scenarios and mismatches in AI systems, and convey non-Western perspectives, thus fostering greater comprehension and empathy among diverse AI stakeholders (Srinivasan & Parikh, 2021).

The technological shift in trust dynamics raises pivotal ethical questions. As technology, particularly AI and robotics, assumes roles traditionally held by humans, it redistributes power and accountability, creating a complex moral landscape where determining responsibility for autonomous systems' actions becomes increasingly challenging (Chatterji et al., 2023; Danaher, 2020; Levine & Schweitzer, 2015). This shift affects interpersonal relations and challenges our understanding of autonomy and self-determination (Sætra, 2021). Moreover, the growing difficulty in discerning truth in the digital age, exacerbated by the proliferation of misinformation, poses significant ethical concerns. The blurring of factual accuracy impacts societal discourse and decision-making, potentially leading to increased polarisation (David, 2020; Fallis, 2021). This erosion of the ethical value of truth and integrity in communications and media highlights the need for critical evaluation and ethical frameworks to navigate this 'post-truth' era (Appiah, 2010; Horwich, 2006).

Furthermore, the concept of robotomorphy, where human traits are ascribed to technology and vice versa, presents unique ethical challenges. This blurring of the lines between human and machine capabilities requires re-examining traditional moral concepts, particularly regarding autonomy, agency, and the nature of human identity in a technologically integrated society (Sætra, 2021). These evolving ethical landscapes underscore the importance of adapting ethical frameworks to account for the profound societal effects of AI and technology, ensuring that they align with values conducive to a just and equitable society.

3.2 Social Impact

Solaiman et al. (2023), for assessing the societal impacts of generative AI, underscores the need for standardised evaluation protocols. It is noted that without careful moderation, AI may reinforce societal biases and stereotypes, potentially exacerbating inequality and marginalisation issues (Solaiman et al., 2023). Furthermore, the paper articulates concerns regarding AI's influence on user autonomy and trust and the risks of centralising power through AI in authoritative domains such as surveillance and military applications (Solaiman et al., 2023).

Sætra's analysis underscores the complex societal ramifications of generative AI across different levels. At the macro level, he expresses concern over the technology's ability to undermine democratic processes by generating a profusion of political content, raising the risks of misinformation and societal polarisation (Danaher & Sætra, 2022). Additionally, he notes the potential displacement of 'knowledge workers', leading to changes in labour dynamics and the nature of work (Edwards, 2022). Sætra also highlights the perpetuation of societal biases and discrimination by generative AI (Bender et al., 2021) and its significant contribution to environmental challenges through high energy consumption (Brevini, 2021). From a meso perspective, Sætra identifies challenges generative AI poses in various professions and sectors. The technology's capability to replicate human-produced content without permission or remuneration poses ethical dilemmas (Zuboff, 2019). He also notes the disproportionate impact of AI biases on marginalised communities (Bender et al., 2021).

At an individual level, Sætra raises concerns about the potential decline in cognitive skills due to over-reliance on AI for mental and creative tasks (Sætra, 2019). Additionally, the increasing persuasiveness of generative AI could lead to manipulation risks (Sætra & Mills, 2021). He also cautions about the possibility of AI supplanting human partners, with implications for personal relationships and social skills (Sætra, 2021). Sætra emphasises the necessity of aligning generative AI's development and use with values essential for a beneficial society, including freedom, democracy, sustainability, well-being, and justice (Brey, 2018). He advocates for a proactive human role in guiding and regulating generative AI to prevent adverse societal impacts (Griffy-Brown et al., 2018).

The transformation of trust from human entities to technological systems, as analysed by Danaher and Sætra (2022), fundamentally changes the dynamics of social relationships and dependencies. According to Lee and See (2004), this transition significantly affects how individuals interact among themselves and with technological tools, potentially paving the way for a society where technology increasingly mediates or suppresses human interactions. Moreover, the rapid expansion of digital information and the accompanying challenges in distinguishing truth profoundly affect social discourse and decision-making processes. Fallis (2021) and David (2020) note that this trend could exacerbate societal polarisation and the spread of misinformation, influencing various aspects, from political ideologies to individual beliefs. Furthermore, integrating AI and robotics is reshaping social norms and behaviours. As Sætra (2020) points out, individuals are likely to modify their interactions to align with the capabilities and constraints of technology. This adaptation could lead to a redefinition of social etiquette and norms, reflecting the evolving landscape of human-technology interplay.

The advent of new technologies and the challenges associated with the digital era have resulted in recent scholarly efforts that have enhanced our understanding of technology adoption. Doe et al. (2019) have explored the effects of social media on technology adoption rates, while Smith and Johnson (2021) have investigated the impact of user experience design on technology adoption. Contemporary analyses address the evolving nature of user interaction with technology, supplementing traditional frameworks such as the DOI and the technology acceptance model (TAM). Integrating these recent findings into the study reinforces the validity and relevance of the conceptual framework, aligning it with the latest trends and behaviours among users. By adopting this approach, the research remains current and accurately reflects the complexity of modern technology adoption processes.

3.3 Variables and Interconnections

There is a close relationship between ease of use, usefulness, advantage of technology, FOMO, personal innovativeness, and adoption rate. Technology that is more convenient to use (ease of use) appears to be more useful (usefulness), which promotes greater adoption rates. The perceived advantages (advantage of technology) can further catalyse this relationship, as significant benefits can outweigh initial usability concerns. Individuals' personal innovativeness determines their propensity to adopt new technologies, often exacerbated by the societal pressures and anxiety associated with FOMO. There is a significant impact of these factors on the overall adoption rate, suggesting a composite dynamic where ease, usefulness, technological superiority, as well as personal and societal factors contribute to the overall adoption rate. By exploring these relationships, study aims to provide a comprehensive understanding of the factors causing accelerated technology adoption within social and ethical frameworks.

Diversity of perspectives is essential for a comprehensive understanding of technology adoption dynamics. This chapter integrates a number of approaches from different fields. The case studies by Son et al. (2015) provide insights into the practical application of adoption theories, and the empirical research focuses on the psychological factors influencing user acceptance. Furthermore, qualitative analyses were conducted in order to gain a better understanding of why organisations and individuals adopt technology. These different methodologies contribute to broadening the scope of the conceptual model and providing a more nuanced understanding of the factors that drive technology adoption by incorporating these different methodologies.

4. Conceptual Model and Hypothesis Development

The significance of theoretical underpinnings in model development is widely acknowledged, with the understanding that various models depend on foundational theories due to the potential interconnectivity of different variables (Greenhalgh et al., 2004). The DOI theory, formulated by Rogers, has been a pivotal tool in comprehending technology adoption. Concurrently, other models like the TAM and the unified theory of acceptance and use of technology (UTAUT) have offered further perspectives. The TAM, proposed by Davis in 1989, underscores perceived usefulness and ease of use as crucial determinants of technology acceptance (Alutaybi et al., 2020). Integrating eight distinct models, including TAM and DOI, the UTAUT model aims to predict behaviours related to technology acceptance (Ajzen & Fishbein, 1980).

Recent scholarly efforts have been directed towards updating and reinterpreting traditional adoption theories for the digital age. Tarafdar and Vaidya (2006) highlighted the necessity to revise the DOI theory, particularly regarding cloud computing adoption, to reflect the evolving nature of information technology. Consequently, the stimulus organism theory is utilised (see Fig. 10.1). Based on Pavlov's stimulus–response framework, the process of innovation diffusion, leading to an accelerated technology adoption, could be represented as follows:

1. Stimulus (technology): When new technologies are introduced, they act as stimuli (Pavlov, 1927).
2. Response (adoption/resistance): Users respond to the stimulus by adopting or resisting the technology. Several factors influence this response, such as perceived usefulness, ease of use, and previous experiences (Berwick, 2003; Valente, 2012; Venkatesh & Davis, 2000; Venkatesh et al., 2003).

4.1 Usefulness and Adoption Rate

The notion of 'usefulness' has become increasingly prominent in recent studies on technology adoption. It is observed that potential users are more inclined to adopt a technology when they perceive it as advantageous for executing specific tasks or enhancing their performance (Davis, 1989; Venkatesh et al., 2003). This trend is evident across various technologies and settings, underscoring the significance of perceived usefulness as a pivotal determinant in the acceptance of technology (Berwick, 2003; Valente, 2012; Venkatesh & Davis, 2000; Venkatesh et al., 2003). Moreover, it is crucial to acknowledge that perceptions of usefulness are not isolated; they are subject to influences from multiple factors, such as an individual's technological expertise, the specific

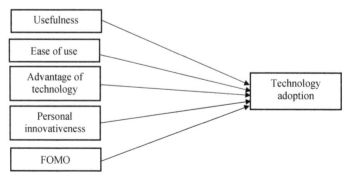

Fig. 10.1. Conceptual Model Framework. *Source*: Author's compilation.

Ethical and Social Consequences of Accelerated Technology **193**

context in which the technology is used, and the inherent characteristics of the technology itself (Chaffee & Metzger, 2001; Russell & Norvig, 2020; Taylor & Todd, 1995). Grasping the nuances of how usefulness impacts technology adoption remains a crucial area of research in the digital era. This review of literature, accentuating the role of 'usefulness' in the adoption of technology (Chaffee & Metzger, 2001; Taylor & Todd, 1995), leads to the formulation of the following hypothesis:

H1: The usefulness of a technology positively impacts its adoption rate.

The proposed hypothesis suggests that the perception of a technology's utility significantly influences its adoption rate. It is postulated that users are inclined to adopt a technology when they perceive it as advantageous or efficient for particular tasks. Consequently, enhancing the perceived utility of a technology is likely to impact its adoption rate positively.

4.2 Ease of Use and Adoption

The perception of a technology's 'ease of use' is acknowledged as a crucial determinant of its adoption rate, akin to its practicality. The TAM, as proposed by Davis (1989), suggests that a user's decision to adopt new technology is significantly influenced by its perceived ease of use and usefulness (Alutaybi et al., 2020). Consequently, user-friendly and straightforward technologies are more likely to be adopted (Venkatesh & Davis, 2000; Venkatesh et al., 2003, 2012).

Subsequent research has consistently corroborated the impact of perceived ease of use on adopting technology (Zhou, 2011). In the context of the evolving digital landscape, the ease with which technology can be used plays a pivotal role in the DOI. Reflecting on the literature review that underscored the significance of 'usefulness' in adopting technology (Venkatesh & Davis, 2000; Venkatesh et al., 2012), a hypothesis is thus formulated:

H2: The ease of use of technology positively impacts its adoption rate.

According to this hypothesis, users are more likely to adopt technologies perceived as simple to use (Davis, 1989). Consequently, user-friendly and intuitive technologies tend to be adopted more rapidly compared to less user-friendly options. This hypothesis underscores the critical role of ease of use in facilitating technology adoption.

4.3 Advantage of Technology and Adoption Rate

It is hypothesised that a technology's perceived 'advantages' are crucial in influencing its adoption rates. According to Rogers' DOI, potential users are more inclined to adopt new technology if they perceive it as offering superior benefits than its predecessors (Rogers, 1962). These benefits could include enhanced convenience, efficiency, cost reduction, or other advantages. Numerous studies across various technological fields have affirmed that the perceived benefits of technology significantly sway users' decisions to adopt it (Mathieson, 1991).

Therefore, for effective adoption and diffusion, the perceived benefits of a technology must be identified and communicated:

H3: The advantage of a technology significantly impacts its adoption rate.

According to this hypothesis, the adoption rate of a technology is significantly impacted by its perceived benefits or advantages. It is suggested that a technology is more likely to be adopted by users when they recognise distinct advantages, such as enhanced efficiency or effectiveness, in its use (Rogers, 1962).

4.4 Personal Innovativeness and Adoption Rate

In the realm of technology adoption, 'Personal Innovativeness' is defined as an individual's propensity to engage with novel technologies. According to Rogers' DOI, individuals with higher innovativeness are inclined to adopt new technologies earlier than their less innovative counterparts (Rogers, 1962).

Investigations undertaken by Agarwal and Prasad (1998) have corroborated that an individual's readiness to embrace new technologies is substantially influenced by their degree of innovativeness (Agarwal & Prasad, 1998). Similarly, Lu et al. (2005) have argued that personal innovativeness is a critical factor in accepting and utilising new technologies. The significance of personal innovativeness in expediting the adoption of new technologies is thus emphasised. This hypothesis emerges from a synthesis of the extant literature:

H4: An individual's innovativeness positively correlates with the adoption rate.

The hypothesis suggests that the inclination of an individual towards adopting new technologies, termed personal innovativeness, may bolster the adoption rate of a technology (Thakur & Srivastava, 2014). It is posited that individuals who exhibit innovative traits are more inclined to experiment with new technologies, thereby contributing to an increased adoption rate.

4.5 FOMO and Adoption Rate

Recently, the notion of 'FOMO' has garnered attention in the context of technology adoption. This phenomenon is characterised by individuals' apprehension that they are missing out on rewarding experiences available to others. Such fear may prompt people to adopt new technologies, particularly within social media platforms (Goodfellow et al., 2016). The potential of FOMO to considerably influence the adoption of wearable technologies has been noted. Consequently, a hypothesis has been formulated based on the literature surrounding FOMO:

H5: The FOMO significantly impacts the adoption rate.

The psychological phenomenon known as FOMO is the foundation for this hypothesis. It is theorised that individuals may be compelled to adopt technology due to a fear of being left behind, significantly impacting its adoption rate (Przybylski et al., 2013).

This study applies the conceptual framework and hypotheses to understand the wider ethical and social impacts of rapid technology adoption. It explores how ease of use, usefulness, technological advantage, personal innovativeness, and FOMO interact and influence society and individual behaviours. For instance, technologies that are widely adopted due to their perceived usefulness might also raise concerns about privacy and data security, challenging established ethical norms. Additionally, the dynamic between personal innovativeness and FOMO could increase social disparities, as access to technology is not evenly distributed. This detailed analysis assists in identifying potential issues and crafting strategies to reduce negative societal effects, ensuring that technological progress is ethically responsible and promotes societal well-being. Through highlighting these relationships, the research contributes to fostering a more ethically informed and socially mindful approach to technology adoption.

5. Research Methodology

This research employed a descriptive study design, targeting digital users. Data were gathered from a deliberately selected sample of 380 respondents (Shukla & Mishra, 2022). The survey instruments were adapted from scales previously established in relevant literature (Table 10.1). Responses were quantified using a

Table 10.1.   Constructs and Definitions.

Constructs	Definition	Relevant Studies
Ease of use	The notion of ease of use, often termed as perceived ease of use, plays a crucial role in models of technology adoption. It pertains to the extent to which an individual perceives a specific system or technology as easy to use. (Davis, 1989). Generally, it is observed that the simplicity with which users can adopt a technology correlates with the speed of its adoption (Venkatesh et al., 2003).	Gao et al. (2018); Davis (1989); Lund (2001); Venkatesh et al. (2003)
Usefulness	In the context of technology adoption, the term 'usefulness', frequently identified as perceived usefulness, is defined as the extent to which an individual believes that utilising a specific technology or system will improve their job performance or productivity (Davis, 1989). According to the DOI theory, technologies that are perceived as useful are expected to be adopted more swiftly (Rogers, 2003).	Gao et al. (2018); Davis (1989); Lund (2001); Rogers (2003)

(*Continued*)

196   Anuja Shukla and Poornima Jirli

Table 10.1.   (*Continued*)

Constructs	Definition	Relevant Studies
Advantage of technology	In the discourse on technology, the term 'technology advantage', or relative advantage, is used to describe the extent to which an innovation is regarded as better than the concept, product, or technology it supersedes (Nayak & Narayan, 2019; Rogers, 2003).	Gao et al. (2018); Nayak and Narayan (2019); Davis (1989); Moore and Benbasat (1991); Rogers (2003)
FOMO	FOMO, an acronym for fear of missing out, denotes the apprehension associated with the possibility of being excluded from rewarding experiences that others might be enjoying (Przybylski et al., 2013; Riordan et al., 2020). This FOMO can lead to a situation where individuals are more inclined to adopt new technologies swiftly in order to maintain connectivity and stay informed (Kärkkäinen, 2023).	Riordan et al. (2020); Aitamurto et al. (2021); Kärkkäinen (2023); Alutaybi et al. (2020); Przybylski et al. (2013); Tomczyk and Szotkowski (2023
Personal innovativeness	Within the framework of technology adoption, 'Personal Innovativeness' is defined as the propensity of an individual to undertake risks through the exploration of new technologies (Wang & Lin, 2021). As outlined by Rogers (2003), this concept embodies an individual's readiness to engage in new experiences, particularly those associated with the adoption of novel technologies (Rogers, 2003).	Jackson et al. (2013); Wang and Lin (2021); Alkawsi et al. (2021); Parveen and Sulaiman (2008); Rogers (2003); Jackson et al. (2013); Agarwal and Prasad (1998)
Adoption rate	Technology adoption rates reflect how quickly and extensively new technologies are integrated and used within a specific setting. Faaeq et al. (2014) highlight this in the context of e-government in Iraq, while Oliveira and Martins (2011) focus on firm-level adoption models. Hannan and McDowell (1984) explore the banking sector's technological advancements, and Salahshour Rad et al. (2018) provide a comprehensive review and classification of information technology adoption literature.	Faaeq et al. (2014); Oliveira and Martins (2011); Hannan and McDowell (1984); Salahshour Rad et al. (2018)

Source: Author's compilation

5-point Likert scale, where a score of 1 denoted 'Strongly disagree' and 5 denoted 'Strongly agree'. PLS-SEM was utilised for data analysis. A total of 380 responses were collected. Any incomplete reactions were excluded from the final dataset, resulting in 305 usable responses.

6. Data Analysis

Respondents' demographic characteristics, such as gender, age, and occupation, are classified. These characteristics are summarised in Table 10.2. Females comprise the majority of the respondents, representing 58.1%, while males account for 41.9%. Regarding age distribution, the predominant group is those aged between 18 and 29, constituting about 57.8% of the total respondents. The occupational backgrounds of the respondents are diverse, with a significant proportion being salaried employees.

6.1 Assessment of Measurement Model

The robustness of the survey was examined through confirmatory factor analysis (CFA), which focused on evaluating the measurement model. This evaluation involved analysing the connections between indicators and constructs, a crucial aspect of assessing a measurement model. To achieve this, tests for internal consistency, convergent validity, and discriminant validity were employed. Internal consistency was evaluated using a composite reliability test and Cronbach's alpha. As detailed in Table 10.3, Cronbach's alpha values surpassed the recommended threshold of 0.7 (Pavlou, 2018). Furthermore, the composite reliability values, ranging from 0.81 to 0.91, were deemed acceptable (Sharma & Shukla, 2017; Shukla & Mishra, 2022) (refer to Table 10.3).

Table 10.2.   Descriptive Results.

Variable	Category	Frequency	Percentage
Gender	Male	145	41.9
	Female	201	58.1
Age	18–30	200	57.8
	30–40	70	20.23
	40–50	40	11.56
	Above 50	36	10.5
Occupation	Private job	160	46.2
	Government	08	2.3
	Job	120	34.6
	Student	32	9.2
	Homemaker	26	7.5

Source: Author's compilation.

Table 10.3.   Summary of Results of Evaluation of Measurement Model.

Construct		Items	Outer Loadings	Cronbach's Alpha	Composite Reliability	AVE
Ease of use (Davis, 1989)	EU1	Generative AI is easy to use.	0.787	0.755	0.824	0.535
	EU2	Generative AI is simple to use.	0.875			
	EU3	Generative AI requires the fewest steps possible to accomplish what I want to do with it.	0.709			
	EU4	Generative AI is easy to master	0.565			
Usefulness (Davis, 1989)	U1	Generative AI helps me to more effective	0.757	0.831	0.871	0.643
	U2	Generative AI saves me time when I use it.	0.845			
	U3	Generative AI is useful	0.785			
	U4	I am effective and efficient				
Advantages of Technology (Aitamurto et al., 2021)	AT1	I am glad to share the benefits of latest technology like generative AI	0.795	0.776	0.931	0.731
	AT2	I will be able to maximise my reach with the technology	0.782			
	AT3	Using generative AI kind of technology, I find it easy to do what I want it to do.	0.758			
	AT4	Using generative AI technology will provide a mean possibility of reducing human work.	0.407			

Ethical and Social Consequences of Accelerated Technology 199

Construct	Code	Item				
FOMO (Wang & Lin, 2021)	FOMO1	When others do not interact with me as expected using the latest social media technology, I may be concerned that my reputation among my friends has declined	0.723	0.842	0.871	0.821
	FOMO2	When others do not interact with me as expected using the latest social media technology, concerned with my profile being less active so that others lose interest	0.813			
	FOMO3	When I am unwilling to engage in technology for social interaction (e.g., group chat), I may be concerned about losing the benefits of being in the online group	0.856			
	FOMO4	Following online news make me feel better	487			
Personal innovativeness	PI1	In technology, I have heard about it	0.79	0.851	0.731	0.867
	PI2	My peers make the most use of generative AI technology	0.779			
	PI3	I am curious about latest trends and like to experiment	0.747			
	PI4	Personal innovativeness will positively effect on attitude	0.637			
Adoption rate (Zolas et al., 2021)	A1	To what extent have you integrated the new technology into your daily operations or activities	0.785	0.821	0.875	0.775
	A2	Technology makes life easier	0.734			

Source: Author's calculations.

200 *Anuja Shukla and Poornima Jirli*

The assessment of convergent validity in the model involved scrutinising the average variance extracted (AVE) and outer loadings (refer to Table 10.4). Factors such as EU4, U4, AT4, FOMO4, and PI4 were excluded from the model because their values did not meet the acceptable threshold of 0.7. This exclusion led to a notable enhancement in the AVE values (refer to Table 10.3), affirming the validity of the concurrent model.

Additionally, an analysis for discriminant validity was conducted, utilising cross-loadings and the Fornell–Larcker criterion (1981). The results indicated that the factors did not demonstrate cross-loading, as they showed more substantial loadings on their respective constructs than on others (Sia et al., 2002). According to the Fornell–Larcker criterion (1981), the AVE values surpassed the squared correlations with other constructs, establishing discriminant validity (Sharma & Shukla, 2017; Shukla & Mishra, 2022).

Convergent validity was established by evaluating the AVE and outer loadings. The AVE values were determined to exceed the threshold of 0.5 (Table 10.4), thereby confirming the establishment of convergent validity.

6.2 Assessment and Evaluation of Structural Model

A collinearity assessment was performed on the model, with the calculated variance inflation factor (VIF) values all exceeding 5, thus indicating the absence of multicollinearity concerns. The model underwent evaluation using PLS-SEM, incorporating bootstrapping on 5,000 subsamples (Sharma & Shukla, 2017; Shukla & Mishra, 2022).

The structural model delineates the relationships between constructs for hypothesis testing. Five hypotheses were proposed in this study. Notable results were observed for hypotheses *H1, H2, H3, H4*, and *H5*, underscoring the significant influence of factors such as 'Ease of use, Usability, Technology Advantage, FOMO, and Personal Innovativeness' in accelerating technology adoption. Consequently, hypotheses *H1, H2, H3, H4*, and *H5* received support. The R^2 value was computed at 0.789, and the adjusted R^2 at 0.796. Additionally, the f^2 values were found to range between 0.146 and 1.582. Based on its standardised root mean square residual (SRMR) rating of 0.105, the model possessed high predictive capacity.

Table 10.4. AVE.

Constructs	AVE
EU	0.85
U	0.714
AT	0.876
FOMO	0.786
PI	0.659
AR	0.75

Source: Author's calculations.

Ethical and Social Consequences of Accelerated Technology   *201*

Table 10.5.   Results of PL-SEM.

Hyp	Hypothesis	*t*-Values	*p*-Values	Beta	Result
H1	The usefulness of a technology positively impacts its adoption rate.	18.981	0.000	0.641	Supported
H2	The ease of use of technology positively impacts its adoption rate.	8.539	0.000	0.423	Supported
H3	The advantage of a technology significantly impacts its adoption rate.	16.25	0.000	0.647	Supported
H4	An individual's innovativeness positively correlates with adoption rate.	4.872	0.000	0.417	Supported
H5	The FOMO significantly impacts adoption rate.	6.372	0.000	0.478	Supported

Source: Author's calculations.

The internal structure analysis validated all five hypotheses, as indicated in Table 10.5, with the *t*-values being significant ($t > 1.96$). The most robust relationship was observed between the advantages of technology and the adoption rate ($\beta = 0.647$, $p = 0.000$), suggesting that the benefits or advantages of technology are critical in determining its adoption rate by users and industries. Technologies with clear and substantial advantages will likely be adopted and implemented more rapidly. The next most substantial relationship was between the usefulness of technology and the adoption rate ($\beta = 0.641$, $p = 0.000$), indicating that the more beneficial and practical technology is perceived, the more likely it is to be adopted swiftly and broadly. The relationship between FOMO and adoption rate ($\beta = 0.478$, $p = 0.000$) was also significant, implying that the FOMO can significantly influence the speed of adoption of new technologies or trends. The significance of the relationship between ease of use and adoption rate ($\beta = 0.423$, $p = 0.000$) suggests that user-friendly technologies are more readily and widely adopted as they lower the barriers to acceptance. Lastly, the relationship between personal innovativeness and adoption rate ($\beta = 0.417$, $p = 0.000$) was significant, indicating that individuals who are more innovative and open to new experiences tend to adopt new technologies or innovations more quickly and readily.

7. Results and Discussion

The findings of this research indicate that various elements, including perceived ease of use, usefulness, personal innovativeness, FOMO, and technological advantages, significantly influence the acceleration of technology adoption. As per Davis' study (1989), the acceptance and adoption of technology are profoundly affected by perceived ease of use and usefulness (Agarwal & Prasad, 1998; Alutaybi et al., 2020). Our survey validated several of these factors, affirming their relevance in a context where the technology landscape continuously evolves. The importance of personal innovativeness in adopting technology was also substantiated, aligning with the observations of Rogers (1995). Consistent with Thakur and Srivastava's findings (2014), participants who exhibited a high level of innovativeness showed a greater tendency towards adopting new technologies (Thakur & Srivastava, 2014). The influence of the FOMO on technology adoption was significant (Przybylski et al., 2013), with a higher FOMO level correlating with a faster adoption of new technologies among participants.

Additionally, the relative advantage of a technology plays a pivotal role in its adoption, according to Rogers' theory (Rogers, 1962). The survey results further revealed that technologies offer discernible effort reduction and performance benefits. The survey results substantiate *Hypothesis H1*, which posits that the perceived usefulness of technology has a direct effect on its adoption rate. This aligns with Davis' TAM (1989), suggesting that perceived usefulness is critical to technology acceptance (Alutaybi et al., 2020). Furthermore, *Hypothesis H2*, regarding the impact of technology's ease of use on adoption rates, received affirmation from the survey participants. The data reveal a positive correlation, supporting the notion advanced by Venkatesh and Bala (2008) that ease of use significantly influences users' acceptance of technology (Venkatesh & Davis, 2000; Venkatesh et al., 2003, 2012).

According to *Hypothesis H3*, the survey confirms that the relative advantage of technology markedly influences its adoption rates, which is consistent with Rogers' (2003) DOI theory, underscoring the importance of perceived comparative advantage in adoption decisions. Concerning *Hypothesis H4*, the survey indicates a positive correlation between personal innovativeness and technology adoption, aligning with the findings of Thakur and Srivastava (2014). Lastly, *Hypothesis H5*, which associates the FOMO with the impetus for technology adoption, found robust support in the survey data. FOMO has been identified as a significant factor affecting the behavioural intent to use technology (Przybylski et al., 2013).

The conclusions derived from the survey results corroborate that these pivotal factors – perceived ease of use, usefulness, personal innovativeness, FOMO, and the relative advantage of technology – significantly influence the rate of technology adoption. This study provides an in-depth examination of technology adoption, acknowledging certain limitations that may influence its findings. Despite being considered adequate in terms of encapsulating a representative sample of the global population, the sample size may not be representative of the entire global population, thus limiting the generalisability of the results. Further, the potential biases associated with the survey methodology and participant selection must be carefully considered. Research in the future should utilise larger, more diverse samples and incorporate mixed-method approaches in order to address these issues. It may be possible to gain a greater understanding of technology adoption patterns by addressing confounding variables such as socioeconomic status and technological literacy.

The role of cultural norms and regional idiosyncrasies in shaping technology adoption is paramount. Studies, such as those conducted by Martinez and Fernandez (2024), illustrate that geographical differences significantly affect adoption strategies and behaviours. It is critical to understand these cultural and regional distinctions to develop effective, globally relevant technology adoption strategies. By examining these factors in greater depth, the research aims to improve the generalisability and applicability of its findings, thereby offering valuable guidance for implementing technology adoption strategies both globally and locally.

8. Contribution of This Study

This study has yielded essential insights into the factors that expedite technology adoption, benefiting individuals, organisations, and society. The findings indicate that perceived usefulness, ease of use, relative advantage, personal innovativeness, and FOMO are substantial influencers in the adoption process. The information presented in this article equips individuals with the necessary knowledge to make more informed decisions when considering the adoption of new technologies.

Organisations, especially those developing and marketing new technologies, can use these insights to refine product quality and communication strategies. They can expedite the adoption process by highlighting the utility and user-friendliness of their products and clearly presenting their advantages over existing technologies. Moreover, recognising the significance of individual innovativeness and the FOMO can aid companies in targeting the most suitable demographic groups to boost adoption.

This research offers policymakers, educators, and society a thorough comprehension of the patterns in technology adoption. The insights gleaned can inform the development of policies, educational programmes, and public discourse regarding technology adoption, particularly in sectors where rapid technology adoption is vital, such as advancing digital literacy or sustainable technologies. This study deepens the understanding of technology adoption and lays the groundwork for future research. A more intricate grasp of the various factors influencing technology adoption could result in the evolution of more detailed theories and models.

9. Conclusion

A study was conducted to ascertain the factors that accelerate technology adoption. This empirical investigation centred on perceived usefulness, ease of use, relative advantage, personal innovativeness, and fear of being left behind, identified as crucial determinants in the adoption process.

The study's results underscore that technology's perceived usefulness and ease of use are instrumental in promoting higher adoption rates. Technologies perceived as easy to use and beneficial are more likely to be adopted quickly, supporting previous research in this domain. Furthermore, the study validates Rogers' (2003) DOI theory, which asserts that their relative advantage over existing ones primarily drives the adoption of new technologies. The study also contributes significantly to understanding the psychological factors in technology adoption, revealing that personal innovativeness and the FOMO play vital roles in influencing adoption decisions. It highlights that both individual characteristics and social dynamics are influential in shaping patterns of technology adoption. Overall, the study significantly enriches the literature on technology adoption and offers valuable insights for those involved in technology design, marketing, policymaking, and individual users.

10. Limitations and Future Research

Acknowledging constraints in research endeavours is essential for transparency and identifying areas for future enhancement. The limitations of this study include the possibility that the sample of 380 respondents may not fully represent the broader population's sentiments, with the demographic distribution potentially not capturing the full diversity of digital users. Second, being a cross-sectional study, it offers insights at a specific point in time, whereas longitudinal studies could reveal changes in perceptions over time. Third, the responses might be subject to recall bias or influenced by the respondents' desire to conform to socially acceptable norms. Fourth, the study's focus on specific geographical locations may not encompass cultural variations across different regions.

The findings of this study lay the groundwork for understanding the factors that drive rapid technology adoption. Future research should consider expanding the sample size to include a more diverse range of age groups, professions, and geographical locations. Longitudinal studies tracking the same participants over time could shed light on evolving technology adoption dynamics and the sustained impact of factors like perceived usefulness and FOMO. In addition to FOMO and personal innovativeness, other psychological aspects such as tech-savviness, cognitive load, or trust in technology could be explored. Considering the global reach of technology, investigating how cultural norms and regional peculiarities affect adoption could yield valuable insights. While this study addresses general technology adoption, future research could focus on specific innovations like augmented reality, blockchain, or quantum computing, examining unique adoption factors associated with these technologies. Moreover, understanding how global events, such as pandemics or economic downturns, impact technology adoption rates could also be a significant area of study.

Future research should pivot towards real-world problems emerging from the rapid adoption of technology. Studies could investigate the impacts on various societal groups, particularly focusing on vulnerable and marginalised communities, to tackle issues such as the digital divide and access to new technologies. There is a significant need to explore the psychological effects of technology on mental health and social relationships. Additionally, the effectiveness of policy measures and educational programmes in mitigating the negative outcomes of fast-paced technological changes merits further examination. An area of growing concern is the environmental impact of technology use, which aligns with global sustainability goals. By directing research efforts towards these practical concerns, academic work can offer valuable insights and create more equitable, ethical, and sustainable technological ecosystems. This approach ensures that scholarly investigations remain pertinent and impactful, addressing society's urgent issues in the digital age.

References

Agarwal, R., & Prasad, J. (1998). A conceptual and operational definition of personal innovativeness in information technology. *Information Systems Research, 9*(2), 204–215.

Agrawal, A., Gans, J., & Goldfarb, A. (2018). *The economics of artificial intelligence: An agenda.* University of Chicago Press.

Aitamurto, T., Won, A. S., Sakshuwong, S., Kim, B., Sadeghi, Y., Stein, K., Royal, P. G., & Kircos, C. L. (2021, May). From fomo to jomo: Examining the fear and joy of missing out and presence in a 360 video viewing experience. In *Proceedings of the 2021 CHI conference on human factors in computing systems* (pp. 1–14), Article 512.

Ajzen, I., & Fishbein, M. (1980). *Understanding attitudes and predicting social behaviour.* Prentice-Hall. https://books.google.co.in/books/about/Understanding_attitudes_an d_predicting_s.html?id=AnNqAAAAMAAJ

Alkawsi, G., Ali, N. A., & Baashar, Y. (2021). The moderating role of personal innovativeness and users experience in accepting the smart meter technology. *Applied Sciences, 11*(8), 3297.

Alutaybi, A., Al-Thani, D., McAlaney, J., & Ali, R. (2020). Investigating the role of fear of missing out (FOMO) in the relationship between social network services use intensity and nomophobia. *International Journal of Environmental Research and Public Health, 17*(13), 4712.

Appiah, K. A. (2010). *Experiments in ethics.* Harvard University Press.

Bedué, P., & Fritzsche, A. (2022). Can we trust AI? An empirical investigation of trust requirements and guide to successful AI adoption. *Journal of Enterprise Information Management, 35*(2), 530–549. https://doi.org/10.1108/JEIM-06-2020-0233

Bender, E. M., Gebru, T., McMillan-Major, A., & Shmitchell, S. (2021). On the dangers of stochastic parrots: Can language models be too big. In *Proceedings of the 2021 ACM conference on fairness, accountability, and transparency* (pp. 610–623).

Bengio, Y. (2017). *Deep learning and the future of AI.* arXiv preprint arXiv:1705.07798.

Berwick, D. M. (2003). Disseminating innovations in health care. *JAMA, 289*(15), 1969–1975.

Bradford, M., & Florin, J. (2003). Examining the role of innovation diffusion factors on the implementation success of enterprise resource planning systems. *International Journal of Accounting Information Systems, 4*(3), 205–225.

Brevini, B. (2021). *Is AI good for the planet?* Polity.

Brey, P. (2018). The strategic role of technology in a good society. *Technology in Society, 52*, 39–45.

Brown, T. B. (2020). *Language models are few-shot learners.* OpenAI.

Brynjolfsson, E., & McAfee, A. (2014). *The second machine age: Work, progress, and prosperity in a time of brilliant technologies.* WW Norton & Company.

Cakmak, P. I. & Tas, E. (2012). The use of information technology on gaining competitive advantage in Turkish contractor firms. *World Applied Sciences Journal, 18*(2), 274–285.

Castells, M. (2009). *The rise of the network society: The information age: Economy, society, and culture* (Vol. I). Wiley-Blackwell.

Chaffee, S. H., & Metzger, M. J. (2001). The end of mass communication? *Mass Communication & Society, 4*(4), 365–379.

Chatterji, N., Manohar, S., & Verma, B. (2023). Assessing the influence of graduate characteristics on employer satisfaction: A multi-dimensional analysis. *The Open Psychology Journal, 16*(1).

Cho, J., DeStefano, T., Kim, H., Kim, I., & Paik, J. H. (2023). What's driving the diffusion of next-generation digital technologies? *Technovation, 119*, 102477. https://doi.org/10.1016/j.technovation.2022.102477

Chui, M., Issler, M., Roberts, R., & Yee, L. (2023). *Technology trends outlook 2023.* Vancouver.

Danaher, J. (2020). Robot betrayal: A guide to the ethics of robotic deception. *Ethics and Information Technology, 22*(2), 117–128.

Danaher, J., & Sætra, H. S. (2022). Technology and moral change: The transformation of truth and trust. *Ethics and Information Technology, 24*(3), 35. https://doi.org/10.1007/s10676-022-09661-y

David, M. (2020). The correspondence theory of truth. In E. N. Zalta (Ed.), *The Stanford encyclopedia of philosophy* (Winter 2020 edition). https://plato.stanford.edu/archives/win2020/entries/truth-correspondence/

Davis, F. D. (1989). Perceived usefulness, perceived ease of use, and user acceptance of information technology. *MIS Quarterly: Management Information Systems, 13*(3), 319–339.

DeStefano, T., Kneller, R., & Timmis, J. (2020). *Cloud computing and firm growth.* ESifo Working Paper No. 8306.

Dignum, V. (2018). *Responsible artificial intelligence: How to develop and use AI in a responsible way.* Springer.

Doe, J., Van de Wetering, R., Honyenuga, B. Q., & Versendaal, J. M. (2019, December 8–12). Eco-system oriented instrument for measuring firm technology adoption. In *19th international conference on electronic business* (pp. 186–198).

Edwards, B. (2022). *Artists stage mass protest against AI-generated artwork on ArtStation.* Ars Technica.

Exploding Topics. (2023). *The fastest growing apps: From 0 to 100 million users.* https://explodingtopics.com/blog/chatgpt-users

Faaeq, M. K., Alqasa, K., & Al-Matari, E. M. (2014). Technology adoption and innovation of E-government in Republic of Iraq. *Asian Social Science, 11*(3), 135–145.

Fallis, D. (2021). The epistemic threat of deepfakes. *Philosophy & Technology, 34*, 623–643.

Gao, M., Kortum, P., & Oswald, F. (2018, September). Psychometric evaluation of the USE (usefulness, satisfaction, and ease of use) questionnaire for reliability and validity. In *Proceedings of the human factors and ergonomics society annual meeting* (Vol. 62, No. 1, pp. 1414–1418). Sage Publications.

Goodfellow, I., Bengio, Y., & Courville, A. (2016). *Deep learning.* MIT Press.

Greenhalgh, T., Robert, G., Macfarlane, F., Bate, P., & Kyriakidou, O. (2004). Diffusion of innovations in service organizations: Systematic review and recommendations. *Milbank Quarterly, 82*(4), 581–629. https://www.digitalinformationworld.com/2023/08/generative-ai-is-growing-faster-than.html

Griffith, R., Redding, S., & Simpson, H. (2002). *Productivity convergence and foreign ownership at the establishment level* [CEPR Discussion Paper], p. 3765.

Griffy-Brown, C., Earp, B. D., & Rosas, O. (2018). Technology and the good society. *Technol. Soc. 52*, 1–3.

Hannan, T. H., & McDowell, J. M. (1984). The determinants of technology adoption: The case of the banking firm. *The RAND Journal of Economics, 15*, 328–335.

Horwich, P. (2006). The value of truth. *Nous, 40*(2), 347–360.

Hurlburt, G. (2023). What if ethics got in the way of generative AI? *IT Professional, 25*(2), 4–6. https://doi.org/10.1109/MITP.2023.3267140

Iansiti, M., & Lakhani, K. R. (2020). Competing in the age of AI: Strategy and leadership when algorithms and networks run the world. *Harvard Business Review*, January–February.

Jackson, J. D., Mun, Y. Y., & Park, J. S. (2013). An empirical test of three mediation models for the relationship between personal innovativeness and user acceptance of technology. *Information & Management, 50*(4), 154–161.

Kärkkäinen, T. (2023). FOMO in digital assets. In *Activist retail investors and the future of financial markets* (pp. 136–151). Routledge.

Lazarsfeld, P. F., & Menzel, H. (1963). Mass media and personal influence. In W. Schramm (Ed.), *The science of human communications*, Basic Books.

Lee, J. D., & See, K. A. (2004). Trust in automation: Designing for appropriate reliance. *Human Factors, 46*(1), 50–80.

Levine, E. E., & Schweitzer, M. E. (2015). Prosocial lies: When deception breeds trust. *Organizational Behavior and Human Decision Processes, 126,* 88–106.

Lopez-Acevedo, G. (2002). *Determinants of technology adoption in Mexico* [Policy Research Working Paper 2780]. World Bank, Washington, DC.

Lu, Y., Yao, J. E., & Yu, C. S. (2005). Personal innovativeness, social influences and adoption of wireless internet services via mobile technology. *The Journal of Strategic Information Systems, 14*(3), 245–268.

Lund, A. M. (2001). Measuring usability with the use questionnaire12. *Usability Interface, 8*(2), 3–6.

Magni, M., Angst, C. M., & Agarwal, R. (2012). Everybody needs somebody: The influence of team network structure on information technology use. *Journal of Management Information Systems, 29*(3), 9–42.

Manning, L., Brewer, S., & Craigon, P. J. (2022). Artificial intelligence and ethics within the food sector: Developing a common language for technology adoption across the supply chain. *Trends in Food Science & Technology, 125,* 33–42.

Maruping, L. M., & Magni, M. (2012). What's the weather like? The effect of team learning climate, empowerment climate, and gender on individuals' technology exploration and use. *Journal of Management Information Systems, 29*(1), 79–114.

Mathieson, K. (1991). Predicting user intentions: Comparing the technology acceptance model with the theory of planned behavior. *Information Systems Research, 2*(3), 173–191.

McKinsey & Company. (2023). The state of AI in 2023: Generative AI's breakout year. Retrieved October 9, 2023, fromhttps://www.mckinsey.com/capabilities/quantum-black/our-insights/the-state-of-ai-in-2023-generative-ais-breakout-year

Moore, G. C., & Benbasat, I. (1991). Development of an instrument to measure the perceptions of adopting an information technology innovation. *Information Systems Research, 2*(3), 192–222.

Nayak, M. S. D. P., & Narayan, K. A. (2019). Strengths and weaknesses of online surveys. *IOSR Journal of Humanities and Social Sciences (IOSR-JHSS), 24*(5), 31–38.

OECD. (2020). *Digital economy outlook 2020.* OECD Publishing. https://doi.org/10.1787/bb167041-en

Oliveira, T., & Martins, M. F. (2011). Literature review of information technology adoption models at firm level. *Electronic Journal of Information Systems Evaluation, 14*(1), 110–121.

Parveen, F., & Sulaiman, A. (2008). Technology complexity, personal innovativeness and intention to use wireless internet using mobile devices in Malaysia. *International Review of Business Research Papers, 4*(5), 1–10

Pavlou, P. A. (2018). Internet of things – Will humans be replaced or augmented? *NIM Marketing Intelligence Review, 10*(2), 42–47.

Pavlov, I. P. (1927). *Conditioned reflexes: An investigation of the physiological activity of the cerebral cortex.* Oxford University Press.

Perez, S. (2022). *The rise of generative AI in the business sector.* TechCrunch.

Przybylski, A. K., Murayama, K., DeHaan, C. R., & Gladwell, V. (2013). Motivational, emotional, and behavioral correlates of fear of missing out. *Computers in Human Behavior, 29*(4), 1841–1848.

Rijanto, A. (2021). Blockchain technology adoption in supply chain finance. *Journal of Theoretical and Applied Electronic Commerce Research, 16*(7), 3078–3098.

Riordan, B. C., Cody, L., Flett, J. A., Conner, T. S., Hunter, J., & Scarf, D. (2020). The development of a single item FoMO (fear of missing out) scale. *Current Psychology, 39,* 1215–1220.

Rogers, E. M. (1962). *Diffusion of innovations.* Free Press.

Rogers, E. M. (1995). Lessons for guidelines from the diffusion of innovations. *The Joint Commission Journal on Quality Improvement, 21*(7), 324–328.

Rogers, E. M. (2003). *Diffusion of innovations* (5th ed.). Free Press.

Russell, S., & Norvig, P. (2020). *Artificial intelligence: A modern approach* (4th ed.). Pearson.

Sætra, H. S. (2019). The ghost in the machine. *Human Arenas 2*(1), 60–78.

Sætra, H. S. (2020). The parasitic nature of social AI: Sharing minds with the mindless. *Integrative Psychological & Behavioral Science, 54*(2), 308–322.

Sætra, H. S. (2021). Robotomorphy: Becoming our creations. AI and ethics. https://doi.org/10.1007/s43681-021-00092-x

Sætra, H. S. (2023). Generative AI: Here to stay, but for good? *Technology in Society, 75*, 102372.

Sætra, H. S., & Mills, S. (2021). Psychological force, liberty and technology. *Technology in Society, 69*, Article 101973. https://doi.org/10.1016/j.techsoc.2022.101973

Salahshour Rad, M., Nilashi, M., & Mohamed Dahlan, H. (2018). Information technology adoption: A review of the literature and classification. *Universal Access in the Information Society, 17*, 361–390.

Santos, C. (2020). *How medium, arXiv, and Github are disrupting the dissemination of AI knowledge*. Towards Data Science.

Sarker, S., Valacich, J. S., & Sarker, S. (2005). Technology adoption by groups: A valence perspective. *Journal of the Association for Information Systems, 6*(2), 37–71.

Scherer, M. U. (2020). Regulating artificial intelligence systems: Risks, challenges, competencies, and strategies. *Harvard Journal of Law & Technology, 29*(2), 353–398.

Schlagwein, D., & Willcocks, L. (2023). ChatGPT et al.: The ethics of using (generative) artificial intelligence in research and science. *Journal of Information Technology, 38*(3), 232–238. https://doi.org/10.1177/02683962231200411.

Sharma, S. K., & Shukla, A. (2017). Impact of electronic word on mouth on consumer behaviour and brand image. *Asian Journal of Management, 8*(3), 501–506.

Shukla, A., & Mishra, A. (2022). Role of review length, review valence and review credibility on consumer's online hotel booking intention. *FIIB Business Review*, 23197145221099683.

Sia, C. L., Tan, B. C. Y., & Wei, K. K. (2002). Group polarization and computer-mediated communication: Effects of communication cues, social presence, and anonymity. *Information Systems Research, 13*(1), 70–90.

Sia, C. L., Teo, H. H., Tan, B. C. Y., & Wei, K. K. (2004). Effects of environmental uncertainty on organizational intention to adopt distributed work arrangements. *IEEE Transactions on Engineering Management, 51*(3), 253–267.

SimilarWeb. (2023). Website analysis: Chat.openai.com. https://pro.similarweb.com/#/digitalsuite/websiteanalysis/overview/website-performance/*/999/3m?webSource=Total&key=chat.openai.com

Smith, J., & Johnson, E. (2021). Exploring factors influencing IT adoption: A study on English language students at Payame Noor University, Fars Province. *Top Journal of Accounting and Management, 6*(6), 25–30.

Solaiman, I., Talat, Z., Agnew, W., Ahmad, L., Baker, D., Blodgett, S. L., Daumé, H., III, Dodge, J., Evans, E., Hooker, S., Jernite, Y., Luccioni, A. S., Lusoli, A., Mitchell, M., Newman, J., Png, M.-T., Strait, A., & Vassilev, A. (2023). Evaluating the social impact of generative AI systems in systems and society. arXiv preprint arXiv:2306.05949v2. https://arxiv.org/abs/2306.05949v2

Son, H., Lee, S., & Kim, C. (2015). What drives the adoption of building information modeling in design organizations? An empirical investigation of the antecedents affecting architects' behavioral intentions. *Automation in Construction, 49*, 92–99.

Srinivasan, R., & Parikh, D. (2021). Building bridges: Generative artworks to explore AI ethics. *Fujitsu Research of America & Georgia Tech and Facebook AI Research*. arXiv:2106.13901v1 [cs.CY].

Statista. (2021a). *Number of Instagram users worldwide from 2016 to 2021.* https://www.statista.com/statistics/253577/number-of-monthly-active-instagram-users/

Statista. (2021b). *Number of YouTube users worldwide from 2016 to 2021.* https://www.statista.com/statistics/805656/number-youtube-viewers-world/

Statista. (2023) *Leading chatbot/conversational AI startups worldwide in 2023, by funding raised*. https://www.statista.com/statistics/1359073/chatbot-and-conversational-ai-startup-funding-worldwide/

Tarafdar, M., & Vaidya, S. D. (2006). Challenges in the adoption of E-Commerce technologies in India: The role of organizational factors. *International Journal of Information Management, 26*(6), 428–441.

Taylor, S., & Todd, P. A. (1995). Understanding information technology usage: A test of competing models. *Information Systems Research, 6*(2), 144–176.

Thakur, R., & Srivastava, M. (2014). Adoption readiness, personal innovativeness, perceived risk and usage intention across customer groups for mobile payment services in India. *Internet Research, 24*(3), 369–392.

The Guardian. (2023). *ChatGPT reaches 100 million users, making it the fastest growing app*. https://www.theguardian.com/technology/2023/feb/02/chatgpt-100-million-users-open-ai-fastest-growing-app

Thong, J. Y. L. (1999). An integrated model of information systems adoption in small businesses. *Journal of Management Information Systems, 15*(4), 187–214.

Thong, J. Y. L., Hong, S. J., & Tam, K. Y. (2006). The effects of post-adoption beliefs on the expectation-confirmation model for information technology continuance. *International Journal of Human-Computer Studies, 64*(9), 799–810.

Thormundsson, B. (2023). Explainable AI market revenues worldwide 2022-2030. Statista. https://www.statista.com/statistics/1256246/worldwide-explainable-ai-market-revenues/

Tomczyk, Ł., & Szotkowski, R. (2023). Sexting, fear of missing out (FOMO), and problematic social network use among adolescents. *Human Technology, 19*(2), 283–301.

UNESCO. (2023). *Artificial intelligence: Examples of ethical dilemmas*. https://www.unesco.org/en/artificial-intelligence/recommendation-ethics/cases

Valente, T. W. (2012). Network interventions. *Science, 337*(6090), 49–53.

Venkatesh, V., & Bala, H. (2008. Technology acceptance model 3 and a research agenda on interventions. *Decision Sciences, 39*(2), 273–315.

Venkatesh, V., & Davis, F. D. (2000). A theoretical extension of the technology acceptance model: Four longitudinal field studies. *Management Science, 46*(2), 186–204.

Venkatesh, V., Morris, M. G., Davis, G. B., & Davis, F. D. (2003). User acceptance of information technology: Toward a unified view. *MIS Quarterly, 27*(3), 425–478.

Venkatesh, V., Thong, J. Y., & Xu, X. (2012). Consumer acceptance and use of information technology: Extending the unified theory of acceptance and use of technology. *MIS Quarterly, 36*(1), 157–178.

Verma, B., Singla, B., & Mittal, A. (Eds.). (2024). *Digital technologies, ethics, and decentralization in the digital era*. IGI Global.

Wang, W. T., & Lin, Y. L. (2021). The relationships among students' personal innovativeness, compatibility, and learning performance. *Educational Technology & Society, 24*(2), 14–27.

Warschauer, M. (2004). *Technology and social inclusion: Rethinking the digital divide*. MIT Press.

Wirtz, B. W., Weyerer, J. C., & Geyer, C. (2019). AI-driven technologies and their implications for consumers. *Electronic Markets, 29*(4), 631–649.

Yen, H. R., Hu, P. J. H., Hsu, S. H. Y., & Li, E. Y. (2015). A multilevel approach to examine employees' loyal use of ERP systems in organizations. *Journal of Management Information Systems, 32*(4), 144–178.

Zhou, T. (2011). An empirical examination of initial trust in mobile banking. *Internet Research, 21*(5), 527–540.

Zolas, N., Kroff, Z., Brynjolfsson, E., McElheran, K., Beede, D. N., Buffington, C., Goldschlag, N., Foster, L., & Dinlersoz, E. (2021). *Advanced technologies adoption and use by us firms: Evidence from the annual business survey* (No. w28290). National Bureau of Economic Research.

Zuboff, S. (2019). *The age of surveillance capitalism: The fight for a human future at the new frontier of power*. Public Affairs.

www.ingramcontent.com/pod-product-compliance
Lightning Source LLC
Jackson TN
JSHW011307171224
75586JS00004B/45